THE SHAKESPEARE PARALLEL TEXT SERIES REVISED

S0-AXR-568

ROMEO AND JULIET

Edited by
Janie B. Yates-Glandorf, Ph.D.

Perfection Learning® Corporation
Logan, Iowa 51546-0500

Publisher's Note

This edition of *Romeo and Juliet* provides two complete versions of the play. On the left is Shakespeare's original language. Even with extensive footnotes, the syntax and vocabulary of Elizabethan English is difficult for modern readers. Therefore, a line-by-line prose paraphrase is printed beside the original text. This paraphrase is not intended as a replacement for the original but as an aid to understanding. As students become more familiar with the play, they often move from reliance on the paraphrase to confident reading of Shakespeare's original language.

Cover image of Shakespeare: Heather Cooper
Cover art: English engraving, 19th century,
            The Granger Collection

Special contents of this edition
© 1998 Perfection Learning® Corporation
1000 North Second Avenue, P.O. Box 500
Logan, Iowa 51546-0500
Published in the U.S.A.
Paperback ISBN 0-7891-2252-9
Cover Craft® ISBN 0-7807-7038-2

1 2 3 4 5 6 PP 06 05 04 03 02

Shakespeare's Life

Many great authors can be imagined as living among the characters in their works. Historical records reveal how these writers spoke, felt, and thought. But Shakespeare is more mysterious. He never gave an interview or wrote an autobiography—not

Young Will Shakespeare's schoolroom   British Travel Association

even one of his letters survives. What we know about his life can be told very briefly.

Shakespeare was born in April 1564. The exact date of his birth is unknown, but he was baptized on April 26 in the Stratford-upon-Avon church. His father, John, was a prominent local man who served as town chamberlain and mayor. Young William attended grammar school in Stratford, where he would have learned Latin—a requirement for a professional career—and some Greek.

In 1582, William married Anne Hathaway. He was 18; she was 26. At the time of their marriage, Anne was already three months pregnant with their first daughter, Susanna. In 1585, the couple had twins, Judith and Hamnet. Hamnet died before reaching adulthood, leaving Shakespeare no male heir.

Even less than usual is known about Shakespeare's life between 1585 and 1592. During that time, he moved to London and became an actor and playwright. He left his family behind in Stratford. Although he surely visited them occasionally, we have little evidence about what Shakespeare was like as a father and a husband.

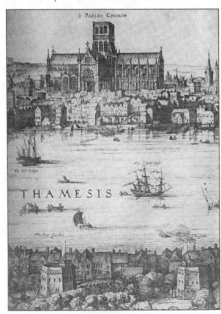

Thames River flowing past St. Paul's Cathedral, the Bear Garden, and the Globe Theatre   Visscher's View of London (1616)

Several of his early plays were written during this time, including *The Comedy of Errors*, *Titus Andronicus*, and the three parts of *Henry VI*. In those days, working in the theater was rather like acting in soap operas today—the results may be popular, but daytime serials aren't recognized as serious art. In fact, many people were opposed to even allowing plays to be performed. Ministers warned their congregations of the dangers of going to plays.

But Shakespeare and his friends were lucky. Queen Elizabeth I loved plays. She protected acting companies from restrictive laws and gave them her permission to perform. Shakespeare wrote several plays to be performed for the queen, including *Twelfth Night*.

After Elizabeth's death in 1603, Shakespeare's company became known as the King's Men. This group of actors performed for James I, who

Queen Elizabeth I   Library of Congress

had ruled Scotland before becoming King of England. Perhaps to thank James for his patronage, Shakespeare wrote *Macbeth*, which included two topics of strong interest to the king—Scottish royalty and witchcraft.

Unlike many theater people, Shakespeare actually earned a good living. By 1599, he was part-owner of the Globe, one of the newest theaters in London. Such plays as *Othello*, *Hamlet*, and *King Lear* were first performed there.

In 1610 or 1611, Shakespeare moved back to the familiar surroundings of Stratford-upon-Avon. He was almost 50 years old, well past middle age by 17th-century standards. Over the years, he'd invested

in property around Stratford, acquiring a comfortable estate and a family coat of arms.

But Shakespeare didn't give up writing. In 1611, his new play *The Tempest* was performed at Court. In 1613, his play *Henry VIII* premiered. This performance was more dramatic than anyone expected. The stage directions called for a cannon to be fired when "King Henry" came on stage. The explosion set the stage on fire, and the entire theater burned to the ground.

Shakespeare died in 1616 at the age of 52. Scholars have wondered why he willed his "second-best bed" to his widow, but he also left Anne his plays and a comfortable income. His gravestone carried this inscription:

**GOOD FRIEND FOR JESUS SAKE FORBEAR
TO DIG THE DUST ENCLOSED HERE!
BLEST BE THE MAN THAT SPARES THESE STONES,
AND CURST BE HE THAT MOVES MY BONES.**

This little verse, so crude that it seems unlikely to be Shakespeare's, has intrigued countless scholars and biographers.

Anyone who loves Shakespeare's plays and poems wants to know more about their author. Was he a young man who loved Anne Whateley but was forced into a loveless marriage with another Anne? Did he teach school in Stratford, poach Sir Thomas Lucy's deer, or work for a lawyer in London? Who is the "dark lady" of his sonnets?

But perhaps we are fortunate in our ignorance. Orson Welles, who directed an all-black stage production of *Macbeth* in 1936, put it this way: "Luckily, we know almost nothing about Shakespeare.... and that makes it so much easier to understand [his] works.... It's an egocentric, romantic, 19th-century conception that the artist is more interesting and more important than his art."

This is the only known portrait of Shakespeare painted while he was alive.

In Shakespeare's world, there can be little question of which is truly important, the work or the author. Shakespeare rings up the curtain and then steps back into the wings, trusting the play to a cast of characters so stunningly vivid that they sometimes seem more real than life.

Juliet and Her Romeo

Romeo's name comes first in the play's title, but Juliet is the stronger character. She, not Romeo, makes all the important decisions in the play. She is even the first to propose marriage.

Two facts about Juliet tend to surprise today's audiences and readers. One is that she is only 13. The other is that the part was probably first played by a teenaged boy.

On Shakespeare's stage, female roles were acted by boys. One of the most famous was John Rice, who created the roles of Lady Macbeth and Cleopatra. These parts made him something of a celebrity. Rice was even invited to make a special appearance before King James I.

The part of Juliet was probably first played by Robert Goffe. He probably played Juliet opposite the famous tragic actor Richard Burbage. The older actor later created Hamlet, Macbeth, Othello, and King Lear. But in *Romeo and Juliet*, Goffe got the meatier role.

Juliet was first played by a woman in 1662. Samuel Pepys, who was in the audience, thought that Mrs. Saunderson gave a terrible performance. However, since that time, the role has almost always been performed by a woman. During the 19th century, women sometimes even played the part of Romeo. The most famous female Romeo was the American actress Charlotte Cushman, who was also known for her Hamlet.

In Shakespeare's time, women were not allowed to play dramatic roles. However, they could marry at a much earlier age than is acceptable today. In Elizabethan England, a girl could legally marry at the age of 12. For boys, the legal age was 14. Wealthy families sometimes arranged marriages to protect their fortunes, but early marriages were not common. The average wealthy woman in Elizabethan England married at 20, the average wealthy man at 22. Still, nobles carefully guarded the legality of early marriage and sometimes arranged for their children to marry at ages even younger than the law allowed.

The Folger Shakespeare Library

Early marriage was a common enough practice to be quite controversial, as Cedric Watts points out in his critical study of *Romeo and Juliet*. Certain scholarly and medical authorities decried the practice in words similar to those of Juliet's father: "And too soon marr'd are those so early made." The danger of childbirth at such an age was widely recognized. One Elizabethan writer even insisted that women shouldn't marry before reaching the age of 18.

> **Excerpt from the diary of Samuel Pepys (1633–1703)**
> March 1.—To the Opera, and there saw *Romeo and Juliet*, the first time it was ever acted, but it is a play of itself the worst that ever I heard in my life, and the worst acted that ever I saw these people do, and I am resolved to go no more to see the first time of acting, for they were all of them out more or less.

A Political Romance

Audiences often think of *Romeo and Juliet* as a love story and nothing more. In fact, the play has a political dimension which is too frequently overlooked. The politics of *Romeo and Juliet* have their roots deep in the story's earliest Italian sources.

The play's plot goes back to several Italian novels. The first of these was written by Masuccio of Salerno during the 15th century. During the 16th century, Luigi da Porto based another novel on Masuccio's, and Bandello based yet another on Luigi's. All of these novels featured two lovers named Romeo and Giulietta whose happiness is thwarted by their feuding families, the Montecchi and Cappelletti.

During the Italian Renaissance, powerful families often quarreled violently. One feud was between the Cerchi and Donati families in Florence. They began fighting around 1300 and barely stopped for another 50 years. The Cerchi and Donati represented two opposing political factions—the Ghibellines and Guelphs, respectively. The

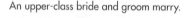

An upper-class bride and groom marry.

Ghibellines (or the White faction) believed in a large Italian empire. The Guelphs (or the Black faction) favored independent city-states under the direction of the pope. Italian fans of Romeo and Giulietta may have seen the lovers as tragic pawns in the struggle over the destiny of Italy itself.

Shakespeare learned their story through Arthur Brookes' narrative poem *The Tragicall Historye of Romeus and Juliet,* published in 1562. He may have used the story of the two Italian lovers to explore a controversy in his own time—the nature of marriage. Should marriages be arranged, or should young people

Renaissance fathers arrange a marriage.

Selection from *Romeus and Juliet* by Arthur Brookes

Love hath inflamed twayne by sodayn sight.
And both do graunt the thing that both desyre.
    They wed in shrift by counsell of a frier.
    Young Romeus clymes fayre Juliets bower by night.
Three monthes he doth enjoy his cheefe delight.
    By Tybalts rage, provoked unto yre,
    He payeth death to Tybalt fro his hyre.
    A banisht man he scapes by secret flight.
New mariage is offred to his wyfe:
    She drinkes a drinke that seemes to reve her
    breath.
    They bury her, that sleping yet hath lyfe.
Her husband heares the tydinges of her death.
    He drinkes his bane and she with Romeus knyfe,
When she awakes, her selfe (alas) she sleath.

choose their spouses? Is marriage simply a practical way to raise children, or should personal happiness be considered?

The controversy about marriage was influenced by religious differences. Catholics tended to see happiness in this world as less important than eternal bliss. Protestants, more concerned

Elizabethan dueling techniques

with worldly success, generally rated marital happiness highly—sometimes even as essential to salvation. But these divisions were by no means simple and clear-cut. The purpose of marriages and the role of parents in arranging them remained quite controversial in Shakespeare's Protestant England. Which viewpoint did Shakespeare himself hold?

Generations of English teachers have advised their students that Shakespeare and his audience were not as sympathetic to the actions of Romeo and Juliet as we are today. The play, they have said, is partly a cautionary tale about the importance of obeying one's parents. But as Cedric Watts points out, the text itself does not support this interpretation.

The love between Romeo and Juliet is necessary to bring about peace between their families. And in the speech that closes the play, Prince Escalus does not place any blame whatsoever upon the young lovers. Instead, he blames their families and even assumes some responsibility for failing to enforce the peace. If Shakespeare had felt that Romeo and Juliet were seriously at fault, surely he would have found a character to voice this viewpoint. Since he did not, we can only assume that, like Escalus, he blamed their families—and more sweepingly, a concept of marriage that did not properly value happiness. To a greater degree than is usually admitted, *Romeo and Juliet* is a play about sexual politics.

There is even an interesting trace of feminism in Shakespeare's play. In most romantic stories of his time, a dashing hero actively woos a beautiful but passive heroine. The hero gets to behave heroically and also to speak splendid lines as he lavishes poetry on his rather witless love object. But Juliet is *at least* Romeo's equal as an initiator of action, and her poetry often surpasses his in beauty. Consider her breathtaking pronouncement in the balcony scene: "My bounty is as boundless as the sea, / My love as deep; the more I give to thee, / The more I have, for both are infinite."

Noble Italian woman

Juliet's strength and assertiveness seem all the more remarkable because her life is so limited. Like a typical well-born Renaissance girl, she can't even come and go as she pleases, much less roam the streets at night as Romeo does with his pals Mercutio and Benvolio. Again and again, we are dazzled by her determination and resourcefulness. Not surprisingly, today's feminist critics frequently take favorable note of Shakespeare's lovers. As Juliet Dusinberre notes, "Shared idolatry can grow into equality, as with Romeo and Juliet...."

The themes of *Romeo and Juliet* and those of Shakespeare's sonnets sometimes echo each other. In the following excerpts, note the emphasis on procreation:

From fairest creatures we desire increase,
That thereby beauty's rose might never die,
But as the riper should by time decease,
His tender heir might bear his memory;
But thou, contracted to thine own bright eyes,
Feed'st thy light's flame with self-substantial fuel,
Making a famine where abundance lies,
Thyself thy foe, to thy sweet self too cruel.

—from "Sonnet 1"

> ROMEO: O, she is rich in beauty, only poor
>   That, when she dies, with beauty dies her store.
> BENVOLIO: Then she hath sworn that she will still
> live chaste?
> ROMEO: She hath, and in that sparing make huge
> waste;
>   For beauty starv'd with her severity
>   Cuts beauty off from all posterity.
>
>   —from *Romeo and Juliet*

The themes of *Romeo and Juliet* and those of Shakespeare's sonnets also sometimes contradict each other. In the following excerpts, notice the contrasting descriptions of the beloved:

> ROMEO: O, she doth teach the torches to burn
> bright!
>   It seems she hangs upon the cheek of night
>   As a rich jewel in an Ethiop's ear;
>   Beauty too rich for use, for earth too dear!
>   So shows a snowy dove trooping with crows,
>   As yonder lady o'er fellows shows.
>
>   —from *Romeo and Juliet*

> My mistress' eyes are nothing like the sun;
> Coral is far more red than her lips' red;
> If snow be white, why then her breasts are dun;
> If hairs be wires, black wires grow on her head.
>
>   —from "Sonnet 130"

Shakespeare's Theater

In Shakespeare's London, a day's entertainment often began with a favorite amusement, bearbaiting. A bear would be captured and chained to a stake inside a pit. A pack of dogs would be released, and they would attack the bear. Spectators placed bets on which would die first. Admission to these pits cost only a penny, so they were very

Dancing captive bear

popular with working-class Londoners.

After the bearbaiting was over, another penny purchased admission to a play. Each theater had its own company of actors, often supported by a nobleman or a member of the royal family. For part of his career, Shakespeare was a member of the Lord Chamberlain's Men. After the death of Queen Elizabeth, King James I became the patron of Shakespeare's company. The actors became known as the King's Men.

Early theaters were located south of the Thames River near the bear garden. (1593)

As part-owner of the Globe Theatre, Shakespeare wrote plays, hired actors, and paid the bills. Since the Globe presented a new play every three weeks, Shakespeare and his actors had little time to rehearse or polish their productions. To complicate matters even more, most actors played more than one part in a play.

Pitkin Pictorials, London

Boys played all the female roles. Most acting companies had three or four youths who were practically raised in the theater. They started acting as early as age seven and played female roles until they began shaving. Shakespeare had a favorite boy actor (probably named John Rice), who played Cleopatra and Lady Macbeth. Actresses would not become part of the English theater for another 50 years.

The audience crowded into the theater at about 2 p.m. The cheapest seats weren't seats at all but standing room in front of the stage. This area, known as the "pit," was occupied by "groundlings" or "penny knaves," who could be more trouble to the actors than they were worth. If the play was boring, the groundlings would throw rotten eggs or vegetables. They talked loudly to their friends, played cards, and even picked fights with each other. One theater was set on fire by audience members who didn't like the play.

The theater was open to the sky, so rain or snow presented a problem. However, the actors were partially protected by a roof known as the "heavens," and wealthier patrons sat in three stories of sheltered galleries that surrounded the pit and most of the main stage.

The main stage, about 25 feet deep and 45 feet wide, projected into the audience, so spectators were closely involved in the action. This stage was rather bare, with only a few pieces of furniture. But this simplicity

De Witt's drawing of the Swan Theatre (1596)

Players on the Globe's apron stage were surrounded by the audience on three sides.

The Folger Shakespeare Library

allowed for flexible and fluid staging. Unlike too many later productions, plays at the Globe did not grind to a halt for scene changes. When one group of actors exited through one doorway and a new group entered through another, Shakespeare's audience understood that a new location was probably being represented.

So the action of the plays was exciting and swift. The Chorus of *Romeo and Juliet* speaks of "the two hours' traffic of our stage," which suggests a rate of performance and delivery that today's actors would find nearly impossible.

Behind the main stage was the "tiring-house" where the actors changed costumes. Above the stage was a gallery that, when it wasn't occupied by musicians or wealthy patrons, could suggest any kind of high place—castle ramparts, a cliff, or a balcony. Although *Romeo and Juliet* was written too early to have been first presented at the Globe, it surely appeared in a theater with many of the same characteristics. In the play's famous "balcony scene," Juliet must have stood in such a gallery. There was possibly also a recessed, curtained area below this gallery where characters could be "revealed"—for example, the sleeping Juliet in the Capulet crypt.

Special effects were common. A trap door in the main stage allowed ghosts to appear. Even more spectacularly, supernatural beings could be lowered from above the stage. For added realism, actors hid bags of

1. **Corridor** A passageway serving the middle gallery.

2. **Entrance** Point leading to the staircase and upper galleries.

3. **Middle Gallery** The seats here were higher priced.

4. **The Heavens** So identified by being painted with the zodiac signs.

5. **Hut** A storage area that also held a winch system for lowering characters to the stage.

6. **Flag** A white flag above the theater meant a show that day.

7. **Wardrobe** A storage area for costumes and props.

8. **Dressing Rooms** Rooms where actors were "attired" and awaited their cues.

9. **Tiring-House Door** The rear entrance or "stage door" for actors or privileged spectators.

10. **Tiring-House** Backstage area providing space for storage and business.

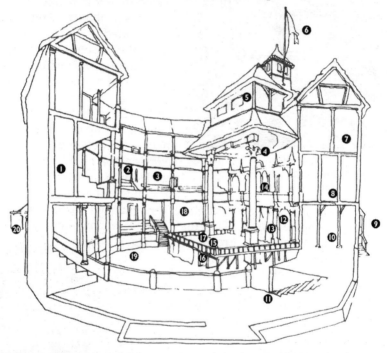

11. **Stairs** Theater goers reached the galleries by staircases enclosed by stairwells.

12. **Stage Doors** Doors opening into the Tiring-House.

13. **Inner Stage** A recessed playing area often curtained off except as needed.

14. **Gallery** Located above the stage to house musicians or spectators.

15. **Trap Door** Leading to the Hell area where a winch elevator was located.

16. **Hell** The area under the stage, used for ghostly comings and goings or for storage.

17. **Stage** Major playing area jutting into the Pit, creating a sense of intimacy.

18. **Lords Rooms** or private galleries. Six pennies let a viewer sit here, or sometimes on stage.

19. **The Pit** Sometimes referred to as "The Yard" where the "groundlings" watched.

20. **Main Entrance** Here the doorkeeper collected admission.

pig's blood and guts under their stage doublets. When pierced with a sword, the bags spilled out over the stage and produced a gory effect. This effect would have added excitement to the duels in *Romeo and Juliet*.

All these staging methods and design elements greatly appealed to Elizabethan audiences and made plays increasingly popular. By the time Shakespeare died in 1616, there were more than 30 theaters in and around London.

What would Shakespeare, so accustomed to the rough-and-tumble stagecraft of the Globe, think of the theaters where his

Elizabethan playwrights used simple props to set the scene; one altar suggested a church. Authors also used familiar comic characters like those above to set the tone for their plays.

The Wits
(1672–73)

plays are performed today? He would probably miss some of the vitality of the Globe. For centuries now, his plays have been most often performed on stages with a frame called the "proscenium arch," which cleanly separates the audience from the performers. This barrier tends to cast a peculiar shroud of privacy over his plays so that his characters do not seem to quite enter our world.

But with greater and greater frequency, Shakespeare's plays are being performed out-of-doors or in theaters with three- or four-sided stages. And a replica of the Globe Theatre itself opened in London in 1996, only about 200 yards from the site of the original. This new Globe may prove an exciting laboratory where directors and actors can test ideas about Elizabethan staging. Their experiments may change our ideas about how Shakespeare's plays were performed and give new insights into their meaning.

Reading *Romeo and Juliet*

Using This Parallel Text

This edition of *Romeo and Juliet* is especially designed for readers who aren't familiar with Shakespeare. If you're fairly comfortable with his language, simply read the original text on the left-hand page. When you come to a confusing word or passage, refer to the modern English version on the right or the footnotes at the bottom.

If you think Elizabethan English doesn't even sound like English, read a passage of the modern version silently. Then read the same passage of the original. You'll find that Shakespeare's language begins to come alive for you. You may choose to work your way through the entire play this way.

As you read more of the play, you'll probably find yourself using the modern version less and less. Remember, the parallel version is meant to be an aid, not a substitute for the original.

••

Romeo and Juliet Timeline

1562	Arthur Brookes publishes *The Tragicall Historye of Romeus and Juliet*
1564	Shakespeare is baptized
1568	Elizabeth I becomes Queen of England
1572	Shakespeare begins grammar school
1576	Opening of The Theatre, the first permanent playhouse in England
1580	Drake sails around the world
1582	Shakespeare marries Anne Hathaway
1583	Shakespeare's daughter Susanna is baptized
1585	Shakespeare's twins baptized
1588	Spanish Armada is defeated

If you read only the modern version, you'll cheat yourself out of Shakespeare's language—his quick-witted puns, sharp-tongued insults, and mood-making images.

Here are some other reading strategies that can increase your enjoyment of the play.

Looking Ahead

Knowing some historical background makes it easier to understand what's going on in the play. In the preface of this edition, you will find information about Elizabethan England, Renaissance Italy, and some of the characters in the play. It also won't hurt your enjoyment of the play to find and read a synopsis of *Romeo and Juliet* before reading the play.

Getting the Beat

Shakespeare typically used a rhythmic pattern called **iambic pentameter.** *Iambic* means that the first syllable is unstressed and the second is stressed. *Pentameter* refers to a series of five. You can feel this five-beat rhythm by tapping your hands according to the accents of the syllables in the line below.

I **KNOW** not **HOW** to **TELL** thee **WHO** I **AM.**
My **NAME,** dear **SAINT,** is **HATE**ful **TO** my**SELF,**
Be**CAUSE** it **IS** an **EN**e**MY** to **THEE.** (II.ii.58-60)

· ·

1592–94	Plague closes all of London's theaters
1594	*Titus Andronicus* becomes first printed Shakespeare play
1594	Shakespeare joins the Lord Chamberlain's Men
1599	Lord Chamberlain's Men build the Globe Theatre; Shakespeare is part-owner of the building
1609	Shakespeare's Sonnets, written in 1598, published for the first time The King's Men acquire the Blackfriars Playhouse
1610	Shakespeare retires to Stratford
1613	Globe Theatre burns to the ground
1616	William Shakespeare dies at the age of 52
1623	Shakespeare's wife Anne dies First Folio published

Speak and Listen

Remember that plays are written to be acted, not read silently. Reading out loud—whether in a group or alone—helps you "hear" the meaning. Listening to another reader will also help your comprehension. You might also enjoy listening to a recording of the play by professional actors.

Clues and Cues

Shakespeare was sparing in his use of stage directions. In fact, many of those in modern editions were added by later editors. Added stage directions are usually indicated by brackets. For example, [aside] tells the actor to give the audience information that the other characters can't hear.

Sometimes a character's actions are suggested by the lines themselves. In Act V, Scene iii, Romeo approaches the Capulets' tomb and speaks to it, saying, "I enforce thy rotten jaws to open." From this, we know that he is using his crowbar to open the tomb.

Stick to the Point

If you can't figure out every word, don't get discouraged. The people in Shakespeare's audience couldn't either. For one thing, Shakespeare loved to play with words. He made up new combinations, like *fat-guts* and *mumble-news*. He often changed one part of speech to another, as in "cursing cries and deep *exclaims.*" To make matters worse, the actors probably spoke at a rate of 140 words per minute. But the audience didn't strain to catch every word. They went to a Shakespeare play for the same reasons we go to a movie—to get caught up in the story and the acting, to have a great laugh or a good cry.

written early in Shakespeares career
love story | tragedy
setting - Italy early 1300s
Julia - 13
Romeo - 16

The Tragedy of Romeo and Juliet

CHARACTERS

ESCALUS: Prince of Verona
PARIS: a young nobleman, related to the prince
MONTAGUE and CAPULET: heads of two families who are feuding
An OLD MAN of the Capulet family
ROMEO: son of Montague
MERCUTIO: a relative of the prince and Romeo's friend
BENVOLIO: Montague's nephew, Romeo's friend and cousin
TYBALT: Lady Capulet's nephew
FRIAR LAURENCE and FRIAR JOHN: Franciscan priests
BALTHASAR: Romeo's servant
ABRAHAM: Montague's servant
SAMPSON and GREGORY: Capulet's servants
PETER: servant to Juliet's nurse
A Pharmacist
Three Musicians
Paris's Page; another page
An Officer

LADY MONTAGUE: Montague's wife
LADY CAPULET: Capulet's wife
JULIET: Capulet's daughter
Nurse to Juliet

Chorus (speaker/narrator)

Citizens of Verona: several men and women who are relatives of the feuding families, masqueraders, guards, watchmen, and attendants

SCENE: Verona, Mantua (in Italy)

PROLOGUE

Two households, both alike in dignity,
   In fair Verona, where we lay our scene,
From ancient grudge break to new mutiny,
   Where civil blood makes civil hands unclean.
5   From forth the fatal loins of these two foes
   A pair of star-cross'd lovers take their life;
Whose misadventur'd piteous overthrows
   Doth with their death bury their parents' strife.
The fearful passage of their death-mark'd love,
10   And the continuance of their parents' rage,
Which, but their children's end, nought could remove,
   Is now the two hours' traffic of our stage;
The which if you with patient ears attend,
What here shall miss, our toil shall strive to mend.

1) where play set
2) reveals problems
   they will face
3) Tell how play ends,

PROLOGUE

Enter CHORUS

CHORUS

Two equally respected families,
    living in lovely Verona, where our play is set,
break out in renewed violence due to an old grudge.
    The townspeople soil their hands with each other's blood.
5 The son of one enemy and the daughter of the other,
    victims of unfavorable fate, commit suicide.
Their unfortunate, pitiful deaths
    bury their parents' quarrel.
This sad story of their ill-fated love,
10   and of their parents' continuing anger,
which nothing except their children's deaths could end,
    you will see acted in the next two hours on our stage.
If you will listen patiently,
our play will fill in what is missing from the
    prologue.

Sunday- hot day

Act I, Scene i: [*Verona. A public place*]. *Enter* SAMPSON *and* GREGORY, *of the house of Capulet, with swords and bucklers.*

SAMPSON
Gregory, on my word, we'll not carry coals.

GREGORY
No, for then we should be colliers.

SAMPSON
I mean, an we be in choler, we'll draw.

GREGORY
Ay, while you live, draw your neck out of collar.

5 SAMPSON
I strike quickly, being mov'd.

GREGORY
But thou art not quickly mov'd to strike.

SAMPSON
A dog of the house of Montague moves me.

GREGORY
To move is to stir, and to be valiant is to stand; therefore, if thou art mov'd, thou run'st away.

SAMPSON
10   A dog of that house shall move me to stand. I will take the wall of any man or maid of Montague's.

GREGORY
That shows thee a weak slave; for the weakest goes to the wall.

SAMPSON
'Tis true; and therefore women, being the weaker vessels, are ever thrust to the wall; therefore I will push Montague's men
15   from the wall, and thrust his maids to the wall.

GREGORY
The quarrel is between our masters and us their men.

SAMPSON
'Tis all one, I will show myself a tyrant. When I have fought with the men, I will be cruel with the maids; I will cut off their heads.

---

2 *colliers* are coal sellers.   10 *take the wall* a drainage ditch ran down the center of many streets. The person of superior rank was usually granted the privilege of walking closest to the wall since this was the cleanest route.

Act I, Scene i: A public street in Verona. SAMPSON *and* GREGORY, *servants of* CAPULET, *enter carrying swords and shields.*

SAMPSON
Gregory, I swear it, we'll not endure insults.

GREGORY
No, for then we would be insult-sufferers.

SAMPSON
I mean, if we get angry, we'll draw our swords.

GREGORY
Yes, and if you want to live, draw your head out of the hangman's rope.

SAMPSON
5   I strike quickly when I'm angry.

GREGORY
But you're not likely to get angry quickly.

SAMPSON
A dog from Montague's house makes me angry.

GREGORY
To be angry is to move, to be brave is to stand still. Therefore, if you're angry, you'll run away.

SAMPSON
10   A dog of that house shall move me to be brave. I will walk near the wall if any of Montague's servants pass by.

GREGORY
That shows you're a weak slave, for the weakest is pushed to the wall.

SAMPSON
That's true, and therefore, women, being the weaker sex, are always being pushed against the wall. So I will push Montague's men away
15   from the wall, and his maidens to the wall.

GREGORY
The quarrel is not only between our masters, but between us and their servants, as well.

SAMPSON
It's all the same quarrel. I'll prove myself a tyrant. After I've fought with the men, I'll be cruel to the maidens. I'll cut off their heads.

GREGORY
The heads of the maids?

SAMPSON
20   Ay, the heads of the maids, or their maidenheads; take it in what sense thou wilt.

GREGORY
They must take it in sense that feel it.

SAMPSON
Me they shall feel while I am able to stand; and 'tis known I am a pretty piece of flesh.

GREGORY
25   'Tis well thou art not fish; if thou hadst, thou hadst been poor John. Draw thy tool; here comes two of the house of Montagues.

> *Enter two other serving-men* ABRAHAM *and* BALTHASAR.

SAMPSON
My naked weapon is out. Quarrel! I will back thee.

GREGORY
How! turn thy back and run?

SAMPSON
Fear me not.

GREGORY
30   No, marry; I fear thee!

SAMPSON
Let us take the law of our sides; let them begin.

GREGORY
I will frown as I pass by, and let them take it as they list.

SAMPSON
Nay, as they dare. I will bite my thumb at them; which is disgrace to them, if they bear it.

ABRAHAM
35   Do you bite your thumb at us, sir?

---

20 *maidenheads*   Sampson is making one of many bawdy puns in his exchange with Gregory. He means he will rob the girls of their virginity.   30 *marry*   originally meant "Virgin Mary," but by Shakespeare's day, it had become an exclamation comparable to "really," "indeed," etc.

GREGORY
The heads of the maidens?

SAMPSON
20   Yes, the heads of the maidens, or their maidenheads. Take it in any sense you like.

GREGORY
They must take it in the sense they feel it.

SAMPSON
They'll feel me as long as I'm able to stand, and everyone knows I'm a real man.

GREGORY
25   It's a good thing you're not a fish. If you were, you would not give much satisfaction.—Draw your weapon! Here comes two of Montague's servants.

Enter ABRAHAM *and* BALTHASAR, *two servants.*

SAMPSON
My bare sword is out. Start a quarrel! I'll back you up.

GREGORY
How will you back me up? By turning your back and running?

SAMPSON
Don't be afraid of me.

GREGORY
30   Afraid, indeed! Don't be ridiculous.

SAMPSON
We'll get the law on our side. Let them begin.

GREGORY
I'll make a sour face as I pass by, and let them take it as they choose.

SAMPSON
No—as they dare. I'll thumb my nose at them. That will insult them, if they notice it.

ABRAHAM
35   Are you thumbing your nose at us, sir?

SAMPSON
I do bite my thumb, sir.

ABRAHAM
Do you bite your thumb at us, sir?

SAMPSON
[*Aside to* GREGORY] Is the law of our side, if I say ay?

GREGORY
No.

SAMPSON
40   No, sir, I do not bite my thumb at you, sir; but I bite my thumb, sir.

GREGORY
Do you quarrel, sir?

ABRAHAM
Quarrel, sir? No, sir.

SAMPSON
But if you do, sir, I am for you. I serve as good a man as you.

ABRAHAM
45   No better.

SAMPSON
Well, sir.

Enter BENVOLIO.

GREGORY
Say "better"; here comes one of my master's kinsmen.

SAMPSON
Yes, better, sir.

ABRAHAM
You lie.

SAMPSON
50   Draw, if you be men. Gregory, remember thy swashing blow.
[*They fight*].

SAMPSON
I'm thumbing my nose, sir.

ABRAHAM
Are you thumbing your nose at us, sir?

SAMPSON (*to Gregory*)
Is the law on our side if I say yes?

GREGORY
No.

SAMPSON
40   No, sir. I'm not thumbing my nose at you, sir. I'm just thumbing my
nose, sir.

GREGORY
Are you trying to start a fight, sir?

ABRAHAM
A fight sir? No, sir.

SAMPSON
If you do start a quarrel, I'm ready. My master is as good as your master.

ABRAHAM
45   But he's no better.

SAMPSON
Well—sir—

Enter BENVOLIO.

GREGORY
You should say "better." Here comes one of my master's relatives.

SAMPSON (*to Abraham*)
My master is better, sir.

ABRAHAM
You're a liar.

SAMPSON
50   Draw your swords, if you're real men. Gregory, give him your
crushing blow.
They fight.

BENVOLIO
  Part, fools!
  Put up your swords; you know not what you do.

  [*Beats down their swords.*]

  Enter TYBALT.

TYBALT
  What, art thou drawn among these heartless hinds?
  Turn thee, Benvolio, look upon thy death.

BENVOLIO
55   I do but keep the peace. Put up thy sword,
  Or manage it to part these men with me.

TYBALT
  What, drawn, and talk of peace! I hate the word
  As I hate hell, all Montagues, and thee.
  Have at thee, coward!

  [*They fight*].

  Enter three or four Citizens *and* OFFICERS, *with clubs
  or partisans.*

OFFICERS
60   Clubs, bills, and partisans! Strike! Beat them down!
  Down with the Capulets! down with the Montagues!

  Enter CAPULET *in his gown, and* LADY CAPULET.

CAPULET
  What noise is this? Give me my long sword, ho!

LADY CAPULET
  A crutch, a crutch! why call you for a sword?

CAPULET
  My sword, I say! Old Montague is come,
65   And flourishes his blade in spite of me.

  Enter MONTAGUE *and* LADY MONTAGUE.

MONTAGUE
  Thou villain Capulet, —Hold me not, let me go.

BENVOLIO
> Stop it, you fools!
> Put your swords away. You don't know what you're
>   doing.
>> *He strikes down their swords.*
>> *Enter* TYBALT.

TYBALT
> Are you fighting with these cowards?
> Turn around, Benvolio. I'm going to kill you.

BENVOLIO
55   I'm only trying to make peace. Put away your sword,
> or use it to get these men away from me.

TYBALT
> You have your sword drawn and you talk about peace!
>   I hate the word peace,
> as I hate hell, all Montagues, and you.
> Fight, coward!
>> *They fight.*
>> *Enter officers and and three or four citizens*
>>   *with clubs and pikes.*

OFFICERS
60   Clubs, axes, and pikes! Strike! Beat them down!
> Down with the Capulets! Down with the Montagues!
>> *Enter* CAPULET, *in his robe, and* LADY CAPULET.

CAPULET
> What's all this noise? Give me my sword!

LADY CAPULET
> You need a crutch! Why are you asking for a sword?

CAPULET
> Give me my sword, I said. Old Montague is coming,
65   and he is waving his sword in defiance of me.
>> *Enter* MONTAGUE *and* LADY MONTAGUE.

MONTAGUE
> You're a villain, Capulet! (*To Lady Montague*) Don't hold me, let me go!

LADY MONGATUE
      Thou shalt not stir one foot to seek a foe.

      Enter PRINCE ESCALUS, *with his train.*

PRINCE ESCALUS
      Rebellious subjects, enemies to peace,
      Profaners of this neighbour-stained steel,—
70   Will they not hear?—What ho! you men, you beasts,
      That quench the fire of your pernicious rage
      With purple fountains issuing from your veins,
      On pain of torture, from those bloody hands
      Throw your mistemper'd weapons to the ground,
75   And hear the sentence of your moved prince.
      Three civil brawls, bred of an airy word,
      By thee, old Capulet, and Montague,
      Have thrice disturb'd the quiet of our streets,
      And made Verona's ancient citizens
80   Cast by their grave beseeming ornaments
      To wield old partisans, in hands as old,
      Cank'red with peace, to part your cank'red hate;
      If ever you disturb our streets again
      Your lives shall pay the forfeit of the peace.
85   For this time, all the rest depart away.
      You, Capulet, shall go along with me;
      And, Montague, come you this afternoon,
      To know our farther pleasure in this case,
      To old Free-town, our common judgement-place.
90   Once more, on pain of death, all men depart.

      [*Exeunt all but Montague, Lady Montague, and Benvolio*].

MONTAGUE
      Who set this ancient quarrel new abroach?
      Speak, nephew, were you by when it began?

BENVOLIO
      Here were the servants of your adversary,
      And yours, close fighting ere I did approach.
95   I drew to part them. In the instant came
      The fiery Tybalt, with his sword prepar'd,

LADY MONTAGUE
>You shall not move a foot toward your enemy.
>>*Enter* PRINCE ESCALUS, *with his followers.*

PRINCE
>Rebellious people, enemies to peace,
>Abusers of your swords bloodied with you neighbor's
>>blood—

70 Won't they listen?—Listen to me, you men, you beasts,
>you who quench the fire of your destructive rage
>with purple blood spurting from your veins.
>Unless you want to be tortured, throw those angry
>weapons you hold in your bloody hands to the ground

75 and hear this sentence from me, your angry prince.
>Three fights arising from meaningless insults—
>started by you, old Capulet, and you, old Montague—
>have disturbed the quiet of our streets three times,
>and caused Verona's old men

80 to throw away their proper, dignified ornaments
>and carry old pikes, rusted with peace, in their equally old
>hands to part your deadly hatred.
>If you ever disturb our streets again,
>you will have to die for breaking the peace.

85 For now, all of you go away
>except you, Capulet. You'll go with me.
>And you, Montague, are to come to me this afternoon
>to find out what I am going to do in your case.
>Go to my castle, Freetown, the common judgment place.

90 Once more, unless you want to die, all of you must leave now.
>>*All leave except* MONTAGUE, LADY MONTAGUE
>>*and* BENVOLIO.

MONTAGUE
>Who started up this old quarrel again?
>Speak up, nephew, were you here when it started?

BENVOLIO
>Capulet's servants were here,
>along with your servants, and they were fighting as I came up.

95 I drew my sword to separate them. At that moment,
>the hot-tempered Tybalt arrived, with his sword drawn,

Which, as he breath'd defiance to my ears,
He swung about his head and cut the winds,
Who, nothing hurt withal, hiss'd him in scorn.
100   While we were interchanging thrusts and blows,
Came more and more and fought on part and part,
Till the Prince came, who parted either part.

LADY MONGATUE
O, where is Romeo? Saw you him to-day?
Right glad I am he was not at this fray.

BENVOLIO
105   Madam, an hour before the worshipp'd sun
Peer'd forth the golden window of the east,
A troubled mind drave me to walk abroad;
Where, underneath the grove of sycamore
That westward rooteth from the city's side,
110   So early walking did I see your son.
Towards him I made, but he was ware of me
And stole into the covert of the wood.
I, measuring his affections by my own,
Which then most sought where most might not be found,
115   Being one too many by my weary self,
Pursued my humour not pursuing his,
And gladly shunn'd who gladly fled from me.

MONTAGUE
Many a morning hath he there been seen,
With tears augmenting the fresh morning's dew,
120   Adding to the clouds more clouds with his deep sighs;
But all so soon as the all-cheering sun
Should in the farthest east begin to draw
The shady curtains from Aurora's bed,
Away from light steals home my heavy son,
125   And private in his chamber pens himself,
Shuts up his windows, locks fair daylight out,
And makes himself an artificial night.
Black and portentous must this humour prove
Unless good counsel may the cause remove.

breathing defiance in my ears,
swinging his sword about my head, and slicing the winds.
But the winds, not being hurt, hissed at him in scorn.
100 While we were exchanging blows,
more and more people came to fight on each side
until the prince came and stopped the fighting.

LADY MONTAGUE
Where is Romeo? Have you seen him today?
I am glad he wasn't at this fight.

BENVOLIO
105 Madam, about an hour before the wonderful sun
peered out of the golden east,
a troubled mind drove me to take a walk.
Underneath a grove of sycamore trees,
west of the city,
110 I saw your son walking at that early hour.
I went toward him, but he saw me,
and he slipped into a thicket in the woods.
Sensing that he felt the same way I did—
wanting to get away from everyone
115 and feeling I was one too many by my weary self—
I chose to pursue my own desire rather than to pursue him.
I as glady shunned him as he fled from me.

MONTAGUE
He has been seen there many mornings,
adding tears to the moisture of the fresh morning dew
120 and adding more clouds to clouds with his deep sighs.
But as soon as the sun, which cheers everything,
begins in the far east to draw
the dark curtains from dawn's bed,
my sad son creeps home, away from this light.
125 He secludes himself alone in his room,
shutting his windows, locking the lovely daylight
outside,
and creating an artificial night.
His mood will become dark and ominous
unless good advice can remove the cause of his
sadness.

BENVOLIO

130   My noble uncle, do you know the cause?

MONTAGUE

I neither know it nor can learn of him.

BENVOLIO

Have you importun'd him by any means?

MONTAGUE

Both by myself and many other friends;
But he, his own affections' counsellor,
135   Is to himself—I will not say how true—
But to himself so secret and so close,
So far from sounding and discovery,
As is the bud bit with an envious worm
Ere he can spread his sweet leaves to the air
140   Or dedicate his beauty to the sun.
Could we but learn from whence his sorrows grow,
We would as willingly give cure as know.

Enter ROMEO.

BENVOLIO

See, where he comes! So please you, step aside;
I'll know his grievance, or be much deni'd.

MONTAGUE

145   I would thou wert so happy by thy stay
To hear true shrift. Come, madam, let's away.

[*Exeunt Montague and Lady*].

BENVOLIO

Good morrow, cousin.

ROMEO

                                    Is the day so young?

BENVOLIO

But new struck nine.

ROMEO

150   Ay me! sad hours seem long.
Was that my father that went hence so fast?

BENVOLIO

130   My noble uncle, do you know the reason for his behavior?

MONTAGUE

I do not know it, and I cannot learn it from him.

BENVOLIO

Have you pleaded with him in any way?

MONTAGUE

I have tried, and so have many friends,
but he is the counselor of
135   his own emotions, though I will not say how well
    (he plays counselor).
He is so secret and close-mouthed,
so far from being found out and cured,
that he's like a bud bitten by a deadly worm before
the bud can spread its sweet leaves to the air
140   or offer its beauty to the sun.
If we could just learn what causes his sorrow,
we would willingly cure it as know about it.
    Enter ROMEO.

BENVOLIO

Here he comes. If you will, please step aside
and I'll find out what's wrong with him. If I
    don't, you can deny any connection with me.

MONTAGUE

145   Stay. I hope you'll be lucky enough
to hear his true confession. (*To Lady Montague*)
    Come, madam, let's go.
    Exit LORD *and* LADY MONTAGUE.

BENVOLIO

Good morning, cousin.

ROMEO

Is it still morning?

BENVOLIO

The clock just struck nine.

ROMEO

150   Alas, the hours seem so long.
Was that my father who left here so quickly?

BENVOLIO
It was. What sadness lengthens Romeo's hours?

ROMEO
Not having that which, having, makes them short.

BENVOLIO
In love?

ROMEO
155   Out—

BENVOLIO
Of love?

ROMEO
Out of her favour, where I am in love.

BENVOLIO
Alas, that love, so gentle in his view,
Should be so tyrannous and rough in proof!

ROMEO
160   Alas, that love, whose view is muffled still,
Should, without eyes, see pathways to his will!
Where shall we dine? O me! What fray was here?
Yet tell me not, for I have heard it all.
Here's much to do with hate, but more with love
165   Why, then, O brawling love! O loving hate!
O anything, of nothing first create!
O heavy lightness! serious vanity!
Mis-shapen chaos of well-seeming forms!
Feather of lead, bright smoke, cold fire, sick health!
170   Still-waking sleep, that is not what it is!
This love feel I, that feel no love in this.
Dost thou not laugh?

BENVOLIO
                    No, coz, I rather weep.

ROMEO
Good heart, at what?

---

165 *brawling love, etc.*   lines 181-188 are paradoxes called oxymorons in which contradictions are stated. Oxymorons commonly occurred in the "artificial" love poetry in Shakespeare's day. Romeo's love for Rosaline is not deep, so he is speaking "artificially."

BENVOLIO
Yes, it was. What sadness lengthens your hours, Romeo?

ROMEO
Not having something that, if I had it, would make
the hours seem short.

BENVOLIO
Are you in love?

ROMEO
155 Out—

BENVOLIO
Of love?

ROMEO
The one I love doesn't love me.

BENVOLIO
It's too bad that love, so gentle in appearance,
should be so tyrannous and rough when being experienced.

ROMEO
160 It's too bad that love, whose sight is blindfolded,
can still see ways to work his will even without his eyes.
(*Pause*) Where shall we eat? (*Pause*) My, what
fight happened here?
On second thought, don't tell me, for I've heard it all.
It has much to do with hate, but more with love.
165 Why, then, O brawling love! O loving hate!
O anything, first created out of nothing!
O heavy lightness! Serious frivolity!
Deformed chaos of outwardly pretty forms!
Lead feather, bright smoke, cold fire, sick health!
170 Ever-wakeful sleep, that is not what it is!
I take no joy from this love I feel.
Are you laughing at me?

BENVOLIO
No, cousin, I'm crying.

ROMEO
Dear, good-hearted friend, why?

BENVOLIO

175   At thy good heart's oppression.

ROMEO

Why, such is love's transgression.
Griefs of mine own lie heavy in my breast,
Which thou wilt propagate to have it prest
With more of thine. This love that thou hast shown
180   Doth add more grief to too much of mine own.
Love is a smoke made with the fume of sighs;
Being purg'd, a fire sparkling in lovers' eyes;
Being vex'd, a sea nourish'd with lovers' tears,
What is it else? A madness most discreet,
185   A choking gall, and a preserving sweet.
Farewell, my coz.

BENVOLIO

                    Soft! I will go along.
An if you leave me so, you do me wrong.

ROMEO

Tut, I have left myself; I am not here.
190   This is not Romeo; he's some otherwhere.

BENVOLIO

Tell me in sadness, who is that you love?

ROMEO

What, shall I groan and tell thee?

BENVOLIO

                    Groan! why, no;
But sadly tell me who.

ROMEO

195   Bid a sick man in sadness make his will,—
Ah, word ill urg'd to one that is so ill!
In sadness, cousin, I do love a woman.

BENVOLIO

I aim'd so near when I suppos'd you lov'd.

ROMEO

A right good mark-man! And she's fair I love.

BENVOLIO

175   Because of your good heart's grief.

ROMEO

This is love's sin.
My own griefs make my heart heavy
which will only increase if burdened
with your sorrow, too. The love which you have
    shown me
180   adds more grief to my own too heavy sorrow.
Love is a smoke rising from the fumes of sighs;
when the air is cleared, love is a fire sparkling in
    lovers' eyes.
When frustrated, love is a sea fed by lovers' tears.
What else is love? A very wise insanity,
185   a choking bitterness, and a lasting sweet.
Goodbye, cousin.

BENVOLIO

Wait! I'll go with you.
If you leave me, you'll do me wrong.

ROMEO

Nonsense, I've lost myself; I'm not here.
190   This isn't Romeo, he's somewhere else.

BENVOLIO

Tell me in all seriousness, who is it that you love?

ROMEO

Do you want me to groan and tell you?

BENVOLIO

Groan? No,
but tell me, seriously, who you love.

ROMEO

195   You want a sick man, in seriousness, to make his will.
That's not good advice for someone who is so ill!
In all seriousness, cousin, I do love a woman.

BENVOLIO

I assumed that when I learned you were in love.

ROMEO

You're right on the mark! And the one I love is
    beautiful.

BENVOLIO

200　A right fair mark, fair coz, is soonest hit.

ROMEO

Well, in that hit you miss. She'll not be hit
With Cupid's arrow; she hath Dian's wit;
And, in strong proof of chastity well arm'd,
From Love's weak childish bow she lives unharm'd.

205　She will not stay the siege of loving terms,
Nor bide th' encounter of assailing eyes,
Nor ope her lap to saint-seducing gold.
O, she is rich in beauty, only poor
That, when she dies, with beauty dies her store.

BENVOLIO

210　Then she hath sworn that she will still live chaste?

ROMEO

She hath, and in that sparing make huge waste;
For beauty starv'd with her severity
Cuts beauty off from all posterity.
She is too fair, too wise, wisely too fair,

215　To merit bliss by making me despair.
She hath forsworn to love, and in that vow
Do I live dead that live to tell it now.

BENVOLIO

Be rul'd by me, forget to think of her.

ROMEO

O, teach me how I should forget to think.

BENVOLIO

220　By giving liberty unto thine eyes;
Examine other beauties.

ROMEO

　　　　　　　　　　　'Tis the way
To call hers, exquisite, in question more.
These happy masks that kiss fair ladies' brows,

225　Being black, puts us in mind they hide the fair;
He that is strucken blind cannot forget

BENVOLIO

200   A bright clean target, cousin, is the easiest to hit.

ROMEO

Well, you missed the target that time. She won't be hit
with love's arrow. She has the same views as Diana,
    the moon goddess.
She's well protected in her armor of virginity.
She's safe from love's weak, childish bow.

205   She will not listen to my loving words,
or let me look at her with love in my eyes,
or allow herself to be seduced.
O, she is rich in beauty; only poor
in that when she dies, her treasure will die with her beauty.

BENVOLIO

210   Then has she sworn that she'll always live as a virgin?

ROMEO

She has, and in being stingy, she is horribly wasteful.
For when beauty is starved by severe attitudes,
it is cut off from all future generations.
She's too beautiful, too wise, too wisely beautiful

215   to earn her way to heaven by making me suffer.
She vows she will not love, and because of that vow,
I'm dead, though I live to tell the fact now.

BENVOLIO

Listen to me: forget her.

ROMEO

O, teach me how to forget to think!

BENVOLIO

220   Just set your eyes free
to look at other beautiful women.

ROMEO

That would just be another way
to make me recall her unparalleled beauty.
Those fortunate masks that kiss beautiful ladies' foreheads,

225   being black, make us remember that they hide the beautiful.
The man who is struck blind can't forget

The precious treasure of his eyesight lost.
Show me a mistress that is passing fair,
What doth her beauty serve, but as a note
230   Where I may read who pass'd that passing fair?
Farewell! Thou canst not teach me to forget.

BENVOLIO
I'll pay that doctrine, or else die in debt.
        [*Exeunt.*]

Scene ii: [*A street.*] *Enter* CAPULET, PARIS, *and the Clown*
[*a* SERVANT].

CAPULET
But Montague is bound as well as I,
In penalty alike; and 'tis not hard, I think,
For men so old as we to keep the peace.

PARIS
Of honourable reckoning are you both;
5   And pity 'tis you liv'd at odds so long.
But now, my lord, what say you to my suit?

CAPULET
But saying o'er what I have said before.
My child is yet a stranger in the world;
She hath not seen the change of fourteen years.
10   Let two more summers wither in their pride,
Ere we may think her ripe to be a bride.

PARIS
Younger than she are happy mothers made.

CAPULET
And too soon marr'd are those so early made.
The earth hath swallow'd all my hopes but she;
15   She is the hopeful lady of my earth;
But woo her, gentle Paris, get her heart,
My will to her consent is but a part;
And she agree, within her scope of choice

the precious treasure of his lost eyesight.
Show me a woman who's surpassingly beautiful,
and I'll ask what good is her beauty except as a note
230   where I could read who is still more beautiful than
      that beauty?
Goodbye! You can't teach me to forget her.

BENVOLIO
    I'll make you change your mind, or else die trying.
      They exit.

    Act I, Scene ii: A street. Enter CAPULET, PARIS, *and
    the clown (a servant).*

CAPULET
    Montague is under bond, just like me,
    and facing the same punishment. It shouldn't be
      hard, I think,
    for men as old as we are to keep the peace.

PARIS
    You both have honorable reputations,
5   and it's a pity you've been fighting for so long.
    But now, my lord, what do you say about my proposed
      marriage to your daughter Juliet?

CAPULET
    By saying again what I told you before:
    my child is too young to know the rules of society.
    She isn't quite fourteen years old yet;
10   it will be two more years
    before I think she'll be ready to be married.

PARIS
    Younger girls than she have become happy mothers.

CAPULET
    Yes, and they were disfigured by that early childbirth.
    All of my children are dead except her;
15   she is the only hope I have in the world.
    But go ahead and try to win her heart, gentle Paris;
    my wishes only partially guarantee her consent.
    If she agrees,

Lies my consent and fair according voice.
20   This night I hold an old accustom'd feast,
Whereto I have invited many a guest,
Such as I love; and you, among the store
One more, most welcome, makes my number more.
At my poor house look to behold this night
25   Earth-treading stars that make dark heaven light.
Such comfort as do lusty young men feel
When well-apparell'd April on the heel
Of limping winter treads, even such delight
Among fresh female buds shall you this night
30   Inherit at my house. Hear all, all see,
And like her most whose merit most shall be;
Which on more view of, many, mine being one,
May stand in number, though in reckoning none.
Come, go with me. [*To Servant.*] Go, sirrah, trudge about
35   Through fair Verona; find those persons out
Whose names are written there, and to them say
My house and welcome on their pleasure stay.

[*Exeunt Capulet and Paris*].

SERVANT
Find them out whose names are written here! It is written that
the shoemaker should meddle with his yard and the tailor with
40   his last, the fisher with his pencil and the painter with his nets;
but I am sent to find those persons whose names are here writ,
and can never find what names the writing person hath here writ.
I must to the learned.—In good time.

Enter BENVOLIO *and* ROMEO.

BENVOLIO
Tut, man, one fire burns out another's burning,
45   One pain is less'ned by another's anguish;
Turn giddy, and be holp by backward turning;
One desperate grief cures with another's languish.
Take thou some new infection to thy eye,
And the rank poison of the old will die.

---

39 *shoemaker should meddle with his yard*   the servant, a comic character, has everything
backwards. He means: the shoemaker's leather, the tailor's wool, the fisherman's nets, and
the artist's pencil.

I'll go along with her wishes.

20 Tonight, I am going to give my annual masquerade banquet,
and I have invited many guests
who are people I love. You are invited, too.
One more very welcome guest makes the company all the richer.
At my humble house tonight, you'll see

25 the most beautiful maidens of Verona that make the night bright.
Such joy as red-blooded young men feel
when well-dressed spring treads on the heel
of limping winter, just such joy
among the lovely young maidens will you find tonight

30 at my house. Listen to everything, look at everything,
and like the lady best who is most worthy.
My daughter will be among the ladies,
but she may not be the one you choose when you have seen them all.
Come with me. (*To the Servant*) Go, servant, walk about

35 beautiful Verona; find the people
whose names are on these invitations and say to them
that I will be pleased to welcome them to my house tonight.
    Exit CAPULET *and* PARIS.

SERVANT
    I'm to find those whose names are written here! I've heard that
    the shoemaker should work with his wool, and the tailor with

40 his leather, the fisherman with his pencil, and the
        painter with his net.
    But I have to find the people whose names are written here,
    and will never find them because I can't read.
    I must find someone who can read. Here's help already!
        Enter BENVOLIO *and* ROMEO.

BENVOLIO
    Come on, Romeo. One fire burns out another fire;

45   one person's pain is lessened by someone else's misery;
    become dizzy from spinning, and be helped by reversing the direction;
        one terrible grief can be cured by someone else's pain.
    Find a new infection in your eye,
    and the poison of the old infection will die.

ROMEO

50   Your plaintain-leaf is excellent for that.

BENVOLIO

For what, I pray thee?

ROMEO

For your broken shin.

BENVOLIO

Why, Romeo, art thou mad?

ROMEO

Not mad, but bound more than a madman is;

55   Shut up in prison, kept without my food,

Whipp'd and tormented and—God-den, good fellow.

SERVANT

God gi' god-den. I pray, sir, can you read?

ROMEO

Ay, mine own fortune in my misery.

SERVANT

Perhaps you have learn'd it without book.

60   But, I pray, can you read anything you see?

ROMEO

Ay, if I know the letters and the language.

SAMPSON

Ye say honestly. Rest you merry!

ROMEO

Stay, fellow; I can read.

(*Reads.*) "Signior Martino and his wife and daughters; County

65   Anselme and his beauteous sisters; the lady widow of Vitruvio;

Signior Placentio and his lovely nieces; Mercutio and his brother

Valentine; mine uncle Capulet, his wife, and daughters; my fair

niece Rosaline; Livia; Signior Valentio and his cousin Tybalt;

Lucio and the lively Helena." A fair assembly: wither should they

70   come?

SERVANT

Up.

ROMEO

50   The plaintain leaf is a good remedy for that.

BENVOLIO

    For what, I ask you?

ROMEO

    For your wounded shin (when I kick you).

BENVOLIO

    Romeo, are you crazy?

ROMEO

    No, I'm not crazy, but a madman is freer than I am.

55   I'm shut up in prison, given no food,
    whipped, tortured, and—(*Sees the Servant*)—Good
      evening, good fellow.

SERVANT

    And a good evening to you. Sir, can you read?

ROMEO

    Yes, that's my one happiness in my unhappiness.

SERVANT

    Perhaps you memorize.

60   Can you read anything you see?

ROMEO

    Yes, if I know the letters and the language.

SERVANT

    You're an honest fellow. Have a nice day!

ROMEO

    Wait, fellow, I can read.
    (*Romeo takes the list and reads.*) "Signior
      Martino and his wife and daughters; Count

65   Anselme and his beautiful sisters; Vitruvio's widow;
    Signior Placentio and his lovely nieces; Mercutio and his brother
    Valentine; my uncle Capulet, with his wife and daughters; my lovely
    niece Rosaline; Livia; Signior Valentio and his cousin Tybalt;
    Lucio; and the lively Helena." (*Returns the paper
      to the Servant.*) This is a beautiful group of people. Where are they to

70   go?

SERVANT

    Up.

ROMEO
Whither? To supper?

SERVANT
To our house.

ROMEO
Whose house?

SERVANT
75   My master's.

ROMEO
Indeed, I should have ask'd you that before.

SERVANT
Now I'll tell you without asking. My master is the great rich
Capulet; and if you be not of the house of Montagues, I pray,
come and crush a cup of wine. Rest you merry!   [*Exit.*]

BENVOLIO
80   At this same ancient feast of Capulet's
Sups the fair Rosaline whom thou so loves,
With all the admired beauties of Verona.
Go thither; and with unattainted eye
Compare her face with some that I shall show,
85   And I will make thee think thy swan a crow.

ROMEO
When the devout religion of mine eye
    Maintains such falsehood, then turn tears to fires;
And these, who, often drown'd, could never die,
    Transparent heretics, be burnt for liars!
90   One fairer than my love! The all-seeing sun
Ne'er saw her match since first the world begun.

BENVOLIO
Tut, you saw her fair, none else being by,
Herself pois'd with herself in either eye;
But in that crystal scales let there be weigh'd
95   Your lady's love against some other maid
That I will show you shining at this feast,
And she shall scant show well that now seems best.

ROMEO
  Where?

SERVANT
  To dinner, to our house.

ROMEO
  Whose house?

SERVANT
75 My master's.

ROMEO
  Of course, I should have asked you that before.

SERVANT
  Now I'll tell you without your asking. My master is the very rich
  Capulet, and if you're not a Montague, I invite you
  to come and have a drink of wine. Bless you!
       SERVANT *exits.*

BENVOLIO
80 At this party of Capulet's,
  the beautiful Rosaline that you love so much will dine
  with all of the beautiful girls of Verona.
  Go there, and with an unprejudiced eye,
  compare her face to some of the others I'll show you.
85 I'll make you think your swan is a crow.

ROMEO
  When the devout belief of my eyes
     asserts such a lie, then my tears will turn to fires;
  and these eyes, often drowned in tears, could never die.
     Transparent unbelievers should be burned for lying!
90 Someone more beautiful than my love? The all-seeing sun
  has never seen my love's equal since the world began.

BENVOLIO
  Ha! You think she's beautiful because, having no one
     to compare her with,
  you only saw her balanced in each of your eyes.
  But in your two eyes, those crystal scales of yours, weigh
95 your lady's love against another lady
  whom I will show you at this party,
  and your Rosaline will scarcely look good who now
     seems the fairest to you.

ROMEO
I'll go along no such sight to be shown,
But to rejoice in splendour of mine own.   [*Exeunt.*]

Scene iii: [*A room in Capulet's house.*] *Enter* LADY CAPULET *and* NURSE.

LADY CAPULET
Nurse, where's my daughter? Call her forth to me.

NURSE
Now, by my maidenhead at twelve year old,
I bade her come. What, lamb! What, ladybird!
God forbid—Where's this girl? What, Juliet!

        Enter JULIET.

JULIET
5   How now! Who calls?

NURSE
                      Your mother.

JULIET
                          Madam, I am here.
What is your will?

LADY CAPULET
This is the matter.—Nurse, give leave a while,
10 We must talk in secret.—Nurse, come back again;
I have rememb'red me, thou's hear our counsel.
Thou know'st my daughter's of a pretty age.

NURSE
Faith, I can tell her age unto an hour.

LADY CAPULET
She's not fourteen.

NURSE
15   I'll lay fourteen of my teeth,—
And yet, to my teen be it spoken, I have but four,—

ROMEO
I'll go with you, not to find a lovelier girl,
but to rejoice in the beauty of my own Rosaline.
They exit.

Act I, Scene iii: A room in Capulet's house. Enter LADY CAPULET
and the NURSE.

LADY CAPULET
Nurse, where's my daughter? Tell her to come to me.

NURSE
Now by my virginity, when I was twelve years old
I told her to come. (*Calls to Juliet*) Lamb! Ladybird!
Heavens above, where is that girl? Juliet!
Enter JULIET.

JULIET
5   What is it? Who's calling?

NURSE
Your mother.

JULIET
Madam. I am here.
What do you want?

LADY CAPULET
I'll tell you.—Nurse, leave us for awhile,
10   we must talk in secret. (*Pause*)—Nurse, come back again.
I just remembered that you are to hear our plan.
You know my daughter is at the marrying age.

NURSE
Indeed. Heavens, I can tell her age to the exact hour.

LADY CAPULET
She's not quite fourteen.

NURSE
15   I would wager fourteen of my teeth—
and yet it is my misfortune to admit I have only four—

She's not fourteen. How long is it now
To Lammas-tide?

LADY CAPULET
A fortnight and odd days.

NURSE
20   Even or odd, of all days in the year,
Come Lammas-eve at night shall she be fourteen.
Susan and she—God rest all Christian souls!—
Were of an age. Well, Susan is with God;
She was too good for me. But, as I said,
25   On Lammas-eve at night shall she be fourteen;
That shall she, marry; I remember it well.
'Tis since the earthquake now eleven years,
And she was wean'd,—I never shall forget it—
Of all the days of the year, upon that day;
30   For I had then laid wormwood to my dug,
Sitting in the sun under the dove-house wall;
My lord and you were then at Mantua;—
Nay, I do bear a brain;—but, as I said,
When it did taste the wormwood on the nipple
35   Of my dug and felt it bitter, pretty fool,
To see it tetchy and fall out wi' the dug!
Shake, quoth the dove-house; 'twas no need, I trow,
To bid me trudge.
And since that time it is eleven years;
40   For then she could stand high-lone; nay, by the rood,
She could have run and waddled all about;
For even the day before, she broke her brow;
And then my husband—God be with his soul!
'A was a merry man—took up the child.
45   "Yea," quoth he, "dost thou fall upon thy face?
Thou wilt fall backward when thou hast more wit;
Wilt thou not, Jule?" and, by my holidame,
The pretty wretch left crying and said, "Ay."
To see, now, how a jest shall come about!
50   I warrant, an I should live a thousand years,

that she's not fourteen. How many days
   until Lammastide?

LADY CAPULET
   A bit over two weeks.

NURSE
20   Even or odd, of all the days of the year,
on the evening of July thirty-first she'll be fourteen.
Susan and she—God rest all Christian souls!—
were the same age. Well, Susan is with God.
She was too good for me. But as I said,
25   on the evening of July thirty-first, Juliet will be fourteen.
To think she might get married—I remember her
   birth well.
It is now eleven years since the earthquake
and since she was weaned—I'll never forget it.
Of all the days of the year, I remember that day.
30   I'd used a bitter herb on my breast (to wean her),
and I was sitting in the sun next to the dovehouse wall.
You and my lord were in Mantua at the time—
I do have a good memory—but as I said,
when the baby tasted the herb on the nipple
35   of my breast and found out it was bitter, the pretty
   little thing
became fretful and didn't want to nurse any more!
Then the dovehouse shook from the earthquake. There
   was no need
for anyone to have to tell me to run away.
Since that time it's been eleven years,
40   for by then she could stand up alone—indeed, I swear
   by the cross,
she could run and waddle all around.
Just the day before, she'd fallen on her forehead,
and then my husband—God rest his soul,
he was a happy man—picked her up.
45   He said, "Did you fall on your face?
You'll fall backward when you know more,
won't you, Juliet?" And I swear,
the pretty child stopped crying and said, "Yes."
To see now how a joke turns out!
50   I swear, if I live a thousand years,

I never should forget it, "Wilt thou not, Jule?" quoth he;
And, pretty fool, it stinted and said, "Ay."

LADY CAPULET
Enough of this; I pray thee, hold thy peace.

NURSE
Yes, madam; yet I cannot choose but laugh
55   To think it should leave crying and say, "Ay."
And yet, I warrant, it had upon it brow
A bump as big as a young cock'rel's stone;
A perilous knock; and it cried bitterly.
"Yea," quoth my husband, "fall'st upon thy face?
60   Thou wilt fall backward when thou comest to age;
Wilt thou not, Jule?" It stinted and said, "Ay."

JULIET
And stint thou too, I pray thee, nurse, say I.

NURSE
Peace, I have done. God mark thee to his grace!
Thou wast the prettiest babe that e'er I nurs'd.
65   An I might live to see thee married once,
I have my wish.

LADY CAPULET
Marry, that "marry" is the very theme
I came to talk of. Tell me, daughter Juliet,
How stands your dispositions to be married?

JULIET
70   It is an honour that I dream not of.

NURSE
An honour! were not I thine only nurse,
I would say thou hadst suck'd wisdom from thy teat.

LADY CAPULET
Well, think of marriage now; younger than you,
Here in Verona, ladies of esteem,
75   Are made already mothers. By my count,
I was your mother much upon these years
That you are now a maid. Thus then in brief:
The valiant Paris seeks you for his love.

I'll never forget it. "Won't you, Juliet?" he asked.
And the pretty child stopped crying and said, "Yes."

LADY CAPULET
That's enough, nurse, please be quiet.

NURSE
Yes, madam. (*Laughing*) But I can't help laughing
55   to think that she would stop crying and say "Yes."
And yet, I swear, she had a bump on her forehead
as big as a rooster's comb.
She took a bad fall, and she cried bitterly.
"So, you fell on your face?" said my husband.
60   "You'll fall backward when you are older,
won't you, Juliet?" And she stopped crying and said,
    "Yes."

JULIET
And you must stop, too. I beg you nurse.

NURSE
Enough, I'm finished. God bless you.
You were the prettiest baby I've ever nursed.
65   If I can live to see you married,
I'll have my wish.

LADY CAPULET
Indeed, marriage is the very subject I came to talk about.
Tell me, Juliet,
how do you feel about getting married?

JULIET
70   It's an honor I've never dreamed of.

NURSE
An honor? If I weren't your only nurse,
I'd say that you sucked wisdom from your nurse's breast.

LADY CAPULET
Well, think about marriage now. There are younger
    women than you,
ladies of esteem living here in Verona,
75   who are mothers already. If I count correctly,
I became your mother at the same age
you are now. So, in short,
the brave Paris wants you to be his love.

NURSE

A man, young lady! Lady, such a man

80   As all the world—why, he's a man of wax.

LADY CAPULET

Verona's summer hath not such a flower.

NURSE

Nay, he's a flower; in faith, a very flower.

LADY CAPULET

What say you? Can you love the gentleman?

This night you shall behold him at our feast;

85   Read o'er the volume of young Paris' face

And find delight writ there with beauty's pen;

Examine every married lineament

And see how one another lends content,

And what obscur'd in this fair volume lies

90   Find written in the margent of his eyes.

This precious book of love, this unbound lover,

To beautify him, only lacks a cover.

The fish lives in the sea, and 'tis much pride

For fair without the fair within to hide.

95   That book in many's eyes doth share the glory,

That in gold clasps locks in the golden story;

So shall you share all that he doth possess,

By having him, making yourself no less.

NURSE

No less! nay, bigger; women grow by men.

LADY CAPULET

100   Speak briefly, can you like of Paris' love?

JULIET

I'll look to like, if looking liking move;

But no more deep will I endart mine eye

Than your consent gives strength to make it fly.

Enter SERVANT.

SERVANT

Madam, the guests are come, supper serv'd up, you call'd, my

NURSE
A man, young lady! Lady, he's such a man
80   as the entire world—why, he's the handsomest model of a man!

LADY CAPULET
There's not a summer flower in Verona that can match him.

NURSE
He is a flower, truly—a real flower.

LADY CAPULET
What do you say, Juliet? Do you think you can love
    the gentleman?
Tonight you'll see him at our banquet.
85   Read young Paris' face carefully,
and you'll find delight written there with beauty's pen.
Examine each different feature
and see how one feature complements the others.
Read the concealed inner qualities of character
90   written in the margin of his shining eyes.
This precious book of love, this unbound lover,
only needs a wife to make him more handsome.
The fish lives in the sea, and it's wonderful that
something beautiful is hidden in something beautiful.
95   In many people's eyes, a book is also glorious
when golden clasps on the cover bind a good story.
You too will share everything Paris has.
By marrying him, you'll not lower your position.

NURSE
No less! No, you'll be even bigger! Women get pregnant.

LADY CAPULET (*To Juliet*)
100   Tell me, briefly, can you accept Paris as a lover?

JULIET
I will look at him with the intention of liking
    him, if looking can make me like him,
but I won't look any further
than you wish me to look.
            Enter SERVANT.

SERVANT (*To Lady Capulet*)
Madam, the guests have come, supper is served, you
    have been called, my

105   young lady ask'd for, the nurse curs'd in the pantry, and
everything in extremity. I must hence to wait; I beseech you,
follow straight.   [*Exit.*]

LADY CAPULET
    We follow thee. Juliet, the County stays.

NURSE
    Go, girl, seek happy nights to happy days.   [*Exeunt.*]

Scene iv: [*A street.*] *Enter* ROMEO, MERCUTIO, BENVOLIO,
with five or six other Maskers, Torch-bearers.

ROMEO
    What, shall this speech be spoke for our excuse?
    Or shall we on without apology?

BENVOLIO
    The date is out of such prolixity.
    We'll have no Cupid hoodwink'd with a scarf,
5   Bearing a Tartar's painted bow of lath,
    Scaring the ladies like a crow-keeper;
    Nor no without-book prologue, faintly spoke
    After the prompter, for our entrance;
    But let them measure us by what they will,
10   We'll measure them a measure and be gone.

ROMEO
    Give me a torch. I am not for this ambling;
    Being but heavy, I will bear the light.

MERCUTIO
    Nay, gentle Romeo, we must have you dance.

ROMEO
    Not I, believe me. You have dancing shoes
15   With nimble soles; I have a soul of lead
    So stakes me to the ground I cannot move.

---

1 *speech*   the custom at one time had been to give a formal introduction to
masqueraders.

105   young lady's presence has been requested, the nurse
       is being cursed in the kitchen (because she isn't
       helping), and
    everything is happening at once. I must go
       immediately to serve. I beg you
    to follow me immediately.

LADY CAPULET
    We'll follow you. (SERVANT *exits*) Juliet, the
      Count is waiting.

NURSE
    Go, girl, find happy nights to go with your happy days.
      They leave.

Act I, Scene iv: A street. Enter ROMEO, MERCUTIO, *and*
BENVOLIO, *with five or six other masqueraders, torch-bearers.*

ROMEO
    Shall I give a formal speech to introduce us?
    Or shall we just enter without any introduction?

BENVOLIO
    Those speeches are out of fashion.
    We don't want a blindfolded Cupid,
5   carrying his painted bow,
    scaring ladies like a scarecrow.
    And we don't want an impromptu prologue softly spoken
    behind a prompter for our entrance.
    Let the people measure us as they want to;
10   we'll dance one dance and be gone.

ROMEO
    Give me a torch. I'm not for this leisurely dancing.
    Since I'm so weighted down with sadness, I'll carry the torch.

MERCUTIO
    No, gentle Romeo, we want you to dance.

ROMEO
    Not me, believe me. You have dancing shoes
15   with light soles; I have a soul of lead
    which holds me to the ground so I can't move.

MERCUTIO
> You are a lover; borrow Cupid's wings,
> And soar with them above a common bound.

ROMEO
> I am too sore enpierced with his shaft
20 To soar with his light feathers, and so bound
> I cannot bound a pitch above dull woe.
> Under love's heavy burden do I sink.

MERCUTIO
> And, to sink in it, should you burden love;
> Too great oppression for a tender thing.

ROMEO
25 Is love a tender thing? It is too rough,
> Too rude, too boist'rous, and it pricks like thorn.

MERCUTIO
> If love be rough with you, be rough with love;
> Prick love for pricking, and you beat love down.—
> Give me a case to put my visage in, [*Puts on a mask.*]
30 A visor for a visor! what care I
> What curious eye doth quote deformities?
> Here are the beetle brows shall blush for me.

BENVOLIO
> Come, knock and enter; and no sooner in,
> But every man betake him to his legs.

ROMEO
35 A torch for me; let wantons light of heart
> Tickle the senseless rushes with their heels,
> For I am proverb'd with a grandsire phrase:
> I'll be a candle-holder, and look on.
> The game was ne'er so fair, and I am done.

MERCUTIO
40 Tut, dun's the mouse, the constable's own word.
> If thou art Dun, we'll draw thee from the mire
> Or, save your reverence, love, wherein thou stickest
> Up to the ears. Come, we burn daylight, ho!

---

35 *torch* this is a pun on "carrying the torch" for Rosaline. There are several puns here: sole/soul, Cupid's bows, and leaps. 40 *dun* Mercutio makes a number of puns on the word dun: the proverb "dun's the mouse" (keep quiet), dark, done, and the proverb "Dun is in the mire" (a horse is stuck in the mud).

MERCUTIO
    You are a lover. Borrow Cupid's wings
    and fly with them above an ordinary dance leap.

ROMEO
    I'm too painfully pierced with Cupid's arrow
20   to fly with his light feathers, and so bound to the ground,
    I cannot leap even an inch above dull sorrow.
    I'm sinking under love's heavy burden.

MERCUTIO
    And to sink in it would burden love.
    That's too heavy a burden for so tender a thing as
        love.

ROMEO
25   Is love a tender thing? It's too rough,
    too rude, too rowdy, and it pricks like a thorn.

MERCUTIO
    If love is rough with you, be rough with love.
    If love pricks you, prick it back, and you'll beat
        love down.
    Give me a mask to cover my face. (*Puts on a mask*)
30   A mask for an ugly face! What do I care
    if a curious eye notices my ugliness?
    The beetlelike eyebrows on this mask shall cover my
        embarrassment.

BENVOLIO
    Come, knock, and let's go in. And when we get in,
    every man is to dance.

ROMEO
35   Give me a torch. Let mischievous, light-hearted men
    dance over the floor coverings.
    I take the advice of the old proverb which says,
    "I'll be an onlooker and watch.
    It's better to quit the game while it's still fun!"

MERCUTIO
40   Nonsense, like the sheriff says, be still as a mouse.
    If you're a horse, we'll get you out of the mud,
    or if you'll excuse me, out of love where you're sticking
    up to your ears. Come on, we're burning daylight.

ROMEO
  Nay, that's not so.

MERCUTIO

45   I mean, sir, in delay
  We waste our lights in vain, like lights by day.
  Take our good meaning, for our judgment sits
  Five times in that ere once in our five wits.

ROMEO
  And we mean well in going to this mask;
50   But 'tis no wit to go.

MERCUTIO

                      Why, may one ask?

ROMEO
  I dream'd a dream to-night.

MERCUTIO

                          And so did I.

ROMEO
  Well, what was yours?

MERCUTIO

55   That dreamers often lie.

ROMEO
  In bed asleep, while they do dream things true.

MERCUTIO
  O, then, I see Queen Mab hath been with you.
  She is the fairies' midwife, and she comes
  In shape no bigger than an agate-stone
60   On the fore-finger of an alderman,
  Drawn with a team of little atomies
  Over men's noses as they lie asleep;
  Her waggon-spokes made of long spinners' legs,
  The cover of the wings of grasshoppers,
65   Her traces of the smallest spider web,
  Her collars of the moonshine's wat'ry beams,
  Her whip of cricket's bone, the lash of film,
  Her waggoner a small grey-coated gnat,

---

48 *five wits* common sense, imagination, fantasy, judgment, and reasoning.

ROMEO
>No, that's not true.

MERCUTIO
45
>I mean, sir, that by delaying,
>we waste our time in vain, like using torches by day.
>Take it as I mean it, for judgment is found
>in correct interpretation five times before its
>>found once in our five wits.

ROMEO
>We have good intentions in going to this masquerade
>>dance,
50
>but it isn't intelligent to go.

MERCUTIO
>Why, may I ask?

ROMEO
>I dreamed a dream tonight.

MERCUTIO
>And so did I.

ROMEO
>Well, what was your dream?

MERCUTIO
55
>That dreamers often lie.

ROMEO
>In bed asleep, while they dream true dreams.

MERCUTIO
>O, I see that the fairy, Queen Mab, has been with you.
>She delivers babies for the fairies, and she is
>no bigger than an agate for a ring
60
>on the forefinger of a magistrate.
>She's drawn by a team of tiny creatures
>over men's noses as they lie asleep.
>Her wagon spokes are made of long spiders' legs;
>the cover is made of the wings of grasshoppers;
65
>the harness is made of the smallest spider web;
>her steeds' collars are made of the rays of watery moonbeams;
>her whip is made of cricket's bone; the lash a
>>spider's web;
>her coachman is a small, grey-coated gnat,

70   Not half so big as a round little worm
        Prick'd from the lazy finger of a maid;
        Her chariot is an empty hazel-nut
        Made by the joiner squirrel, or old grub,
        Time out o' mind the fairies' coachmakers.
75   And in this state she gallops night by night
        Through lovers' brains, and then they dream of love;
        On courtiers' knees, that dream on curtsies straight;
        O'er lawyers' fingers, who straight dream on fees;
        O'er ladies' lips, who straight on kisses dream,
        Which oft the angry Mab with blisters plagues,
80   Because their breath with sweetmeats tainted are.
        Sometime she gallops o'er a courtier's nose,
        And then dreams he of smelling out a suit;
        And sometime comes she with a tithe-pig's tail
        Tickling a parson's nose as 'a lies asleep,
85   Then he dreams of another benefice.
        Sometime she driveth o'er a soldier's neck,
        And then dreams he of cutting foreign throats,
        Of breaches, ambuscadoes, Spanish blades,
        Of healths five fathom deep; and then anon
90   Drums in his ear, at which he starts and wakes,
        And being thus frighted swears a prayer or two
        And sleeps again. This is that very Mab
        That plats the manes of horses in the night,
        And bakes the elf-locks in foul sluttish hairs,
95   Which, once untangled, much misfortune bodes.
        This is the hag, when maids lie on their backs,
        That presses them and learns them first to bear,
        Making them women of good carriage.
        This is she—

ROMEO

100   Peace, peace, Mercutio, peace!
        Thou talk'st of nothing.

MERCUTIO

                        True, I talk of dreams,
        Which are the children of an idle brain,

69-70 *worm...maid*   maids were told that if they were lazy, worms would grow in their fingers.

not half as big as a little round worm
70   removed from the finger of a lazy maid.
Her chariot is an empty hazelnut shell
made by a squirrel, or an old worm,
who, ever since anyone could remember, have been the
        fairies' coachmakers.
In this manner she gallops night after night
75   through lovers' brains, and then they dream of love.
She travels over courtiers' knees and they dream of bowing;
over lawyers' fingers, and they dream of fees;
over ladies' lips, and they dream of kisses.
Often the testy Mab puts blisters on the ladies' lips
80   because their breaths smell of too many sweets.
Sometimes she gallops over a courtier's nose,
and then he dreams of finding someone whose cause he
        can support for a fee;
and sometimes she comes with the tail of a pig owed
        to the church
and tickles a minister's nose as he sleeps,
85   so that he dreams of being given another well-paying post.
Sometimes she drives over a soldier's neck,
and he dreams of cutting foreigners' throats,
and of invasions, ambushes, Spanish knives,
and drinking toasts from glasses thirty feet deep.
        Then soon he hears
90   drums and he awakens,
and being frightened by the noise, he says a prayer or two
and goes back to sleep. This is that same Mab
who braids the manes of horses in the night,
and tangles dirty, unkempt hair
95   which, when untangled, means terrible misfortune.
This is the hag which presses maidens down
as they lie on their backs and teaches them to bear up
so they will have good posture. This is the fairy woman—

ROMEO
100   Stop, stop, Mercutio!
You're talking nonsense.

MERCUTIO
True, I'm talking about dreams,
which are the children of an idle brain,

Begot of nothing but vain fantasy,
105   Which is as thin of substance as the air
And more inconstant than the wind, who wooes
Even now the frozen bosom of the north,
And, being anger'd, puffs away from thence,
Turning his face to the dew-dropping south.

BENVOLIO
110   This wind you talk of blows us from ourselves.
Supper is done, and we shall come too late.

ROMEO
I fear, too early; for my mind misgives
Some consequence yet hanging in the stars
Shall bitterly begin his fearful date
115   With this night's revels, and expire the term
Of a despised life clos'd in my breast
By some vile forfeit of untimely death.
But He that hath the steerage of my course
Direct my sail! On, lusty gentlemen!

BENVOLIO
120   Strike, drum.

[*They march about the stage.*]

[*Exeunt.*]

Scene v: [*A hall in Capulet's house.*] [Musicians *waiting.*] *Enter*
SERVING-MEN, *with napkins.*

1. SERVANT
Where's Potpan, that he helps not to take away? He shift a
trencher! He scrape a trencher!

2. SERVANT
When good manners shall lie all in one or two men's hands,
and they unwash'd too, 'tis a foul thing.

1. SERVANT
5   Away with the joint-stools, remove the court-cupboard, look

born from nothing but an empty fantasy.
105   Dreams are as thin as the air
and more likely to change than the wind, who is wooing
the frozen heart of the north right now,
and, becoming angry, he puffs away from the north,
turning his face to the rainy south.

BENVOLIO

110   This wind you are talking about blows us away from
      our purpose.
The banquet is about over, and we'll get there too late.

ROMEO

I am afraid we're too early, for I'm afraid
that some unpleasant events, still only destined to happen
will bitterly begin
115   at this party tonight and bring to an end
this hateful life of mine
by some terrible, untimely death.
But God, who steers my life's course,
will give my sail direction. Let's go, merry
      gentlemen!

BENVOLIO

120   Beat your drums.
    They march about the stage and then leave.

*Act I, Scene v: A hall in Capulet's house. Enter servingmen, with
napkins. (Musicians waiting.)*

FIRST SERVANT

Where's Potpan? He's not helping us take the plates
    away. He carries a
wooden platter! He scrapes a wooden plate!

SECOND SERVANT

When household manners rest in the hands of only one
    or two people—
and their hands dirty at that—it's disgusting.

FIRST SERVANT

· 5   Take these folding stools away, remove the sideboard,
    .watch

to the plate. Good thou, save me a piece of marchpane; and, as thou loves me, let the porter let in Susan Grindstone and Nell. Antony and Potpan!

2. SERVANT
Ay, boy, ready.

1. SERVANT
10   You are look'd for and call'd for, ask'd for and sought for, in the great chamber.

3. SERVANT
We cannot be here and there too. Cheerly, boys; be brisk a while, and the longer liver take all.   [*They retire.*]

Enter [CAPULET, *with* JULIET, TYBALT, *and others of his house, meeting*] *the* Guests, ROMEO, *and other* Maskers.

CAPULET
Welcome, gentlemen! Ladies that have their toes
15   Unplagu'd with corns will walk a bout with you.
Ah, my mistresses, which of you all
Will now deny to dance? She that makes dainty,
She, I'll swear, hath corns. Am I come near ye now?
Welcome, gentlemen! I have seen the day
20   That I have worn a visor and could tell
A whispering tale in a fair lady's ear,
Such as would please; 'tis gone, 'tis gone, 'tis gone.
You are welcome, gentlemen! Come, musicians, play.

        [*Music plays, and they dance.*]

A hall, a hall! give room! and foot it, girls.
25   More light, you knaves; and turn the tables up,
And quench the fire, the room is grown too hot.
Ah, sirrah, this unlook'd-for sport comes well.
Nay, sit, nay, sit, good cousin Capulet,
For you and I are past our dancing days.
30   How long is't now since last yourself and I
Were in a mask?

    2. CAPULET

            By'r lady, thirty years.

---

27 *sirrah*   was a term used to address someone socially or (as an intentional put-down) mentally inferior. 27 *unlook'd...well* in Shakespeare's day, party hosts considered themselves honored when uninvited quests appeared.

the silverware. Save me a piece of marzipan, and
if you're really a friend, tell the doorman to let in
   Susan Grindstone and
Nell (for our own party). Antony and Potpan!

SECOND SERVANT
   Yes, boy, get ready.
      Enter THIRD SERVANT.

FIRST SERVANT (*to Third Servant*)
10   We've looked for you, called for you, and searched for you
    in the dance hall.

THIRD SERVANT
   We can't be here and there, too. Be cheerful,
   boys, and be quick. To the one who lives longest go the spoils!
      They exit.
     Enter CAPULET *with* JULIET, TYBALT, *and others*
      of his house to greet the guests, ROMEO *and others in disguise.*

CAPULET
   Welcome, gentlemen! Those ladies who don't have
15   corns on their toes will dance with you.
   Ah, dear ladies, which of you
   will now refuse to dance? If you hesitate,
   I'll swear you have corns. Did any of you think that joke hit home?
   Welcome, gentlemen! I remember the time,
20   when I too wore a mask and
   whispered sweet nothings in a beautiful lady's ear
   to please her. That's all in the past now, long gone!
   You are welcome, gentlemen! Come, musicians, play.
      Music plays and they dance.
   Clear the hall! Make room! Dance, girls!
25   Give us more light, you rascals, and get the tables out of the way.
   Put out the fire—the room has grown too hot.
   Ah, sir, these party-crashers are welcome.
   No, sit down, my good relative Capulet,
   for you and I are past our dancing days.
30   How long has it been since you and I
   wore a mask?

SECOND CAPULET
   I swear, it's been thirty years.

CAPULET
What, man! 'tis not so much, 'tis not so much.
'Tis since the nuptial of Lucentio,
35   Come Pentecost as quickly as it will,
Some five and twenty years; and then we mask'd.

2. CAPULET
'Tis more, 'tis more. His son is elder, sir;
His son is thirty.

CAPULET
                    Will you tell me that?
40   His son was but a ward two years ago.

ROMEO
[*To a Serving-man.*]
What lady's that which doth enrich the hand
Of yonder knight?

SERVANT
I know not, sir.

ROMEO
O, she doth teach the torches to burn bright!
45   It seems she hangs upon the cheek of night
As a rich jewel in an Ethiop's ear;
Beauty too rich for use, for earth too dear!
So shows a snowy dove trooping with crows,
As yonder lady o'er her fellows shows.
50   The measure done, I'll watch her place of stand,
And, touching hers, make blessed my rude hand.
Did my heart love till now? Forswear it, sight!
For I ne'er saw true beauty till this night.

TYBALT
This, by his voice, should be a Montague.
55   Fetch me my rapier, boy. What dares the slave
Come hither, cover'd with an antic face,
To fleer and scorn at our solemnity?
Now, by the stock and honour of my kin,
To strike him dead I hold it not a sin.

CAPULET
>What, it can't be that long, not that long!
>It was last at the wedding of Lucentio,
35 >around Pentecost, whenever that comes,
>some twenty-five years ago that we wore masks.

SECOND CAPULET
>No, longer, it was longer ago than that! Lucentio's
>>son is older, sir.
>His son is thirty.

CAPULET
>How can you say that?
40 >His son was still a minor just two years ago.

ROMEO (*to Servant*)
>Who is the lady who graces the hand
>of that gentleman over there?

SERVANT
>I don't know, sir.

ROMEO
>O, she teaches the torches to burn brightly!
45 >She hangs upon the face of night
>like a rich jewel in an Ethopian's ear—
>her beauty is too rich to be touched, too heavenly
>>for this earth!
>She looks like a snow-white dove dancing among crows,
>she is so much more beautiful than the other
>>ladies.
50 >When this dance is over, I'll see where she stands,
>and I'll make my coarse hand blessed by touching
>>her hand.
>Did I ever love anyone before now? My eyes will
>>swear
>that I never saw real beauty until tonight.

TYBALT (*overhearing Romeo*)
>That man has the voice of a Montague.
55 >Get me my sword, boy. How dare this low-life
>come here, disguised by a comic mask,
>to mock and scorn our banquet?
>Now by my family's good name and reputation,
>I wouldn't hold it a sin to kill him.

CAPULET
60   Why, how now, kinsman! wherefore storm you so?

TYBALT
Uncle, this is a Montague, our foe,
A villain that is hither come in spite
To scorn at our solemnity this night.

CAPULET
Young Romeo is it?

TYBALT
65   'Tis he, that villain Romeo.

CAPULET
Content thee, gentle coz, let him alone,
'A bears him like a portly gentleman;
And, to say truth, Verona brags of him
To be a virtuous and well-govern'd youth.
70   I would not for the wealth of all this town
Here in my house do him disparagement;
Therefore be patient, take no note of him;
It is my will, the which if thou respect,
Show a fair presence and put off these frowns,
75   An ill-beseeming semblance for a feast.

TYBALT
It fits, when such a villain is a guest.
I'll not endure him.

CAPULET
He shall be endur'd.
What, goodman boy! I say he shall; go to!
80   Am I the master here, or you? Go to!
You'll not endure him! God shall mend my soul!
You'll make a mutiny among my guests!
You will set cock-a-hoop! You'll be the man!

TYBALT
Why, uncle, 'tis a shame.

CAPULET
85   Go to, go to;

CAPULET

60   What's wrong, nephew? Why are you so angry?

TYBALT

Uncle, that man is a Montague, our enemy.
He's a villain who has come in hatred
to mock our banquet tonight.

CAPULET

That is young Romeo, isn't it?

TYBALT

65   Yes, it is the villain Romeo.

CAPULET

Calm down, gentle nephew, leave him alone.
He carries himself like a dignified gentleman,
and to tell the truth, Verona's citizens say
that he is a good, well-mannered youth.

70   I would not for all the riches in this town
harm him here in my house.
Be patient and pay no attention to him.
Those are my wishes, which if you'll respect,
you'll put on a cheery face and stop frowning.

75   Your frowns aren't proper at a feast.

TYBALT

My frowns are fitting when you have a villain for a
    guest.
I will not tolerate his presence.

CAPULET

You will tolerate him!
What do you mean, boy? I say he shall stay! Be off!

80   Am I the master here, or are you? Be off!
You'll not stand him? By heaven!
You'll disturb the guests!
You'll bring about a riot! You'll play the big hero!

TYBALT

Uncle, this is a disgrace to us.

CAPULET

85   Enough, enough!

You are a saucy boy. Is't so, indeed?
This trick may chance to scathe you; I know what.
You must contrary me! Marry, 'tis time.—
Well said, my hearts!—You are a princox; go;
90   Be quiet, or—More light, more light!—for shame!
I'll make you quiet.—What, cheerly, my hearts!

TYBALT

Patience perforce with wilful choler meeting
Makes my flesh tremble in their different greeting.
I will withdraw; but this intrusion shall
95   Now seeming sweet convert to bitt'rest gall.
    [*Exit.*]

ROMEO

[*To Juliet.*] If I profane with my unworthiest hand
    This holy shrine, the gentle fine is this:
My lips, two blushing pilgrims, ready stand
    To smooth that rough touch with a tender kiss.

JULIET

100   Good pilgrim, you do wrong your hand too much,
    Which mannerly devotion shows in this;
For saints have hands that pilgrims' hands do touch,
    And palm to palm is holy palmers' kiss.

ROMEO

Have not saints lips, and holy palmers too?

JULIET

105   Ay, pilgrim, lips that they must use in prayer.

ROMEO

O, then, dear saint, let lips do what hands do;
They pray, grant thou, lest faith turn to despair.

JULIET

Saints do not move, though grant for prayers' sake.

ROMEO

Then move not while my prayer's effect I take.
110   Thus from my lips, by thine, my sin is purg'd.
    [*Kissing her.*]

---

97 *holy shrine*   Romeo is referring to Juliet. Some scholars think Romeo is disguised as a pilgrim.

You're a rude boy, aren't you? So this is the way it is?
This suggestion of yours may just hurt you. I know
    what's behind this.
You are compelled to contradict me. I swear it's time—
(*To the dancers*) Well done, friends.—(*To
    Tybalt*) You are impertinent—Go away!
90   Be quiet, or—(*To servants*) More light, give us
    more light! (*To Tybalt*) Shame on you!
I'll shut you up.—(*To dancers*) Have fun, friends.

TYBALT
    The clash of forced self-control when it meets with anger
    makes me shake from the different emotions.
    I'll leave, but Romeo's intrusion,
95   which now seems sweet, will be bitterly regretted.

ROMEO (*to Juliet*)
    If I abuse with my unworthy hand
        your holy shrine, here's the fine I'll pay:
    that my lips, like two blushing pilgrims, stand ready
        to smooth away my rough touch with a tender kiss.

JULIET
100   Good pilgrim, your hands are not rough as you say.
        The touch of your hand is sufficient devotion.
    Even saints greet pilgrims by touching hands,
        and holding hands is the pilgrim's greeting.

ROMEO
    Don't saints have lips, and religious pilgrims, too?

JULIET
105   Yes, pilgrim. They have lips which they use to pray.

ROMEO
    O, then, dear saint, let lips touch as hands do.
    Lips pray, you know, so faith won't turn to despair.

JULIET
    Saints do not usually take action, though they may
        grant favors prayed for.

ROMEO
    Then don't move while I receive what I prayed for.
110   My lips, by yours, will be cleansed of sin.
        He kisses her.

JULIET
Then have my lips the sin that they have took.

ROMEO
Sin from my lips? O trespass sweetly urg'd!
Give me my sin again.
  [*Kissing her again.*]

JULIET
                    You kiss by the book.

NURSE
115   Madam, your mother craves a word with you.

ROMEO
What is her mother?

NURSE
                    Marry, bachelor,
Her mother is the lady of the house,
And a good lady, and a wise and virtuous.
120   I nurs'd her daughter, that you talk'd withal;
I tell you, he that can lay hold of her
Shall have the chinks.

ROMEO
                    Is she a Capulet?
O dear account! my life is my foe's debt.

BENVOLIO
125   Away, be gone; the sport is at the best.

ROMEO
Ay, so I fear; the more is my unrest.

CAPULET
Nay, gentlemen, prepare not to be gone;
We have a trifling foolish banquet towards.
Is it e'en so? Why, then, I thank you all;
130   I thank you, honest gentlemen; good-night.
More torches here! Come on then, let's to bed.
Ah, sirrah, by my fay, it waxes late;
I'll to my rest.
  [*All but Juliet and Nurse begin to go out.*]

JULIET

Now my lips have taken on your sin.

ROMEO

Sin from my lips? That is a sin that is sweetly
    suggested.

Give me my sin again.

    He kisses her again.

JULIET

You kiss as though you researched the subject.

NURSE

115   Madam, your mother wants to speak with you.

ROMEO

Who is her mother?

NURSE

Why, bachelor,

her mother is the lady of this house.

And she is a good lady, as well as being wise and virtuous.

120   I nursed her daughter with whom you spoke.

I tell you, the man who can marry her

will have a lot of money.

ROMEO

Is she a Capulet?

What a costly account! My life is at the mercy of my enemy.

BENVOLIO

125   Let's go. The party is over.

ROMEO

Yes, I'm afraid so; I am worried.

CAPULET

No, gentlemen, don't go.

There's still a modest feast to come.

(*They whisper in his ear*) Is that so? Well then,
    thank you.

130   Thanks to all of you honest gentlemen. Good night.

Bring more torches here! (*Maskers leave.*) Come
    on then, let's go to bed.

Ah, sir, by my faith, it's late.

I'll go to bed.

    All but JULIET *and the* NURSE *leave.*

JULIET
Come hither, nurse. What is yond gentleman?

NURSE
135   The son and heir of old Tiberio.

JULIET
What's he that now is going out of door?

NURSE
Marry, that, I think, be young Petruchio.

JULIET
What's he that follows here, that would not dance?

NURSE
I know not.

JULIET
140   Go, ask his name.—If he be married,
My grave is like to be my wedding-bed.

NURSE
His name is Romeo, and a Montague;
The only son of your great enemy.

JULIET
My only love sprung from my only hate!
145   Too early seen unknown, and known too late!
Prodigious birth of love it is to me
That I must love a loathed enemy.

NURSE
What's this? what's this?

JULIET
                    A rhyme I learn'd even now
150   Of one I danc'd withal.
            [*One calls within,* "Juliet."]

NURSE
                    Anon, anon!
Come, let's away; the strangers all are gone.
            [*Exeunt.*]

JULIET
Come here, nurse. Who is that gentleman?

NURSE
135   The son and heir of old Tiberio.

JULIET
Who is that going out the door now?

NURSE
Indeed, I think that's young Petruchio.

JULIET
Who is the one who is following behind—the one who
would not dance?

NURSE
I don't know.

JULIET
140   Go and ask what his name is. (*To herself*) If he
is married,
my grave will probably be my wedding bed.

NURSE (*leaves and then returns*)
His name is Romeo, Romeo Montague.
He's the only son of your great enemy.

JULIET
My only love springs from my only hate!
145   I saw him too early when I didn't know him, and now
I realize who he is too late!
This is a horrible beginning to love
that I must love a hated enemy.

NURSE
What is this? What are you saying?

JULIET
A rhyme I just learned from someone
150   I just danced with.
            Someone calls Juliet's name from offstage.

NURSE
We're coming!
Come, let's go; the strangers are all gone.
            They exit.

Act II: [*Prologue.*] *Enter* CHORUS.

CHORUS.
    Now old Desire doth in his death-bed lie,
      And young Affection gapes to be his heir;
    That fair for which love groan'd for and would die,
      With tender Juliet match'd is now not fair.
5   Now Romeo is belov'd and loves again,
      Alike bewitched by the charm of looks,
    But to his foe suppos'd he must complain,
      And she steal love's sweet bait from fearful hooks.
    Being held a foe, he may not have access
10   To breathe such vows as lovers use to swear;
    And she as much in love, her means much less
      To meet her new-beloved anywhere.
    But passion lends them power, time means, to meet,
    Temp'ring extremities with extreme sweet.
      [*Exit.*]

Scene i: [*A lane by the wall of Capulet's orchard.*] *Enter*
ROMEO, *alone.*

ROMEO
    Can I go forward when my heart is here?
    Turn back, dull earth, and find thy centre out.
      [*He climbs the wall, and leaps down within it.*]
      Enter BENVOLIO *with* MERCUTIO.

BENVOLIO
    Romeo! my cousin Romeo!

MERCUTIO
                       He is wise;
5   And, on my life, hath stol'n him home to bed.

BENVOLIO
    He ran this way, and leap'd this orchard wall.
    Call, good Mercutio.

Act II: Prologue, enter CHORUS.

CHORUS.
Romeo's old love for Rosaline is now dead,
　and a new love eagerly hopes to win his heart.
That beauty for whom he groaned and wanted to die
　is now no longer beautiful, compared with Juliet.
5　Romeo is loved and he loves again.
　Both have been bewitched by the charm of beauty.
To Juliet, his supposed enemy, he must plead,
　and she must steal love's tempting bait from
　　terrifying hooks.
Since he is considered an enemy, he may not be able
10　to use the vows that lovers typically swear.
Juliet, just as deeply in love, has even fewer means
　to meet her new beloved anywhere.
However, love gives them power, time gives them the
　means to meet,
and their great problems are softened by great
　sweetness.
　　　Exit.

Act II, Scene i: A lane by the wall of Capulet's orchard. ROMEO
enters alone.

ROMEO
How can I leave when my heart is here?
I'll go back and find my heart's delight.
　　He climbs on the wall, then leaps over it.
　　Enter BENVOLIO *and* MERCUTIO.

BENVOLIO
Romeo! My cousin Romeo!

MERCUTIO
He's smart,
5　so I'll bet on my life that he sneaked home to bed.

BENVOLIO
No, he ran this way and jumped over this orchard wall.
Call him, Mercutio.

MERCUTIO

                            Nay, I'll conjure too.
Romeo! humours! madman! passion! lover!
10   Appear thou in the likeness of a sigh!
Speak but one rhyme, and I am satisfied;
Cry but "Ay me!" pronounce but "love" and "dove";
Speak to my gossip Venus one fair word,
One nick-name for her purblind son and heir,
15   Young Adam Cupid, he that shot so trim,
When King Cophetua lov'd the beggar-maid!
He heareth not, he stirreth not, he moveth not;
The ape is dead, and I must conjure him.
I conjure thee by Rosaline's bright eyes,
20   By her high forehead and her scarlet lip,
By her fine foot, straight leg, and quivering thigh,
And the demesnes that there adjacent lie,
That in thy likeness thou appear to us!

BENVOLIO

An if he hear thee, thou wilt anger him.

MERCUTIO

25   This cannot anger him; 'twould anger him
To raise a spirit in his mistress' circle,
Of some strange nature, letting it there stand
Till she had laid it and conjur'd it down.
That were some spite; my invocation
30   Is fair and honest; in his mistress' name
I conjure only but to raise up him.

BENVOLIO

Come, he hath hid himself among these trees
To be consorted with the humorous night.
Blind is his love and best befits the dark.

MERCUTIO

35   If Love be blind, Love cannot hit the mark.
Now will he sit under a medlar tree
And wish his mistress were that kind of fruit
As maids call medlars, when they laugh alone.

---

13 *Venus*   Venus is the Roman goddess of love. Cupid is her son who shoots love's arrows into the breasts of humans to make them fall in love.   15 *Adam*   Adam is believed to be Adam Bell, a famous archer in old ballads.   16 *King Cophetua*   a reference to the old ballad "King Ophetus and the Beggar-Maid."   18 *ape*   Mercutio compares Romeo to a trained

MERCUTIO

No, I'll conjure him up with an incantation.
Romeo! Moody madman! Passionate lover!
10   Appear to us in the form of a sigh!
Give us just one couplet and I'll be satisfied.
Simply exclaim, "Oh, me!" Just say "love" and "dove."
Say one fair word to my friend Venus,
just one nickname for her totally blind son and heir,
15   young Adam Cupid. He's the one who shot so well
causing King Cophetua to love the beggar maid.
He doesn't hear, he doesn't stir, he doesn't move.
The poor fellow is playing dead and I must conjure him up.
I invoke you by Rosaline's bright eyes,
20   by her high forehead and her red lips,
by her fine foot, straight leg, and quivering thigh,
and the regions that lie nearby:
appear to us as yourself!

BENVOLIO

If he hears you, he'll be angry.

MERCUTIO

25   That speech can't anger him. It would anger him
to conjure up a spirit of some strange kind
in his lady love's circle and let it stand there until she conjured it down.
That would make him mad. My invocation
30   is proper and respectable—in his lady love's name,
I conjure only to raise him up.

BENVOLIO

Come on, he has hidden among these trees
so he can melt into the damp night.
His love is blind, and that best suits the dark.

MERCUTIO

35   If love is blind, love cannot hit its target.
Now he'll sit under an apple tree
and wish his lady love were that kind of fruit
that girls call apples when they're in private.

---

ape that plays dead until the trainer gives the command to sit up.   **26-28** *circle...down*   Mercutio's metaphor has a second, sexual meaning, as does the rest of this speech.   **38** *medlars*   an apple-like fruit. Medlars and pears were also vulgar terms for sexual organs in Shakespeare's day.

O, Romeo, that she were, O, that she were
40   An open *et cetera*, thou a poperin pear!
Romeo, good-night; I'll to my truckle-bed;
This field-bed is too cold for me to sleep.
Come, shall we go?

BENVOLIO
                    Go, then; for 'tis in vain
45   To seek him here that means not to be found.
        [*Exeunt* BENVOLIO *and* MERCUTIO].

Scene ii: [*Capulet's orchard.* ROMEO *advances from the wall.*]

ROMEO
He jests at scars that never felt a wound.
        [*Juliet appears above at her window.*]
But, soft! what light through yonder window breaks?
It is the east, and Juliet is the sun.
Arise, fair sun, and kill the envious moon,
5   Who is already sick and pale with grief
That thou, her maid, art far more fair than she.
Be not her maid, since she is envious;
Her vestal livery is but sick and green,
And none but fools do wear it; cast it off.
10   It is my lady, O, it is my love!
O, that she knew she were!
She speaks, yet she says nothing; what of that?
Her eye discourses; I will answer it.—
I am too bold, 'tis not to me she speaks.
15   Two of the fairest stars in all the heaven,
Having some business, do entreat her eyes
To twinkle in their spheres till they return.
What if her eyes were there, they in her head?
The brightness of her cheek would shame those stars,
20   As daylight doth a lamp; her eyes in heaven
Would through the airy region stream so bright
That birds would sing and think it were not night.

---

41 *truckle-bed* (trundle bed) is pushed under a regular bed when not in use. Children slept on this kind of bed. Mercutio is saying he will play the innocent and wash his hands of Romeo. 6 *she* Romeo is referring to the Roman moon goddess, Diana, in this speech. Diana demanded that her female followers remain chaste.

O, Romeo, if only she were that, if she just were
40   an open unmentionable and you a pear.
Romeo, good night. I'm going to my trundle bed.
This ground is too cold for me to sleep on.
Come on, shall we leave?

BENVOLIO
Go on, then. It's useless
45   to look for him when he does not want to be found.
    BENVOLIO *and* MERCUTIO *exit.*

Act II, Scene ii: Capulet's orchard. ROMEO *comes from the wall, just having overheard* MERCUTIO *and* BENVOLIO'S *conversation.*

ROMEO
Mercutio makes fun of scars because he's never felt pain.
    JULIET *appears at her upstairs window, and*
        ROMEO *sees her.*
But wait! What light is coming from that window?
It is the eastern light and Juliet is the sun.
Rise up, beautiful sun, and make the jealous moon invisible.
5   The moon is already sick and pale with grief
because you, Juliet, are more beautiful than she is.
Don't become one of her virgin followers because she is jealous;
her virginity is sickly and anemic.
Only fools wear the uniform of virginity; take off
    that uniform.
10   There stands my lady; O, she is my love!
If only she could know she was my beloved.
She speaks, yet she says nothing. What does that matter?
Her eyes speak; I'll answer them.
I'm being too confident; she's not speaking to me.
15   Two of the most beautiful stars in all the heavens
beg her eyes
to twinkle in their orbits while they are gone.
What if her eyes were in the heavens, and the stars
    in her head?
The brightness of her cheek would shame those stars,
20   as daylight shames a lamp. If her eyes were stars,
the heavens would shine so brightly
that the birds would sing because they would think
    it was day.

See, how she leans her cheek upon her hand!
O, that I were a glove upon that hand,
25   That I might touch that cheek!

JULIET

Ay me!

ROMEO

She speaks!
O, speak again, bright angel! for thou art
As glorious to this night, being o'er my head,
30   As a winged messenger of heaven
Unto the white-upturned wond'ring eyes
Of mortals that fall back to gaze on him
When he bestrides the lazy-pacing clouds
And sails upon the bosom of the air.

JULIET

35   O Romeo, Romeo! wherefore art thou Romeo?
Deny thy father and refuse thy name;
Or, if thou wilt not, be but sworn my love,
And I'll no longer be a Capulet.

ROMEO

[*Aside.*] Shall I hear more, or shall I speak at this?

JULIET

40   'Tis but thy name that is my enemy;
Thou art thyself, though not a Montague.
What's Montague? It is nor hand, nor foot,
Nor arm, nor face, nor any other part
Belonging to a man. O, be some other name!
45   What's in a name? That which we call a rose
By any other word would smell as sweet;
So Romeo would, were he not Romeo call'd,
Retain that dear perfection which he owes
Without that title. Romeo, doff thy name,
50   And for thy name, which is no part of thee,
Take all myself.

See how she leans her cheek on her hand!
I wish I were a glove on her hand
25   so that I could touch her cheek.

JULIET
    Alas!

ROMEO
    She is speaking!
    O, speak again, bright angel, for you,
    up there above my head, are as glorious to the night
30   as is an angel of heaven
    to the white, upturned, wondering eyes
    of humans who stand back to gaze on him
    when he rides upon the slow-moving clouds
    and sails through the air.

JULIET
35   Romeo! Romeo! Why are you, Romeo?
    Reject your father and refuse his name.
    Or if you will not, just swear to be my love, and I
    will no longer be a Capulet.

ROMEO (*to himself*)
    Shall I listen to her any longer, or shall I speak
      to her?

JULIET
40   Not you, but only your family name is my enemy.
    You would be Romeo even if you were not a Montague.
    What is a Montague? It's not a hand or a foot,
    an arm or a face, or any other part
    of a man's body. O, take some other name!
45   What's in a name? The thing which we call a rose
    would smell just as sweet if it had any other name.
    So Romeo—even if he weren't called Romeo—
    would be just as perfect
    without his name. Romeo, get rid of your name,
50   and in place of that name, which isn't part of you,
    take me.

ROMEO

I take thee at thy word.
Call me but love, and I'll be new baptiz'd;
Henceforth I never will be Romeo.

JULIET

55 What man art thou that thus bescreen'd in night
So stumblest on my counsel?

ROMEO

By a name
I know not how to tell thee who I am.
My name, dear saint, is hateful to myself,
60 Because it is an enemy to thee;
Had I it written, I would tear the word.

JULIET

My ears have yet not drunk a hundred words
Of thy tongue's uttering, yet I know the sound.
Art thou not Romeo, and a Montague?

ROMEO

65 Neither, fair maid, if either thee dislike.

JULIET

How cam'st thou hither, tell me, and wherefore?
The orchard walls are high and hard to climb,
And the place death, considering who thou art,
If any of my kinsmen find thee here.

ROMEO

70 With love's light wings did I o'erperch these walls;
For stony limits cannot hold love out,
And what love can do, that dares love attempt.
Therefore thy kinsmen are no stop to me.

JULIET

If they do see thee, they will murder thee.

ROMEO

75 Alack, there lies more peril in thine eye
Than twenty of their swords! Look thou but sweet,
And I am proof against their enmity.

ROMEO

    I'll take you at your word.

    If you'll call me love, I'll be christened again
       to get a new name

    and never again be called Romeo.

JULIET

55   Who is that, hiding there in the dark,

    who is eavesdropping on my private thoughts?

ROMEO

    If I have to use a name,

    I don't know how to tell you who I am.

    My name, dear saint, is hateful to me

60   because it's the name of your enemy.

    If I had written it down, I'd tear up the word.

JULIET

    I have not listened to even a hundred words

    that you've spoken, but I recognize your voice.

    Aren't you Romeo—and a Montague?

ROMEO

65   Neither one, beautiful maiden, if you dislike either.

JULIET

    How did you get here? Tell me. And why?

    The orchard walls are high and hard to climb,

    and this is a place of death to you—considering who
       you are—

    if any of my relatives should find you here.

ROMEO

70   I flew over the walls on the wings of love;

    those strong walls can't keep love out,

    and whatever love can do, love will try.

    Therefore, your relatives can't keep me out.

JULIET

    If they see you, they'll murder you.

ROMEO

75   I see more danger in your eyes

    than in twenty of their swords. If you just look
       sweetly at me,

    I'm protected from their hatred.

JULIET
I would not for the world they saw thee here.

ROMEO
I have night's cloak to hide me from their eyes;
80   And but thou love me, let them find me here.
My life were better ended by their hate,
Than death prorogued, wanting of thy love.

JULIET
By whose direction found'st thou out this place?

ROMEO
By Love, that first did prompt me to inquire;
85   He lent me counsel and I lent him eyes.
I am no pilot; yet, wert thou as far
As that vast shore wash'd with the farthest sea,
I should adventure for such merchandise.

JULIET
Thou know'st the mask of night is on my face,
90   Else would a maiden blush bepaint my cheek
For that which thou hast heard me speak to-night.
Fain would I dwell on form, fain, fain deny
What I have spoke; but farewell compliment!
Dost thou love me? I know thou wilt say "Ay,"
95   And I will take thy word; yet, if thou swear'st,
Thou mayst prove false. At lovers' perjuries,
They say, Jove laughs. O gentle Romeo,
If thou dost love, pronounce it faithfully;
Or if thou think'st I am too quickly won,
100   I'll frown and be perverse and say thee nay,—
So thou wilt woo; but else, not for the world.
In truth, fair Montague, I am too fond,
And therefore thou mayst think my 'haviour light;
But trust me, gentleman, I'll prove more true
105   Than those that have more cunning to be strange.
I should have been more strange, I must confess,
But that thou overheard'st, ere I was ware,
My true love's passion; therefore pardon me,

JULIET
    I would not have them find you here for anything in
        the world.

ROMEO
    The dark night will hide me from their eyes,
80 and if you don't love me, I wish they would find me here.
    It would be better to be killed by their hate,
    than have my death postponed without your love.

JULIET
    Who told you how to get here?

ROMEO
    Love led me, love who first made me wonder which
        way to go.
85 Love gave me advice and I listened.
    I am no ship's pilot, but if you were as far away as
    the most distant land on the most distant sea,
    I'd risk a voyage there to find you.

JULIET
    If the dark didn't hide my face,
90 you'd see that I am blushing
    because of what you've heard me say tonight.
    I'd gladly stand on formalities—gladly, gladly deny
    what you heard me say—but goodbye to proprieties.
    Do you love me? I know you'll say "yes."
95 And I'll believe you. Yet, even if you swear,
    you could turn out to be a liar. They say even Jove
    laughs at the false oaths of lovers! O, gentle Romeo,
    if you love me, honestly admit it.
    Or if you think I am too quickly won by you,
100 I'll frown and be grouchy and say "no,"
    so you'll have to court me; but otherwise I wouldn't
        snub you for any reason.
    To tell the truth, handsome Montague, I'm too fond of you.
    Therefore, you may think my behavior is immodest.
    But trust me, gentle sir, I'll be truer
105 than those who act more clever and pretend coolness.
    I would have been more coy, I must admit,
    but you overheard me before I knew you were here,
    my true love. Please forgive me,

And not impute this yielding to light love,
110   Which the dark night hath so discovered.

ROMEO
Lady, by yonder blessed moon I vow
That tips with silver all these fruit-tree tops—

JULIET
O, swear not by the moon, the inconstant moon,
That monthly changes in her circled orb,
115   Lest that thy love prove likewise variable.

ROMEO
What shall I swear by?

JULIET
Do not swear at all;
Or if thou wilt, swear by thy gracious self,
Which is the god of my idolatry,
120   And I'll believe thee.

ROMEO
If my heart's dear love—

JULIET
Well, do not swear. Although I joy in thee,
I have no joy of this contract to-night;
It is too rash, too unadvis'd, too sudden,
125   Too like the lightning, which doth cease to be
Ere one can say it lightens. Sweet, good-night!
This bud of love, by summer's ripening breath,
May prove a beauteous flower when next we meet.
Good-night, good-night! as sweet repose and rest
130   Come to thy heart as that within my breast!

ROMEO
O, wilt thou leave me so unsatisfied?

JULIET
What satisfaction canst thou have to-night?

ROMEO
Th' exchange of thy love's faithful vow for mine.

and don't think that I fell for you because of a
shallow love
110   which the dark night has revealed.

ROMEO
Lady, I swear by the blessed moon
that gives a silver light to the tops of these fruit trees—

JULIET
O, don't swear by the moon, the fickle moon
that changes monthly in her circular orbit,
115   for fear that your love should prove equally changeable.

ROMEO
What shall I swear by?

JULIET
Don't swear at all;
or, if you have to swear, swear by your gracious self.
You're the god I worship,
120   and I'll believe you.

ROMEO
If my heart's dear love—

JULIET
Well, don't swear. I'm delighted by you,
but I'm not delighted by our pledges tonight.
Our love is too rash, too unadvised, too sudden,
125   too like the lightning which has faded
before you can even say, "It's lightning." Good
    night, my sweet!
Our bud of love, ripened by summer's breath,
may have turned into a beautiful flower by the next
    time we meet.
Good night, good night. May sweet rest and peace
130   come to your heart the way it lies within my breast!

ROMEO
Will you leave me so unsatisfied?

JULIET
What satisfaction can you want tonight?

ROMEO
I want you to exchange love's faithful vows with me.

JULIET

I gave thee mine before thou didst request it;
135   And yet I would it were to give again.

ROMEO

Wouldst thou withdraw it? For what purpose, love?

JULIET

But to be frank, and give it thee again.
And yet I wish but for the thing I have.
My bounty is as boundless as the sea,
140   My love as deep; the more I give to thee,
The more I have, for both are infinite.
        [*Nurse calls within.*]
I hear some noise within; dear love, adieu!
Anon, good nurse! Sweet Montague, be true.
Stay but a little, I will come again.

        [*Exit, above.*]

ROMEO

145   O blessed, blessed night! I am afeard,
Being in night, all this is but a dream,
Too flattering-sweet to be substantial.

        [*Re-enter* JULIET, *above.*]

JULIET

Three words, dear Romeo, and good-night indeed.
If that thy bent of love be honourable,
150   Thy purpose marriage, send me word to-morrow,
By one that I'll procure to come to thee,
Where and what time thou wilt perform the rite;
And all my fortunes at thy foot I'll lay
And follow thee my lord throughout the world.

NURSE

155   (*Within.*) Madam!

JULIET

I come, anon.—But if thou mean'st not well,
I do beseech thee—

JULIET
    I gave you my vow of love before you even asked for it.
135   I wish I could give it again.

ROMEO
    Would you take back your vow of love? Why, my love?

JULIET
    So I can be generous and give it to you again.
    Yet I don't want anything but your love, and I have that.
    My desire to give you love is as broad as the sea,
140   and just as deep; the more love I give you,
    the more I have to give because my love is infinite.
         The NURSE *calls from within.*
    I hear a noise inside. Dear love, goodbye!
    (*To Nurse*) I'm coming, good nurse.—(*To Romeo*)
      Sweet Montague, be true to me.
    Stay here just a little while, and I'll be back.
        JULIET *exits.*

ROMEO
145   O blessed, blessed night! I'm afraid,
    since it is night, that this is all a dream,
    too flattering and sweet to be real.
        Re-enter JULIET *on the balcony.*

JULIET
    Just a few more words, dear Romeo, and then it's
      definitely good night.
    If your love is honorable,
150   and you want to marry me, send me word tomorrow
    by someone I'll send to you.
    Tell me where and what time the wedding will be,
    and I'll lay all my wealth at your feet
    and follow you as my husband anywhere.

NURSE (*calling*)
155   Madam!

JULIET (*to Nurse*)
    I am coming right now.—(*To Romeo*) But if you
      don't have honest intentions,
      I beg you—

NURSE
   (*Within*.) Madam!

JULIET

                    By and by, I come:—
160   To cease thy suit, and leave me to my grief.
       To-morrow will I send.

ROMEO

                    So thrive my soul—

JULIET
       A thousand times good-night!

          [*Exit above*].

ROMEO
       A thousand times the worse, to want thy light.
165   Love goes toward love, as schoolboys from their books,
       But love from love, toward school with heavy looks.

          [*Retiring*.]
          Re-enter JULIET, *above*.

JULIET
       Hist! Romeo, hist! O, for a falconer's voice,
       To lure this tassel-gentle back again!
       Bondage is hoarse, and may not speak aloud;
170   Else would I tear the cave where Echo lies,
       And make her airy tongue more hoarse than mine,
       With repetition of my Romeo's name.
       Romeo!

ROMEO
       It is my soul, that calls upon my name.
175   How silver-sweet sound lovers' tongues by night,
       Like softest music to attending ears!

JULIET
       Romeo!

ROMEO
                    My dear?

---

170 *Echo* was a Greek nymph who fell in love with Narcissus. She pursued him with cries
until she hid for shame in a cave. There she wasted away until only her voice was left.

NURSE (*calling*)
   Madam!

JULIET (*to Nurse*)
   Immediately! I'm coming!
160   (*To Romeo*)—to stop pursuing me and leave me to my
      grief.
   I'll send a messenger tomorrow.

ROMEO
   My soul will live for that—

JULIET
   Good night a thousand times. (*She exits*)

ROMEO
   This night is a thousand times worse without your light.
165   Love is drawn toward love the way schoolboys are
         drawn away from their books;
      but when love is drawn away from love, it's like
         going to school with a scowl.
            He starts to leave.
            JULIET *re-enters on the balcony.*

JULIET (*whispers*)
   Romeo! I wish I had a falconer's voice
   to lure this male falcon back again!
   But being still ruled by others, I can't shout,
170   or else I would yell until I opened the cave where Echo lies.
   Then I'd make her silver voice more hoarse than mine
   by saying my Romeo's name over and over.
   Romeo!

ROMEO
   It's my soul that is calling my name.
175   Lovers' voices sound silver-sweet at night,
   like soft music to receptive listeners.

JULIET
   Romeo!

ROMEO
   Yes, my sweet?

JULIET

                     What o'clock to-morrow
180   Shall I send to thee?

ROMEO

                 By the hour of nine.

JULIET

       I will not fail; 'tis twenty year till then.
       I have forgot why I did call thee back.

ROMEO

       Let me stand here till thou remember it.

JULIET

185   I shall forget, to have thee still stand there,
       Rememb'ring how I love thy company.

ROMEO

       And I'll still stay, to have thee still forget,
       Forgetting any other home but this.

JULIET

       'Tis almost morning, I would have thee gone;—
190   And yet no farther than a wanton's bird,
       That lets it hop a little from her hand,
       Like a poor prisoner in his twisted gyves,
       And with a silk thread plucks it back again,
       So loving-jealous of his liberty.

ROMEO

195   I would I were thy bird.

JULIET

                Sweet, so would I;
       Yet I should kill thee with much cherishing.
       Good-night, good-night! Parting is such sweet sorrow,
       That I shall say good-night till it be morrow.

          [*Exit, above.*]

ROMEO

200   Sleep dwell upon thine eyes, peace in thy breast!
       Would I were sleep and peace, so sweet to rest!

JULIET

    What time tomorrow
180   should I send my messenger to you?

ROMEO

    By nine o'clock.

JULIET

    I will not fail. It will be twenty years until then.
    I forget why I called you back.

ROMEO

    I'll stay here until you remember.

JULIET

185   I'll forget if you stay here
    because I'll only remember how much I love your company.

ROMEO

    I'll stay so you'll forget everything—
    everything except me.

JULIET

    It's almost morning. I wish you would go now—
190   but no farther than a spoiled girl's pet bird
    which is allowed to hop away from her hand just a little
    like a poor prisoner in his twisted chains.
    Then with a silk thread, the girl pulls the bird back again,
    she is so loving, and yet so jealous of his freedom.

ROMEO

195   I wish I were your bird.

JULIET

    Sweetheart, so do I.
    Yet if you were my bird, I'd kill you with too much love.
    Good night, good night! Parting is such sweet sorrow
    that I could say good night through tomorrow.
         JULIET exits.

ROMEO

200   May you sleep well and feel peaceful inside.
    I wish I were your sleep and peace to find such a
        sweet resting place.

Hence will I to my ghostly father's cell,
His help to crave, and my dear hap to tell.

[*Exit.*]

[*Scene iii. Friar Laurence's cell*.*] Enter FRIAR LAURENCE,
with a basket.

FRIAR LAURENCE
The grey-ey'd morn smiles on the frowning night,
Chequ'ring the eastern clouds with streaks of light,
And flecked darkness like a drunkard reels
From forth day's path and Titan's fiery wheels.
5   Now, ere the sun advance his burning eye,
The day to cheer and night's dank dew to dry,
I must up-fill this osier cage of ours
With baleful weeds and precious-juiced flowers.
The earth, that's nature's mother, is her tomb;
10   What is her burying grave, that is her womb;
And from her womb children of divers kind
We sucking on her natural bosom find:
Many for many virtues excellent,
None but for some, and yet all different.
15   O, mickle is the powerful grace that lies
In plants, herbs, stones, and their true qualities;
For nought so vile that on the earth doth live
But to the earth some special good doth give,
Nor aught so good but, strain'd from that fair use,
20   Revolts from true birth, stumbling on abuse.
Virtue itself turns vice, being misapplied;
And vice sometime's by action dignified.

            Enter ROMEO.

Within the infant rind of this weak flower
Poison hath residence and medicine power;
25   For this, being smelt, with that part cheers each part;
Being tasted, slays all senses with the heart.

---

* *cell* is a monk's house separated from the rest of the monastary by some distance.

From here I'll go to my priest
to ask for his help and tell him of my good fortune.
    ROMEO exits.

Act II, Scene iii: Friar Laurence's cell. Enter FRIAR LAURENCE,
with a basket.

FRIAR LAURENCE
    The grey-eyed morning smiles on the frowning night.
    It checkers the eastern clouds with streaks of light,
    and the spotted darkness staggers like a drunk
    from the path of the day and the sun's fiery wheels.
5   Now, before the sun can raise his burning eye
    to cheer up the day and dry up night's dew,
    I must fill this wicker basket
    with deadly weeds and healing flowers.
    The earth, which is the mother of nature, is also a tomb,
10 both a grave and a womb.
    And from earth's womb come all kinds of children
    who suck from her natural breasts.
    Many of earth's children have many excellent uses—
    not one child that doesn't have some use—and yet
        they're all different.
15 Great are the powerful uses that lie
    in plants, herbs, stones, and in their pure qualities.
    For there's nothing that lives on earth that is so bad
    that it doesn't give the earth some special good.
    And there isn't anything so good that when improperly
        used,
20 it stops serving its natural purpose and becomes poisonous.
    Good can turn to bad when it is misused,
    and sometimes evil can be made right by right action.
        Enter ROMEO.
    Within the new bud of this weak flower,
    there lies poison and medicinal power.
25 If you smell this flower, you'll be strengthened all over;
    but if you taste this flower, you die.

Two such opposed kings encamp them still
In man as well as herbs, grace and rude will;
And where the worser is predominant,
30   Full soon the canker death eats up that plant.

ROMEO

Good morrow, father.

FRIAR LAURENCE

Benedicite!

What early tongue so sweet saluteth me?
Young son, it argues a distempered head
35   So soon to bid good morrow to thy bed.
Care keeps his watch in every old man's eye,
And where care lodges, sleep will never lie;
But where unbruised youth with unstuff'd brain
Doth couch his limbs, there golden sleep doth reign;
40   Therefore thy earliness doth me assure
Thou art up-rous'd with some distemp'rature;
Or if not so, then here I hit it right,
Our Romeo hath not been in bed to-night.

ROMEO

That last is true; the sweeter rest was mine.

FRIAR LAURENCE

45   God pardon sin! Wast thou with Rosaline?

ROMEO

With Rosaline, my ghosty father? No!
I have forgot that name, and that name's woe.

FRIAR LAURENCE

That's my good son; but where hast thou been, then?

ROMEO

I'll tell thee ere thou ask it me again.
50   I have been feasting with mine enemy,
Where on a sudden one hath wounded me
That's by me wounded; both our remedies
Within thy help and holy physic lies.
I bear no hatred, blessed man, for, lo,
55   My intercession likewise steads my foe.

Two opposed kings always live
within man, as well as in herbs—virtue and base lust.
Where evil is predominant,
30 the cankerworm will soon eat up that plant.

ROMEO
Good morning, father.

FRIAR LAURENCE
Bless you!
Who is the early riser who greets me so sweetly?
Young man, you must be very worried
35 to be out of bed so early in the morning.
Worry is always present in an old man's life,
and where you find worry, you'll never find sleep.
But when the young and the carefree
lie down to rest, then you'll find sleep is king.
40 So your appearance at this early hour tells me that
something is bothering you.
Or if that's not the case, then this must be right—
Romeo, you've not been to bed tonight.

ROMEO
The last statement is true. I had a sweeter rest
than bed.

FRIAR LAURENCE
45 God forgive your sin! Were you with Rosaline?

ROMEO
With Rosaline, father? No!
I've forgotten that name and all the sorrow it
brought.

FRIAR LAURENCE
That's my good boy. But where have you been then?

ROMEO
I'll tell you before you ask me again.
50 I was dining with my enemies
when all of a sudden, one of them wounded me,
whom I in turn wounded. You have the remedy
to help us both with your holy medicine.
I have no hatred, father, for
55 my request will also benefit my enemy.

FRIAR LAURENCE
Be plain, good son, and homely in thy drift;
Riddling confession finds but riddling shrift.

ROMEO
Then plainly know my heart's dear love is set
On the fair daughter of rich Capulet.
60 As mine on hers, so her is set on mine;
And all combin'd, save what thou must combine
By holy marriage. When and where and how
We met, we woo'd, and made exchange of vow,
I'll tell thee as we pass; but this I pray,
65 That thou consent to marry us to-day.

FRIAR LAURENCE
Holy Saint Francis, what a change is here!
Is Rosaline, that thou didst love so dear,
So soon forsaken? Young men's love then lies
Not truly in their hearts, but in their eyes.
70 Jesu Maria, what a deal of brine
Hath wash'd thy sallow cheeks for Rosaline!
How much salt water thrown away in waste,
To season love, that of it doth not taste!
The sun not yet thy sighs from heaven clears,
75 Thy old groans yet ring in mine ancient ears;
Lo, here upon thy cheek the stain doth sit
Of an old tear that is not wash'd off yet.
If e'er thou wast thyself and these woes thine,
Thou and these woes were all for Rosaline.
80 And art thou chang'd? Pronounce this sentence then:
Women may fall, when there's no strength in men.

ROMEO
Thou chid'st me oft for loving Rosaline.

FRIAR LAURENCE
For doting, not for loving, pupil mine.

ROMEO
And bad'st me bury love.

FRIAR LAURENCE
Good son, speak clearly and simply.
If you confess in riddles, you'll be forgiven in
    riddles.

ROMEO
Then I'll tell you clearly that the girl I love
is the beautiful daughter of rich Capulet.
60   Just as my heart is set on her, her heart is set on me,
and we're totally united, except by the union
of holy marriage that you must perform. When, where,
    and how
we met, fell in love, and exchanged our vows,
I'll tell you later, but I ask you this now:
65   that you agree to marry us today.

FRIAR LAURENCE
Holy Saint Francis! How you have changed!
So, Rosaline, whom you loved so much,
is so quickly forgotten? Then young men's love lies
not in their hearts but in their eyes.
70   Jesus and Mary, what a lot of salt tears
have washed your pale cheeks because of Rosaline!
A lot of salty tears were wasted
to flavor a love that you didn't really feel.
The sun has not yet cleared your signs from the heavens,
75   and your old groans are still ringing in my old ears.
Look, there's still a stain on your cheek
from a tear stain that is not yet washed off.
If ever you were yourself, and that old sorrow was yours,
you and your crying were all for Rosaline.
80   Have you changed? Say this sentence then:
"Women may fall when men don't have the strength to
    catch them."

ROMEO
You often scolded me for loving Rosaline.

FRIAR LAURENCE
For doting on her, not for loving her, my dear student.

ROMEO
You told me to bury my love.

FRIAR LAURENCE

85   Not in a grave,
    To lay one in, another out to have.

ROMEO

    I pray thee, chide me not. Her I love now
    Doth grace for grace and love for love allow;
    The other did not so.

FRIAR LAURENCE

90   O, she knew well
    Thy love did read by rote that could not spell.
    But come, young waverer, come, go with me,
    In one respect I'll thy assistant be;
    For this alliance may so happy prove
95 To turn your households' rancour to pure love.

ROMEO

    O, let us hence; I stand on sudden haste.

FRIAR LAURENCE

    Wisely and slow; they stumble that run fast.

            [*Exeunt.*]

[*Scene iv. A street.*] *Enter* BENVOLIO *and* MERCUTIO.

MERCUTIO

    Where the devil should this Romeo be?
    Came he not home to-night?

BENVOLIO

    Not to his father's; I spoke with his man.

MERCUTIO

    Why, that same pale hard-hearted wench, that Rosaline,
5   Torments him so, that he will sure run mad.

BENVOLIO

    Tybalt, the kinsman of old Capulet,
    Hath sent a letter to his father's house.

FRIAR LAURENCE

85 Not in a grave
where you bury one love to take another one out.

ROMEO

Please, don't scold me. The one I love now
gives me kindness for kindness and love for love.
Rosaline did not.

FRIAR LAURENCE

90 Rosaline knew all too well
that you were merely repeating words that you didn't
mean.
But come, my changeable young man, go with me.
I will help you for just one reason:
this marriage alliance may prove to be so happy

95 that it will turn the hatred of your two households
into love.

ROMEO

Let's go. I insist on being quick about this.

FRIAR LAURENCE

Let's be wise and slow. Those who run too fast
stumble.
They exit.

Act II, Scene iv: A street. Enter BENVOLIO *and* MERCUTIO.

MERCUTIO

Where the devil is Romeo?
Didn't he come home last night?

BENVOLIO

Not to his father's house, according to his servant.

MERCUTIO

That pale-hearted witch, Rosaline,

5 torments him so much that he'll surely go crazy!

BENVOLIO

Tybalt, old Capulet's nephew,
sent a letter to Romeo's house.

MERCUTIO
A challenge, on my life.

BENVOLIO
Romeo will answer it.

MERCUTIO
10   Any man that can write may answer a letter.

BENVOLIO
Nay, he will answer the letter's master, how he dares, being dared.

MERCUTIO
Alas, poor Romeo! he is already dead; stabb'd with a white wench's black eye; run through the ear with a love song; the very pin of his heart cleft with the blind bow-boy's butt-shaft; and is
15   he a man to encounter Tybalt?

BENVOLIO
Why, what is Tybalt?

MERCUTIO
More than prince of cats. O, he's the courageous captain of compliments. He fights as you sing prick-song; keeps time, distance, and proportion; he rests his minim rests, one, two, and the third
20   in your bosom: the very butcher of a silk button; a duellist, a duellist; a gentleman of the very first house, of the first and second cause. Ah, the immortal *passado!* the *punto reverso!* the *hai!*

BENVOLIO
The what?

MERCUTIO
The pox of such antic, lisping, affecting fantasticoes; these new
25   tuners of accent! "By Jesu, a very good blade! a very tall man! a very good whore!" Why, is not this a lamentable thing, grandsire, that we should be thus afflicted with these strange flies, these fashion-mongers, these *perdonami's* who stand so much on the new form, that they cannot sit at ease on the old bench? O, their
30   bones, their bones!

Enter ROMEO.

---

17 *prince of cats* Tybalt or a similar name was the name of the king of the cats in the story "Reynard the Fox."   28 *perdonami's* pardon me's, in Italian.   30 *bones* a pun on the French word "bon" which means "good."

MERCUTIO
That letter contains a challenge to a duel, I'll bet my life.

BENVOLIO
Romeo will answer it.

MERCUTIO
10   Any man who can write may answer a letter.

BENVOLIO
No, I meant Romeo will answer the writer of the letter. He'll take up
the challenge to fight a duel.

MERCUTIO
Poor Romeo, he's already dead. He's been stabbed with that white
maid's black eye; shot through the air with a love song; and the very
center of his heart has been split by Cupid's blunt arrow. Is
15   he the kind of man to fight a duel with Tybalt?

BENVOLIO
Why? Who is Tybalt?

MERCUTIO
He's not just the prince of cats. He's the brave master of all the
laws of etiquette.
He fights as you would sing from a music sheet, keeping time, distance,
and proportion. He observes even the shortest rests—one, two, and
the third
20   is a sword in your breast. He's the butcher of a silk button on his
opponent's shirt. A duelist, a
duelist! He's a gentleman from the best school of fencing and ready to
quarrel over
a trifle. He gives the immortal lunge, the backhanded thrust, the
home thrust!

BENVOLIO
The what?

MERCUTIO
Damn these grotesque, lisping, snobbish fops, these
25   speakers of buzz words! "By Jesus, he was a very good swordsman! A
very brave man!
A very good fellow!" Isn't it terrible, venerable
sir, that we should be plagued with these strange parasites—these
fashion nuts, these courteous fops who so insist on
new fashion that they're not at ease with our old manners and learning?
O their
30   bones, their bones!
        Enter ROMEO.

BENVOLIO
Here comes Romeo, here comes Romeo.

MERCUTIO
Without his roe, like a dried herring: O flesh, flesh, how art thou fishified! Now is he for the numbers that Petrarch flowed in. Laura to his lady was a kitchen-wench (marry, she had a better
35   love to be-rhyme her); Dido a dowdy; Cleopatra a gipsy; Helen and Hero hildings and harlots; Thisbe, a grey eye or so, but not to the purpose. Signior Romeo, *bonjour!* There's a French salutation to your French slop. You gave us the counterfeit fairly last night.

ROMEO
40   Good morrow to you both. What counterfeit did I give you?

MERCUTIO
The slip, sir, the slip; can you not conceive?

ROMEO
Pardon, good Mercutio, my business was great; and in such a case as mine a man may strain courtesty.

MERCUTIO
.   That's as much as to say, such a case as yours constrains a man
45   to bow in the hams.

ROMEO
Meaning, to curtsy.

MERCUTIO
Thou hast most kindly hit it.

ROMEO
A most courteous exposition.

MERCUTIO
Nay, I am the very pink of courtesy.

ROMEO
50   Pink for flower.

MERCUTIO
Right.

33-36 *Petrarch...*   Laura was the subject of the Italian poet Petrarch's sonnets. Queen Dido of Carthage was Aeneas' lover. Cleopatra, ruler of Egypt, captured Antony's and Caesar's affections. Paris' abduction of the beautiful Helen sparked the Trojan War. Hero was Leander's beloved. Thisbe and her lover Pyramus closely compare to Romeo and

BENVOLIO

Here comes Romeo! Here comes Romeo!

MERCUTIO

Looking like a fish that has spawned—like a dried
    herring. O flesh, flesh, how fishy you have
become! Now he's ready to say the kind of poems that Petrarch wrote.
But compared with Rosaline, Petrarch's lady lover was
    just a kitchen maid (even if she did have better
35   love poems written to her). Compared with Rosaline,
    Dido was a drab woman; Cleopatra, deceitful; Helen
and Hero good-for-nothings and loose women; Thisbe's
    shining eyes might be lovely but are not
worth mentioning. Sir Romeo, good day! That's a French hello
for your French pants. You certainly gave us the counterfeit last
night.

ROMEO

40   Good morning to both of you. What counterfeit did I give you?

MERCUTIO

The slip, sir, the slip! Don't you understand?

ROMEO

Excuse me, good Mercutio. I had some serious
    business to take care of, and in a
case such as mine, a man may forget his manners.

MERCUTIO

That's as much as admitting that, in your condition,
45   you have to bow from the hips.

ROMEO

You mean to curtsy.

MERCUTIO

You have interpreted quite graciously.

ROMEO

You gave a very polite explanation.

MERCUTIO

Indeed, I am the height of courtesy.

ROMEO

50   You mean pink for flower.

MERCUTIO

Right.

Juliet.   38 *French slop*   a style of French trousers. Romeo has been up all night and is
still wearing his costume from the night before.   41 *slip*   beside meaning escape, also refers
to counterfeit coins.   49,ff *pink*   means perfection, flower, and a decoration of punched
holes.

ROMEO

Why, then is my pump well flower'd.

MERCUTIO

Sure wit! Follow me this jest now till thou hast worn out thy pump, that, when the single sole of it is worn, the jest may remain, after the wearing, solely singular.

55

ROMEO

O single-sol'd jest, solely singular for the singleness!

MERCUTIO

Come between us, good Benvolio; my wits faint.

ROMEO

Switch and spurs, switch and spurs; or I'll cry a match.

MERCUTIO

Nay, if our wits run the wild-goose chase, I am done, for thou hast more of the wild-goose in one of thy wits than, I am sure, I have in my whole five. Was I with you there for the goose?

60

ROMEO

Thou wast never with me for anything when thou wast not there for the goose.

MERCUTIO

I will bite thee by the ear for that jest.

ROMEO

Nay, good goose, bite not.

65

MERCUTIO

Thy wit is a very bitter sweeting; it is a most sharp sauce.

ROMEO

And is it not, then, well serv'd in to a sweet goose?

MERCUTIO

O, here's a wit of cheveril, that stretches from an inch narrow to an ell broad!

ROMEO

I stretch it out for that word "broad"; which added to the goose, proves thee far and wide a broad goose.

70

---

54 *single-sole* means both weak and unique. 59 *wild-goose chase* is a game of follow-the-leader on horseback. To catch the goose was to conclude the chase. 63 *goose* also was slang for streetwalker. 65 *Nay...not.* is a proverb meaning "spare me." 69 *ell* equals forty-five inches.

ROMEO
Then my shoe is well-flowered.

MERCUTIO
Touche! Now follow this joke until you have worn out your shoe
so that when your single sole is worn out, the
    joke will be remembered
55   after the telling as unique.

ROMEO
What a weak joke, remarkable only for being so pathetic.

MERCUTIO
You'll have to come between us, Benvolio. I can't think of a comeback.

ROMEO
Come on, keep it up, or I'll claim victory!

MERCUTIO
Well, if our wits are on a wild-goose chase, I'm done
    for. I'm certain you
60   have more wild goose in one of your wits than
I have in all five of mine. There—didn't I hit
    home at the end of the game?

ROMEO
You were never with me anywhere if you weren't there
looking for a streetwalker.

MERCUTIO
I'll bite you on the ear for that joke!

ROMEO
65   No, good goose, don't bite me.

MERCUTIO
Your wit is like a tart apple: it makes very sharp sauce.

ROMEO
Doesn't such a sauce go well with a sweet goose like you?

MERCUTIO
O, here's wit of pliable leather. You stretch a
    little joke a long way.

ROMEO
70   I'll stretch my wit to tackle that word "broad"
    which, when added to goose,
proves that you're known far and wide as an out-and-out goose.

MERCUTIO

Why, is not this better now than groaning for love? Now art thou sociable, now art thou Romeo, now art thou what thou art, by art as well as by nature; for this drivelling love is like a great
75   natural, that runs lolling up and down to hide his bauble in a hole.

BENVOLIO

Stop there, stop there.

MERCUTIO

Thou desir'st me to stop in my tale against the hair.

BENVOLIO

Thou wouldst else have made thy tale large.

MERCUTIO

O, thou art deceiv'd; I would have made it short; for I was come
80   to the whole depth of my tale, and meant, indeed, to occupy the argument no longer.

ROMEO

Here's goodly gear!

Enter NURSE *and her man* PETER.

A sail, a sail!

MERCUTIO

Two, two; a shirt and a smock.

NURSE

85   Peter!

PETER

Anon!

NURSE

My fan, Peter.

MERCUTIO

Good Peter, to hide her face; for her fan's the fairer face.

NURSE

God ye good morrow, gentlemen.

MERCUTIO

90   God ye good den, fair gentlewoman.

---

78 *large* also means indecent.
83 *sail* the nurse is quite large and is probably wearing a white apron, so Romeo calls her a "sail."

MERCUTIO
Now, isn't this better than groaning for love? Now you're being
friendly, now you're the Romeo I remember. You're
    Romeo! Now you are what you are, in
learning as well as by temperament. This silly love is like a
75   big idiot running up and down with his tongue hanging
    out, trying to hide his toy in a hole.

BENVOLIO
Stop! Stop!

MERCUTIO
You want me to stop when I don't want to stop.

BENVOLIO
If I hadn't stopped you, you would have told an
    overly long story.

MERCUTIO
You're wrong. I'd have kept it short because I said
80   all I'd meant to say, and really didn't intend to continue
    the discussion any longer.

ROMEO (*sees Juliet's nurse coming*)
Here comes some handsome stuff.
        Enter NURSE *and her servant* PETER.
A sail, a sail!

MERCUTIO
Two sails! A man and a woman.

NURSE
85   Peter!

PETER
At your service!

NURSE
Give me my fan, Peter.

MERCUTIO
Give it to her, good Peter, so she can hide her
    face. Her fan is prettier than her face.

NURSE
Good morning, gentlemen.

MERCUTIO
90   Good afternoon, lovely lady.

NURSE
Is it good den?

MERCUTIO
'Tis no less, I tell ye; for the bawdy hand of the dial is now upon
the prick of noon.

NURSE
Out upon you! what a man are you!

ROMEO
95   One, gentlewoman, that God hath made for himself to mar.

NURSE
By my troth, it is well said; "for himself to mar," quoth 'a!
Gentlemen, can any of you tell me where I may find the young
Romeo?

ROMEO
I can tell you; but young Romeo will be older when you have
100   found him than he was when you sought him. I am the youngest
of that name, for fault of a worse.

NURSE
You say well.

MERCUTIO
Yea, is the worst well? Very well took i' faith; wisely, wisely.

NURSE
If you be he, sir, I desire some confidence with you.

BENVOLIO
105   She will indite him to some supper.

MERCUTIO
A bawd, a bawd, a bawd! So ho!

ROMEO
What hast thou found?

MERCUTIO
No hare, sir; unless a hare, sir, in a lenten pie, that is something
stale and hoar ere it be spent.

   [*Sings.*]

92-93 *bawdy...noon* Mercutio tries to shock the nurse with ribald language.   101 *for fault
of a worse* Romeo means "a better name," but the nurse takes him
seriously.   104 *confidence* the nurse really means "conference." She is using a
malapropism—a word similar to the right word but misused for the sake of

NURSE
Is it afternoon already?

MERCUTIO
It is, I assure you. The naughty hand on the clock is now on
the point of noon.

NURSE
Shame on you! What kind of man are you?

ROMEO
95   He's one, madam, who was made to harm himself.

NURSE
Truly, that was a clever remark. "Made to harm
    himself," did he say?
Gentlemen, can any of you tell me where I can find young
Romeo?

ROMEO
I can tell you. But young Romeo will be older when you have
100 found him than when you started looking for him. I'm the youngest
by the name of Romeo, for lack of a worse name.

NURSE
You speak well.

MERCUTIO
Really, is the "worst" good? You're very perceptive,
    indeed! How intelligent!

NURSE (*to Romeo*)
If you're Romeo, sir, I want to have a confidence with you.

BENVOLIO
105 She'll indite him to supper.

MERCUTIO
A streetwalker, a streetwalker, a streetwalker! I
    found her!

ROMEO
What have you found?

MERCUTIO
Not a streetwalker, sir. Unless a streetwalker is
    like meat in a pie served during Lent—
stale and old before it is eaten.
        He sings.

---

humor. 105 *indite* is a malapropism for "invite." Benvolio is mocking the
nurse. 108 *lenten pie* Lent is a religious period of forty days preceding Easter. Some
Christians do not eat meat during the period (and a lenten or meat pie would go stale before
it was eaten).

110   "An old hare hoar,
            And an old hare hoar,
         Is very good meat in lent;
            But a hare that is hoar
            Is too much for a score,
115   When it hoars ere it be spent."

      Romeo, will you come to your father's? We'll to dinner thither.

ROMEO
      I will follow you.

MERCUTIO
      Farewell, ancient lady; farewell [*singing*] "lady, lady, lady."

      [*Exeunt Mercutio and Benvolio.*]

NURSE
      I pray you, sir, what saucy merchant was this, that was so full
120   of his ropery?

ROMEO
      A gentleman, nurse, that loves to hear himself talk, and will speak
      more in a minute than he will stand to in a month.

NURSE
      An 'a speak anything against me, I'll take him down, an 'a were
      lustier than he is, and twenty such Jacks; and if I cannot, I'll find
125   those that shall. Scurvy knave! I am none of his flirt-gills; I am
      none of his skains-mates.—And thou must stand by too, and
      suffer every knave to use me at his pleasure!

PETER
      I saw no man use you at his pleasure; if I had, my weapon should
      quickly have been out. I warrant you, I dare draw as soon as
130   another man, if I see occasion in a good quarrel, and the law on
      my side.

NURSE
      Now, afore God, I am so vex'd that every part about me quivers.
      Scurvy knave! Pray you, sir, a word: and as I told you, my young
      lady bid me inquire you out; what she bid me say, I will keep
135   to myself. But first let me tell ye, if ye should lead her into a
      fool's paradise, as they say, it were a very gross kind of behaviour,

---

118 *lady, lady, lady*   is a refrain from an old ballad "Chaste Susanna."

110   *An old rabbit harlot,*
           Yes, an old rabbit harlot,
           Is very good meat in Lent.
           But a rabbit that is moldy
           Is not good enough to be paid for
115   *When it rots before it is eaten.*
     Romeo, will you come to your father's house?
     We're going to dinner there.

ROMEO
Yes, I'll follow you.

MERCUTIO (*to Nurse*)
Goodbye, old lady. Goodbye. (*Sings*) "Lady, lady, lady."
     MERCUTIO *and* BENVOLIO *leave.*

NURSE
Tell me, sir, what rude fellow was that who had such
120   a fresh mouth?

ROMEO
He's a gentleman, nurse, who loves to hear himself talk and who'll say
more in a minute than he'll listen to in a month.

NURSE
If he says anything bad about me, I'll beat him up—even if he were
bigger than he is and even if there were twenty such rascals like him.
     And if I can't beat him, I'll find
125   someone who can. Disgusting rascal! I'm not one of his
          flirting women and I'm
not one of his cutthroats. (*To Peter*) And you just stood there and
let every rascal use me as he pleased.

PETER
I didn't see any man use you at his pleasure. If I had, I would have
     drawn my weapon
quickly. I swear, I'm as quick to draw my sword as
130   any man, if I see there's a basis for a good quarrel and if the law is on
my side.

NURSE
I swear to God, I'm so upset that I am shaking all over.
Disgusting rascal! (*To Romeo*) Sir, I must speak to you. As I was telling
     you, my young
lady sent me to find you. What she told me to say, I'll keep
135   to myself. First, let me tell you, if you should
seduce her, it would be a terrible thing to do.

as they say; for the gentlewoman is young, and, therefore, if you
should deal double with her, truly it were an ill thing to be off'red
to any gentlewoman, and very weak dealing.

ROMEO

140   Nurse, commend me to thy lady and mistress. I protest unto
thee—

NURSE

Good heart, and, i' faith, I will tell her as much. Lord, Lord,
she will be a joyful woman.

ROMEO

What wilt thou tell her, nurse? Thou dost not mark me.

NURSE

145   I will tell her, sir, that you do protest; which, as I take it, is a
gentlemanlike offer.

ROMEO

Bid her devise
Some means to come to shrift this afternoon;
And there she shall at Friar Laurence' cell
150   Be shriv'd and married. Here is for thy pains.

NURSE

No, truly, sir; not a penny.

ROMEO

Go to; I say you shall.

NURSE

This afternoon, sir? Well, she shall be there.

ROMEO

And stay, good nurse;—behind the abbey wall
155   Within this hour my man shall be with thee,
And bring thee cords made like a tackled stair;
Which to the high top-gallant of my joy
Must be my convoy in the secret night.
Farewell; be trusty, and I'll quit thy pains.
160   Farewell; commend me to thy mistress.

My mistress is young, and if you
should two-time her, that would be a terrible thing to do
to any lady and very unmanly behavior.

ROMEO
140   Nurse, give my regards to your lady, your mistress. I vow—

NURSE
Good fellow, truly, I'll tell her so. Lord, lord,
she'll be a happy woman.

ROMEO
What will you tell her, nurse? You didn't listen to me.

NURSE
145   I'll tell her, sir, that you made a vow, which, as I understand it, is a
gentlemanlike offer.

ROMEO
Tell her to find
a way to come to confession this afternoon.
There at Friar Laurence's cell
150   she shall receive absolution and be married. Here's
some money for your trouble.

NURSE
No indeed, sir, I won't take a penny.

ROMEO
Not another word! You shall take it.

NURSE
You want her to come this afternoon, sir? Well,
she'll be there. (*Starts to leave*)

ROMEO
Good nurse, wait! My servant will come to you
155   within an hour behind the abbey wall,
and bring you a rope ladder like those used on ships,
which will be my passageway in the dark night
to the peak of my happiness.
Goodbye. Be trustworthy and I'll reward you.
160   Goodbye. Give my love to your mistress.

NURSE

Now God in heaven bless thee! Hark you, sir.

ROMEO

What say'st thou, my dear nurse?

NURSE

Is your man secret? Did you ne'er hear say,
"Two may keep counsel, putting one away"?

ROMEO

165   I warrant thee, my man's as true as steel.

NURSE

Well, sir; my mistress is the sweetest lady—Lord, Lord! when
'twas a little prating thing,—O, there is a nobleman in town, one
Paris, that would fain lay knife aboard; but she, good soul, had
as lief see a toad, a very toad, as see him. I anger her sometimes
170   and tell her that Paris is the properer man; but, I'll warrant you,
when I say so, she looks as pale as any clout in the versal world.
Doth not rosemary and Romeo begin both with a letter?

ROMEO

Ay, nurse; what of that? Both with an R.

NURSE

Ah, mocker! that's the dog's name. R is for the — No; I know
175   it begins with some other letter — and she hath the prettiest sententious of it, of you and rosemary, that it would do you good to
hear it.

ROMEO

Commend me to thy lady.

NURSE

Ay, a thousand times.
        [*Exit Romeo.*]
180   Peter!

PETER

Anon!

NURSE

Before, and apace.
        [*Exeunt.*]

---

172 *rosemary*   was a flower grooms wore at weddings.   172 *begin both with a letter*   the
nurse cannot read, so she does not know one letter from another.   174 *dog's name*   dogs
were called "R" because their growls sounded like the letter.   174-75 *sententious*   the nurse
means sentences; this is another malapropism.

NURSE

>God in heaven bless you.—Listen, sir.

ROMEO

>What did you want to say, dear nurse?

NURSE

>Can your servant keep a secret? Didn't you ever hear the saying, "Two can keep a secret if one is dead?"

ROMEO

165   I assure you that my servant is as trustworthy as steel.

NURSE

>Well, sir—my mistress is the sweetest lady. Lord, lord! When she was just a little chattering thing—O, there's
>   a nobleman in town named
>Paris who's eager to marry Juliet. But she, good soul, would as soon see a toad, a real toad, as to see him. I
>   make her angry sometimes
170   and tell her that Paris is handsomer than you are. But, I swear to you that when I say that, she looks as pale as any rag in the universe. Don't rosemary and Romeo begin with the same letter?

ROMEO

>Yes, nurse. So what? Both begin with an R.

NURSE

>You teaser—R is a dog's name. R is for the—No, I know
175   it begins with some other letter—and she has the prettiest sententious. That letter and you and rosemary.
>   It would do you good to hear them.

ROMEO

>Give my love to your lady.

NURSE

>Yes—a thousand times.
>   ROMEO *leaves.*
180   Peter!

PETER

>Right away!

NURSE

>Go! Go before me and quickly!
>   *They exit.*

[*Scene v. Capulet's orchard.*] *Enter* JULIET.

JULIET
    The clock struck nine when I did send the nurse;
    In half an hour she promis'd to return.
    Perchance she cannot meet him: that's not so.
    O, she is lame! Love's heralds should be thoughts,
5   Which ten times faster glide than the sun's beams
    Driving back shadows over louring hills;
    Therefore do nimble-pinion'd doves draw Love,
    And therefore hath the wind-swift Cupid wings.
    Now is the sun upon the highmost hill
10   Of this day's journey, and from nine till twelve
    Is three long hours, yet she is not come.
    Had she affections and warm youthful blood,
    She would be as swift in motion as a ball;
    My words would bandy her to my sweet love,
15   And his to me;
    But old folks, marry, feign as they were dead,
    Unwieldy, slow, heavy and pale as lead.

        Enter NURSE *and* PETER.
    O God, she comes! O honey nurse, what news?
    Hast thou met with him? Send thy man away.

NURSE
20   Peter, stay at the gate.

        [*Exit Peter.*]

JULIET
    Now, good sweet nurse,—O Lord, why look'st thou sad?
    Though news be sad, yet tell them merrily;
    If good, thou sham'st the music of sweet news
    By playing it to me with so sour a face.

NURSE
25   I am a-weary, give me leave a while.
    Fie, how my bones ache! What a jaunce have I had!

Act II, Scene v: Capulet's orchard. Enter JULIET.

JULIET
    It was nine o'clock this morning when I sent the nurse;
    she promised to return within half an hour.
    Maybe she can't find him. No, that can't be.
    O, she is crippled! Love's messengers should be
        thoughts
5   which can fly ten times faster than the sun's beams
    driving back shadows over darkening hills.
    That's why swift doves pull Venus' chariot,
    and that's why Cupid has wings as swift as the wind.
    Now, the sun is at the highest spot in the sky.
10   From nine o'clock to noon
    is three long hours, and she still hasn't come back.
    If she had the emotions and the warm blood of youth,
    she'd move as fast as a ball.
    My words would speed her to my sweet love,
15   and his words would speed her back to me.
    But many old folks move like they are dead—
    clumsy, slow, heavy, and pale as lead.
        Enter NURSE *and* PETER.
    O God, here she comes! O sweet nurse, what's your news?
    Did you meet him? Send your servant away.

NURSE
20   Peter, wait by the gate.
        PETER *leaves.*

JULIET
    Now, sweet, nurse—O Lord, why do you look sad?
    Even if the news is sad, tell it happily.
    If the news is good, you don't do the music of good
        news justice
    by telling it to me with such a sour face.

NURSE
25   I'm tired; let me rest awhile.
    Oh, how my bones ache! What a rough walk I've had!

JULIET

I would thou hadst my bones, and I thy news.
Nay, come, I pray thee, speak; good, good nurse, speak.

NURSE

Jesu, what haste! Can you not stay a while?
30   Do you not see that I am out of breath?

JULIET

How art thou out of breath, when thou hast breath
To say to me that thou art out of breath?
Th' excuse that thou dost make in this delay
Is longer than the tale thou dost excuse.
35   Is thy news good, or bad? Answer to that;
Say either, and I'll stay the circumstance.
Let me be satisfied, is't good or bad?

NURSE

Well, you have made a simple choice; you know not how to choose
a man. Romeo! no, not he. Though his face be better than any
40   man's, yet his leg excels all men's; and for a hand, and a foot,
and a body, though they be not to be talk'd on, yet they are past
compare. He is not the flower of courtesy, but, I'll warrant him,
as gentle as a lamb. Go thy ways, wench; serve God. What, have
you din'd at home?

JULIET

45   No, no! But all this did I know before. What says he of our marriage? What of that?

NURSE

Lord, how my head aches! What a head have I!
It beats as it would fall in twenty pieces.
My back o' t' other side,—O, my back, my back!
50   Beshrew your heart for sending me about
To catch my death with jauncing up and down!

JULIET

I' faith, I am sorry that thou art not well. Sweet, sweet, sweet
nurse, tell me, what says my love?

JULIET
    I wish you had my bones and I had your news.
    Come on! Please! I beg you tell me good, good nurse. Speak!

NURSE
    Jesus, what a hurry you're in! Can't you wait awhile?
30   Don't you see I'm out of breath?

JULIET
    How can you be out of breath, when you have breath
    to say to me you're out of breath?
    The excuse you're giving for this delay
    is longer than the story you excuse yourself from telling.
35   Is the news good or bad? Answer that!
    Say either good or bad and I'll wait for the details.
    Let me be satisfied: is it good or bad?

NURSE
    Well, you've made a foolish choice; you don't know
      how to choose
    a man. Romeo! No, not him, though he has the
      handsomest face of any
40   man and his leg excels all men's. And for a hand, a foot,
    and a body—though we won't discuss them—they're beyond
    compare. He's not the most courteous, but I'll swear, he's
    as gentle as a lamb. Get along, girl; serve God. Have
    you already eaten at home?

JULIET
45   No, no! But I knew all of this before. What does
      he say about our marriage?
    What about that?

NURSE
    Lord, how my head aches! What a head I have!
    It throbs as if it would split into twenty pieces.
    And then my back—O, my back, my back!
50   Shame on you for sending me out
    to catch my death from jolting up and down!

JULIET
    I'm truly sorry you're not well. Sweet, sweet, sweet
    nurse, tell me, what does my love say?

NURSE

Your love says, like an honest gentleman, and a courteous, and
55   a kind, and a handsome, and, I warrant, a virtuous,—Where is
your mother?

JULIET

Where is my mother! why, she is within;
Where should she be? How oddly thou repliest!
"Your love says, like an honest gentleman,
60   'Where is your mother?' "

NURSE

O God's lady dear!
Are you so hot? Marry, come up, I trow;
Is this the poultice for my aching bones?
Henceforward do your messages yourself.

JULIET

65   Here's such a coil!—Come, what says Romeo?

NURSE

Have you got leave to go to shrift today?

JULIET

I have.

NURSE

Then hie you hence to Friar Laurence' cell;
There stays a husband to make you a wife.
70   Now comes the wanton blood up in your cheeks;
They'll be in scarlet straight at any news.
Hie you to church; I must another way,
To fetch a ladder, by the which your love
Must climb a bird's nest soon when it is dark.
75   I am the drudge and toil in your delight,
But you shall bear the burden soon at night.
Go; I'll to dinner; hie you to the cell.

JULIET

Hie to high fortune! Honest nurse, farewell.

[*Exeunt.*]

NURSE
Your love says, like an honorable gentleman and a
     courteous,
55   kind, handsome, and I swear, a virtuous—where's
     your mother?

JULIET
Where's my mother? Why, she's inside!
Where else would she be? That's an odd reply,
"Your love says, like an honest gentleman,
60   'Where's your mother?' "

NURSE
By the Virgin Mary!
Are you angry? Come now, slow up.
Is this the medicine for my aching bones?
From now on, deliver your messages yourself.

JULIET
65   Such a fuss! Come on, what does Romeo say?

NURSE
Do you have permission to go to confession today?

JULIET
I have.

NURSE
Then hurry to Friar Laurence's cell.
There a husband waits to make you a wife.
70   Now the blood has rushed up into your cheeks.
Another scrap of news and you'll turn scarlet.
Hurry to church! I must go another way.
I have to get a ladder by which your love
can climb to your room when it's dark.
75   I'm the slave and laborer for your delight.
But you shall bear the burden tonight.
Go! I'm off to dinner. Hurry to the cell.

JULIET
I'll hurry to my good fortune. Honest, nurse,
     goodbye.
          They leave.

Scene vi: [*Friar Laurence's cell.*] *Enter* FRIAR LAURENCE
and ROMEO.

FRIAR LAURENCE
So smile the heavens upon this holy act,
That after-hours with sorrow chide us not!

ROMEO
Amen, amen! but come what sorrow can,
It cannot countervail th' exchange of joy
5   That one short minute gives me in her sight.
Do thou but close our hands with holy words,
Then love-devouring Death do what he dare;
It is enough I may but call her mine.

FRIAR LAURENCE
These violent delights have violent ends,
10   And in their triumph die, like fire and powder,
Which as they kiss consume. The sweetest honey
Is loathsome in his own deliciousness
And in the taste confounds the appetite:
Therefore love moderately; long love doth so;
15   Too swift arrives as tardy as too slow.

          Enter JULIET.

Here comes the lady. O, so light a foot
Will ne'er wear out the everlasting flint.
A lover may bestride the gossamer
That idles in the wanton summer air,
20   And yet not fall; so light is vanity.

JULIET
Good even to my ghostly confessor.

FRIAR LAURENCE
Romeo shall thank thee, daughter, for us both.

JULIET
As much to him, else in his thanks too much.

Act II, Scene vi: Friar Laurence's cell. Enter FRIAR LAURENCF
and ROMEO.

FRIAR LAURENCE
   Heavens smile upon this holy act of marriage
   so that sorrow will not come later.

ROMEO
   Amen, amen! But whatever sorrow comes,
   it cannot equal the joy
5 that one short minute in her sight gives me.
   If you will marry us with holy words,
   then let love-destroying death do what he dares.
   It's enough that I may call her mine.

FRIAR LAURENCE
   Violent passions have violent ends,
10 and in triumph they die, like fire and gunpowder,
   which consume one another when they kiss. Even the
      sweetest honey
   tastes sickeningly sweet if eaten to excess
   and will destroy the appetite.
   So love moderately. Love that lasts a long time is
      moderate.
15 To push love too fast can be as bad as being too
      slow to love.
         Enter JULIET.
   Here comes the lady. O, so light a foot as hers
   will never wear out the path.
   A lover may ride upon a spider's thread
   that waves in the wandering summer breeze,
20 and yet not fall. So light is earthly love.

JULIET
   Good evening, father.

FRIAR LAURENCE
   Romeo will kiss you for us both, daughter.

JULIET
   The same greeting to Romeo, otherwise he thanks me
      too much.

ROMEO

    Ah, Juliet, if the measure of thy joy
25   Be heap'd like mine, and that thy skill be more
    To blazon it, then sweeten with thy breath
    This neighbour air, and let rich music's tongue
    Unfold the imagin'd happiness that both
    Receive in either by this dear encounter.

JULIET

30   Conceit, more rich in matter than in words,
    Brags of his substance, not of ornament.
    They are but beggars that can count their worth;
    But my true love is grown to such excess
    I cannot sum up sum of half my wealth.

FRIAR LAURENCE

35   Come, come with me, and we will make short work;
    For, by your leaves, you shall not stay alone
    Till Holy Church incorporate two in one.

       [*Exeunt.*]

Act III, Scene i: [*A public place.*] *Enter* MERCUTIO, BENVOLIO, *and men.*

BENVOLIO

    I pray thee, good Mercutio, let's retire.
    The day is hot, the Capulets abroad,
    And, if we meet, we shall not scape a brawl,
    For now, these hot days, is the mad blood stirring.

MERCUTIO

5   Thou art like one of these fellows that, when he enters the con-
    fines of a tavern, claps me his sword upon the table and says,
    "God send me no need of thee!" and by the operation of the sec-
    ond cup draws him on the drawer, when indeed there is no need.

BENVOLIO

    Am I like such a fellow?

ROMEO
>Ah, Juliet, if you're as happy
25 >as I am, and if you can
>sing better than I do, go ahead and sweeten the air with your voice,
>and let beautiful music
>tell the happiness that both
>of us feel in meeting each other here.

JULIET
30 >True understanding is deeper in meaning than mere words
>and is important for its result, not pretty rhetoric.
>Those who can verbalize their happiness have little
>happiness to speak of. My true love has grown so
>> much that
>I can't tell even half of it in words.

FRIAR LAURENCE
35 >Come! Come with me and we'll make this ceremony short.
>You shall not be alone,
>until the holy church joins you two together.
>>*They exit.*

Act III, Scene i: A public place. Enter MERCUTIO, BENVOLIO
and servants.

BENVOLIO
>Please Mercutio, let's go.
>It's hot, the Capulets are around,
>and if we meet them, there'll be a fight.
>This hot weather makes tempers flare!

MERCUTIO
5 >You're like one of those fellows who enters
>a bar, throws his sword on the table, and says,
>"I pray heaven I'll have no reason to use you!"
>>Then after he has felt the effect of his
>second cup, he'll draw his sword on the waiter who
>> brought his wine for no reason at all.

BENVOLIO
>Am I like that fellow?

MERCUTIO

10   Come, come, thou art as hot a Jack in thy mood as any in Italy,
and as soon moved to be moody, and as soon moody to be moved.

BENVOLIO
And what to?

MERCUTIO
Nay, an there were two such, we should have none shortly, for
one would kill the other. Thou! why, thou wilt quarrel with a man
15   that hath a hair more or a hair less in his beard than thou hast.
Thou wilt quarrel with a man for cracking nuts, having no other
reason but because thou hast hazel eyes. What eye but such an
eye would spy out such a quarrel? Thy head is as full of quarrels
as an egg is full of meat, and yet thy head hath been beaten as
20   addle as an egg for quarrelling. Thou hast quarrell'd with a man
for coughing in the street, because he hath wakened thy dog that
hath lain asleep in the sun. Didst thou not fall out with a tailor
for wearing his new doublet before Easter? with another for tying
his new shoes with old riband? And yet thou wilt tutor me for
25   quarrelling!

BENVOLIO
An I were so apt to quarrel as thou art, any man should buy the
fee-simple of my life for an hour and a quarter.

MERCUTIO
The fee-simple! O simple!

Enter TYBALT, Petruchio, *and others.*

BENVOLIO
By my head, here comes the Capulets.

MERCUTIO
30   By my heel, I care not.

TYBALT
Follow me close, for I will speak to them.
Gentlemen, good den; a word with one of you.

MERCUTIO
And but one word with one of us?
Couple it with something; make it a word and a blow.

---

13 *two* Mercutio is playing on Benvolio's "to."

MERCUTIO

10   Come on, you're as hot-tempered when you're angry as
        any man in Italy.
        You're quick to get angry, and when you get
        angry, you're quick to be moved to—

BENVOLIO
        Moved to do what?

MERCUTIO
        Really, if there were two like you, we'd soon have none because
        one would kill the other. You, why, you would quarrel with a man
15   who has a hair more or a hair less in his beard than you have.
        You'll quarrel with a man for cracking hazelnuts for no other reason
        than that you have hazel eyes. What kind of eye, except one like
        yours, would see the occasion for a quarrel? Your head is as full of
            quarrels
        as an egg is full of yolk, and yet your head has been beaten to a
20   scramble, like an egg, for quarreling. You've quarreled with a man
        for coughing in the street because he woke your dog that
        was lying asleep in the sun. Didn't you quarrel with a tailor
        because he wore his new jacket before Easter? And fought with
            another man for tying
        his new shoes with an old lace? And yet you lecture me about
25   quarreling?

BENVOLIO
        If I were as likely to quarrel as you, someone who bought
        my life would own it for about an hour and a quarter.

MERCUTIO
        Owned it? Stupid!
                Enter TYBALT, PETRUCHIO, *and others.*

BENVOLIO
        I swear by my head, here come the Capulets.

MERCUTIO
30   I swear by my heel, I don't care.

TYBALT (*to his servants*)
        Stay close behind me; I'll speak to them. (*To Mercutio and others*)
        Gentlemen, good afternoon. I wish to speak a word with one of you.

MERCUTIO
        Just one word with one of us? Add something else to that; make it a
        word and a punch in the mouth.

TYBALT

35   You shall find me apt enough to that, sir, an you will give
occasion.

MERCUTIO

Could you not take some occasion without giving?

TYBALT

Mercutio, thou consortest with Romeo,—

MERCUTIO

Consort! what, dost thou make us minstrels? An thou make
40   minstrels of us, look to hear nothing but discords. Here's my
fiddlestick; here's that shall make you dance. 'Zounds, consort!

BENVOLIO

We talk here in the public haunt of men.
Either withdraw unto some private place,
Or reason coldly of your grievances,
45   Or else depart; here all eyes gaze on us.

MERCUTIO

Men's eyes were made to look, and let them gaze;
I will not budge for no man's pleasure, I.

Enter ROMEO.

TYBALT

Well, peace be with you, sir; here comes my man.

MERCUTIO

But I'll be hang'd, sir, if he wear your livery.
50   Marry, go before to field, he'll be your follower;
Your worship in that sense may call him "man."

TYBALT

Romeo, the love I bear thee can afford
No better term than this: thou art a villain.

ROMEO

Tybalt, the reason that I have to love thee
55   Doth much excuse the appertaining rage
To such a greeting. Villain am I none;
Therefore farewell; I see thou know'st me not.

---

39 *consort* means both associate and a company of musicians.   49 *livery*   is the uniform
of a servant. "My man" often referred to a servant.

TYBALT

35   I'll be ready enough to do that, sir, if you'll give
me a reason to do so.

MERCUTIO

Couldn't you take an "occasion" without me giving you
one?

TYBALT

Mercutio, you associate with Romeo—

MERCUTIO

Associate? What do you think we are, musicians?
    If you make

40   musicians of us, you'll hear nothing but sour notes. Here's my
fiddlestick! (*He draws his sword*) This will make
    you dance! By God, associate?

BENVOLIO

We are talking here in public.
Let's move to a private place,
or coolly discuss your grievances,

45   or let's leave. Everyone is staring at us here.

MERCUTIO

Men's eyes were made to look, so let them stare.
I won't budge for anyone.
        Enter ROMEO.

TYBALT

Peace be with you, sir. Here comes my man.

MERCUTIO

But I'll be hanged, sir, if he wears your livery.

50   If you go to the dueling field, he'll certainly follow you.
In that sense, you may call him your follower.

TYBALT

Romeo, the love that I feel for you can find
no better word than this—you're a peasant!

ROMEO

Tybalt, the reason that I have for loving you

55   helps me overcome the anger I should really feel
at such an insult. I'm not a peasant.
Therefore, goodbye. I see you don't really know me.

TYBALT

Boy, this shall not excuse the injuries
That thou hast done me; therefore turn and draw.

ROMEO

60   I do protest I never injur'd thee,
But love thee better than thou canst devise
Till thou shalt know the reason of my love;
And so, good Capulet,—which name I tender
As dearly as mine own,—be satisfied.

MERCUTIO

65   O calm, dishonourable, vile submission!
Alla stoccata carries it away
        [*Draws.*]
Tybalt, you rat-catcher, will you walk?

TYBALT

What wouldst thou have with me?

MERCUTIO

Good king of cats, nothing but one of your nine lives; that I mean
70   to make bold withal, and, as you shall use me hereafter, dry-beat
the rest of the eight. Will you pluck your sword out of his pilcher
by the ears? Make haste, lest mine be about your ears ere it be out.

TYBALT

I am for you.

        [*Drawing.*]

ROMEO

Gentle Mercutio, put thy rapier up.

MERCUTIO

75   Come, sir, your *passado*.

        [*They fight.*]

ROMEO

Draw, Benvolio; beat down their weapons.
Gentlemen, for shame, forbeat this outrage!
Tybalt, Mercutio, the Prince expressly hath
Forbid this bandying in Verona streets.

TYBALT

    Boy, this will not excuse the wrong
    you've done to me. Turn around and draw your sword!

ROMEO

60   I protest, I've never harmed you.
    I love you more than you can understand
    until you know the reason for my love.
    So, good Capulet—a name I value
    as dearly as my own—be satisfied.

MERCUTIO

65   What a calm, dishonorable, disgusting submission to
       an insult!
    Tybalt is getting away with this insult.
       He draws his sword.
    Tybalt, you ratcatcher, will you cross swords with me?

TYBALT

    What do you want of me?

MERCUTIO

    Good king of the cats, I want nothing of you except
       one of your nine lives. That life I mean
70   to take, and then, depending on whether you treat me
       well or badly, I might only thrash
    your other eight. Will you draw your sword from
       your scabbard?
    Hurry, or my sword will beat your ears before yours
       is out.

TYBALT

    I'm ready for you. (*Draws his sword*)

ROMEO

    Gentle Mercutio, put your sword away.

MERCUTIO

75   Come on, sir, give your forward thrust.
       They fight.

ROMEO

    Draw your sword, Benvolio, beat down their weapons.
    Gentlemen, this is shameful! Stop this!
    Tybalt! Mercutio! The prince has specifically
    forbidden fighting in the streets of Verona.

80   Hold, Tybalt! Good Mercutio!

[*Tybalt under Romeo's arm thrusts Mercutio, and flies.*]

MERCUTIO
                    I am hurt.
A plague o' both your houses! I am sped.
Is he gone, and hath nothing?

BENVOLIO
                    What, art thou hurt?

MERCUTIO
85   Ay, ay, a scratch, a scratch; marry, 'tis enough.
Where is my page? Go, villain, fetch a surgeon.

[*Exit Page.*]

ROMEO
Courage, man; the hurt cannot be much.

MERCUTIO
No, 'tis not so deep as a well, nor so wide as a church-door; but
'tis enough, 'twill serve. Ask for me to-morrow, and you shall
90   find me a grave man. I am pepper'd, I warrant, for this world.
A plague o' both your houses! 'Zounds, a dog, a rat, a mouse,
a cat, to scratch a man to death! a braggart, a rogue, a villain,
that fights by the book of arithmetic! Why the devil came you
between us? I was hurt under your arm.

ROMEO
95   I thought all for the best.

MERCUTIO
Help me into some house, Benvolio,
Or I shall faint. A plague o' both your houses!
They have made worms' meat of me. I have it,
And soundly too. Your houses!

[*Exeunt Mercutio and Benvolio*].

ROMEO
100   This gentleman, the Prince's near ally,
My very friend, hath got this mortal hurt
In my behalf; my reputation stain'd

---

90 *grave*   Mercutio is making puns with his last breath. He means grave, as in serious, and
ready for a burial grave.

80   Stop, Tybalt! Please, Mercutio!
            ROMEO *reaches to stop them.* TYBALT *sweeps*
            under ROMEO'S *arm, stabs* MERCUTIO, *and*
            runs away with the rest of his followers.

MERCUTIO
    I'm wounded!
    A curse on both your houses! I'm mortally wounded.
    Is he gone and without even a scrape?

BENVOLIO
    Are you hurt?

MERCUTIO
85   It's just a scratch, a scratch, but it's enough.
    Where's my page? Go, servant, get a doctor.
            The page exits.

ROMEO
    Be brave, man. The wound cannot be deep.

MERCUTIO
    No, it's not as deep as a well, or as wide as a
            church door. But
    it's enough, it will serve. Ask for me tomorrow and you'll
90   find me a grave man. I'm done with this world.
    A curse on both your houses! By God, a dog, a rat, a mouse,
    a cat—he scratches a man to death! A braggart, a rascal, a villain
    who fights according to the manuals. Why the devil did you come
    between us? He stabbed me when you tried to part us.

ROMEO
95   I thought I was doing the right thing.

MERCUTIO
    Help me into a house, Benvolio,
    or I'll faint. Damn both of your houses!
    They have made a corpse of me. I've had it!
    Damn your houses!
            MERCUTIO *and* BENVOLIO *exit.*

ROMEO
100   Mercutio, the prince's cousin
    and my true friend, has been mortally wounded
    defending me—my reputation being slandered

With Tybalt's slander,—Tybalt, that an hour
Hath been my cousin! O sweet Juliet,
105   Thy beauty hath made me effeminate
And in my temper soft'ned valour's steel!

Re-enter BENVOLIO.

BENVOLIO
O Romeo, Romeo, brave Mercutio's dead!
That gallant spirit hath aspir'd the clouds,
Which too untimely here did scorn the earth.

ROMEO
110   This day's black fate on moe days doth depend;
This but begins the woe others must end.

BENVOLIO
Here comes the furious Tybalt back again.

Re-enter TYBALT.

ROMEO
Alive, in triumph! and Mercutio slain!
Away to heaven, respective lenity,
115   And fire-eyed fury be my conduct now!
Now, Tybalt, take the "villain" back again
That late thou gav'st me; for Mercutio's soul
Is but a little way above our heads,
Staying for thine to keep him company.
120   Either thou, or I, or both, must go with him.

TYBALT
Thou, wretched boy, that didst consort him here,
Shalt with him hence.

ROMEO
                    This shall determine that.

[*They fight; Tybalt falls.*]

BENVOLIO
Romeo, away, be gone!
125   The citizens are up, and Tybalt slain.
Stand not amaz'd; the Prince will doom thee death
If thou art taken. Hence, be gone, away!

by Tybalt's insults—from Tybalt who's been my
cousin for only an hour. O sweet Juliet,
105   your beauty has made me act like a woman
and weakened my courage!
                    Re-enter BENVOLIO.

BENVOLIO
     O Romeo, Romeo, brave Mercutio is dead!
     His noble soul has climbed to the clouds.
     He was too young to leave the earth.

ROMEO
110   This day's black fate casts a shadow on the future.
     This is only the beginning of the sorrow to come.

BENVOLIO
     Here comes the furious Tybalt back again.
                    Re-enter TYBALT.

ROMEO
     So, you're living in victory and Mercutio is dead?
     Leave thoughtful mercy to the angels—
115   fiery anger will lead me now.
     Now, Tybalt, take back that insult
     that you gave me just awhile ago. Mercutio's soul
     is hovering just over our heads
     waiting for your soul to keep him company.
120   Either you, or I, or both will soon join him.

TYBALT
     You wretched boy, you who associated with him here,
     will soon be near him again.

ROMEO
     This fight will decide that!
                    They fight, and TYBALT *falls.*

BENVOLIO
     Romeo, run! Get away!
125   People are starting to gather and Tybalt is dead!
     Don't stand there in shock! The prince will
          sentence you to death
     if you're captured. Go on, run!

ROMEO
O, I am fortune's fool!

BENVOLIO
                    Why dost thou stay?

[*Exit Romeo.*]

Enter CITIZENS.

A CITIZEN
130   Which way ran he that kill'd Mercutio?
Tybalt, that murderer, which way ran he?

BENVOLIO
There lies that Tybalt.

A CITIZEN
                    Up, sir, go with me;
I charge thee in the Prince's name, obey.

Enter PRINCE, MONTAGUE, CAPULET, *their*
WIVES, *and all.*

PRINCE ESCALUS
135   Where are the vile beginners of this fray?

BENVOLIO
O noble Prince, I can discover all
The unlucky manage of this fatal brawl.
There lies the man, slain by young Romeo,
That slew thy kinsman, brave Mercutio.

LADY CAPULET
140   Tybalt, my cousin! O my brother's child!
O Prince! O cousin! husband! O, the blood is spilt
Of my dear kinsman! Prince, as thou art true,
For blood of ours, shed blood of Montague.
O cousin, cousin!

PRINCE ESCALUS
145   Benvolio, who began this bloody fray?

BENVOLIO
Tybalt, here slain, whom Romeo's hand did slay!
Romeo that spoke him fair, bid him bethink

ROMEO
>I'm a victim of fate.

BENVOLIO
>Why are you hanging around?
>>ROMEO *exits.*
>>*Enter citizens.*

CITIZEN
130
>Which way did the man run who killed Mercutio?
>Which way did that murderer Tybalt go?

BENVOLIO
>Tybalt is lying there.

CITIZEN
>Come with me, sir.
>I order you in the name of the prince to obey.
>>*Enter the* PRINCE, MONTAGUE, CAPULET, *their*
>>*wives, and others.*

PRINCE
135
>Where are the evil people who started this fight?

BENVOLIO
>O noble, prince, I can reveal
>the whole story of this fatal fight.
>There lies the man that young Romeo killed.
>Tybalt had earlier killed your cousin, Mercutio.

LADY CAPULET
140
>Tybalt, my nephew! My brother's child!
>O prince! O nephew! Husband! The blood
>of my dear nephew has been shed. Prince, by your
>   honor,
>you must execute the Montague who did this!
>My nephew! My nephew!

PRINCE
145
>Benvolio, who started this fight?

BENVOLIO
>Tybalt, who lies here dead, killed by Romeo.
>Romeo spoke courteously and urged Tybalt to consider

How nice the quarrel was, and urg'd withal
Your high displeasure; all this, uttered
150   With gentle breath, calm look, knees humbly bow'd,
Could not take truce with the unruly spleen
Of Tybalt deaf to peace, but that he tilts
With piercing steel at bold Mercutio's breast,
Who, all as hot, turns deadly point to point,
155   And, with a martial scorn, with one hand beats
Cold death aside, and with the other sends
It back to Tybalt, whose dexterity
Retorts it. Romeo he cries aloud,
"Hold, friends! friends, part!" and, swifter than his tongue,
160   His agile arm beats down their fatal points
And 'twixt them rushes; underneath whose arm
An envious thrust from Tybalt hit the life
Of stout Mercutio, and then Tybalt fled;
But by and by comes back to Romeo,
165   Who had but newly entertain'd revenge,
And to't they go like lightning, for, ere I
Could draw to part them, was stout Tybalt slain,
And, as he fell, did Romeo turn and fly.
This is the truth, or let Benvolio die.

LADY CAPULET
170   He is a kinsman to the Montague;
Affection makes him false; he speaks not true.
Some twenty of them fought in this black strife,
And all those twenty could but kill one life.
I beg for justice, which thou, Prince, must give;
175   Romeo slew Tybalt, Romeo must not live.

PRINCE ESCALUS
Romeo slew him, he slew Mercutio;
Who now the price of his dear blood doth owe?

MONTAGUE
Not Romeo, Prince, he was Mercutio's friend;
His fault concludes but what the law should end,
180   The life of Tybalt.

how trivial their disagreement was, and he told Tybalt
it would rouse your anger. Romeo said all of this
150   with gentleness, calmness, and modesty.
But he could not make peace with hot-tempered
Tybalt who was deaf to peace. Instead, Tybalt thrusts
his deadly sword at brave Mercutio's breast.
Mercutio, who was just as angry, turned his sword
point to meet Tybalt's,
155   and with fighting scorn, he beat death away with one hand
and with the other hand, he thrusts
back at Tybalt, who skillfully
returned the thrust. Romeo cried out,
"Stop it, friends! Separate!"And faster than he
could say it,
160   he beat down their weapons with his sword.
Romeo rushed to get between them, but Tybalt
maliciously ran his sword under Romeo's arm and stabbed
brave Mercutio. Then Tybalt fled,
but after awhile, he returned to Romeo.
165   Romeo decided he would avenge Mercutio's death,
and as fast as lightning, they were fighting again.
Before I
could separate them, brave Tybalt was killed,
and as he fell, Romeo turned and ran.
This is the truth, I swear to you on my life.

LADY CAPULET
170   He is related to the Montagues.
His bias makes him lie—he's not telling the truth.
There were twenty of them fighting in this quarrel,
and all twenty of them could only kill one man.
I beg for justice, which you, prince, must give.
175   Romeo killed Tybalt; Romeo must not live!

PRINCE
Romeo killed him, but Tybalt killed Mercutio.
Who has to pay the price for Mercutio's death?

MONTAGUE
Not Romeo, prince. He was Mercutio's friend.
His crime was doing what the law would have done—
180   he killed the murderer Tybalt.

PRINCE ESCALUS
                              And for that offence
         Immediately we do exile him hence.
         I have an interest in your hate's proceeding,
         My blood for your rude brawls doth lie a-bleeding;
185   But I'll amerce you with so strong a fine
         That you shall all repent the loss of mine.
         I will be deaf to pleading and excuses;
         Nor tears nor prayers shall purchase out abuses;
         Therefore use none. Let Romeo hence in haste,
190   Else, when he's found, that hour is his last.
         Bear hence this body and attend our will.
         Mercy but murders, pardoning those that kill.
                    [*Exeunt.*]

Scene ii: [*Capulet's orchard.*] *Enter* JULIET, *alone.*

JULIET
         Gallop apace, you fiery-footed steeds,
         Towards Phoebus' lodging; such a waggoner
         As Phaethon would whip you to the west,
         And bring in cloudy night immediately.
5   Spread thy close curtain, love-performing night,
         That runaway's eyes may wink, and Romeo
         Leap to these arms untalk'd of and unseen!
         Lovers can see to do their amorous rites
         By their own beauties; or, if love be blind,
10   It best agrees with night. Come, civil night,
         Thou sober-suited matron, all in black,
         And learn me how to lose a winning match,
         Play'd for a pair of stainless maidenhoods.
         Hood my unmann'd blood, bating in my cheeks,
15   With thy black mantle, till strange love grow bold,
         Think true love acted simple modesty.
         Come, night; come, Romeo; come, thou day in night;
         For thou wilt lie upon the wings of night,

---

3 *Phaeton* a character from Greek mythology, was the son of Phoebus, the sun god. Phaeton drove his father's chariot of the sun one day. He lost control of the horses and was killed by Zeus to prevent the world's destruction.   6 *runaway's* the meaning of this word is uncertain. Among the interpretations suggested by scholars are observers, horses (Phoebus' horses), the stars, Phaeton, and Cupid.

PRINCE
> For killing Tybalt,
> I immediately exile Romeo.
> I have a personal interest in this fight.
> My relative Mercutio lies bleeding thanks to your fight,
185 and I'm going to penalize you with such a heavy fine
> that all of you will repent the loss of my cousin.
> I'll be deaf to your pleading and excuses.
> Neither your tears nor your prayers will buy forgiveness,
> so don't even try to use them. Let Romeo leave quickly.
190 Otherwise, if he's found, he'll die within the hour.
> Take Tybalt's body and obey my orders.
> Mercy only encourages murders when killers are pardoned.
>> *They exit.*

Act III, Scene ii: Capulet's orchard. Enter JULIET *alone.*

JULIET
> Gallop quickly, you fiery-footed horses,
> to the sun god's house below the horizon. A driver
> like Phaeton would whip you towards the west,
> and bring night immediately.
5 Spread your curtain, love-performing night,
> so watchers' eyes may close and Romeo can
> leap into my arms where no one can see and
>> talk about us.
> Lovers can see to make love
> by the light of their own beauty. Or if love is blind,
10 it best matches the night. Come, courteous night,
> you gravely-dressed woman all in black,
> and teach me how to lose a winning match
> in a game played by two virgins.
> Hide the wild blood fluttering in my cheeks
15 with your black robe until unfamiliar love grows bold
> and believes that enjoying true love is really a modest act.
> Come night! Come Romeo! You're my light in the night.
> You will lie on the wings of night

Whiter than new snow on a raven's back.
20 Come, gentle night, come, loving, black-brow'd night,
Give me my Romeo; and, when he shall die,
Take him and cut him out in little stars,
And he will make the face of heaven so fine
That all the world will be in love with night
25 And pay no worship to the garish sun.
O, I have bought the mansion of a love,
But not possess'd it, and, though I am sold,
Not yet enjoy'd. So tedious is this day
As is the night before some festival
30 To an impatient child that hath new robes
And may not wear them. O, here comes my nurse,

Enter NURSE, *with cords.*

And she brings news; and every tongue that speaks
But Romeo's name speaks heavenly eloquence.
Now, nurse, what news? What hast thou there? The cords
35 That Romeo bid thee fetch?

NURSE

Ay, ay, the cords.

[*Throws them down.*]

JULIET

Ay me! what news? Why dost thou wring thy hands?

NURSE

Ah, well-a-day! he's dead, he's dead, he's dead!
We are undone, lady, we are undone!
40 Alack the day! he's gone, he's kill'd, he's dead!

JULIET

Can heaven be so envious?

NURSE

Romeo can,
Though heaven cannot. O Romeo, Romeo!
Who ever would have thought it? Romeo!

JULIET

45 What devil art thou, that dost torment me thus?

even whiter than freshly fallen snow on a raven's
back.
20 Come, gentle night! Come loving, black-browed night.
Give me my Romeo. And when he dies,
take him and cut him out in little stars,
and he'll make the face of heaven so fine
that all the world will love the night
25 and no longer admire the gaudy sun.
O, I have a handsome husband,
but I have not possessed him yet. Though I am his,
I've not yet been enjoyed. This day is as long
as the night before a holiday
30 to an impatient child who has new clothes
but cannot wear them yet. O, here comes my nurse.
> *Enter* NURSE, *with ropes. She sits down and*
> *wrings her hands.*

And she brings news! Every tongue that says
just Romeo's name speaks with heavenly eloquence.
Nurse, what's the news? What do you have there?
    Are those the ropes
35 that Romeo told you to get?

NURSE
    Yes, yes, the ropes.
> *She throws them down.*

JULIET
    Dear me! What's the news? Why are you wringing
    your hands?

NURSE
    Alas, he's dead, he's dead, he's dead!
    We're ruined, lady, we're ruined!
40 Alas, he's gone, he's killed, he's dead!

JULIET
    Can heaven be so jealous of me that she has to take him?

NURSE
    Romeo can,
    though heaven cannot. O Romeo, Romeo!
    Who would have ever thought it? Romeo!

JULIET
45 What kind of devil are you that you torment me like this?

This torture should be roar'd in dismal hell.
Hath Romeo slain himself? Say thou but ay,
And that bare vowel *I* shall poison more
Than the death-darting eye of cockatrice.
50   I am not I, if there be such an ay;
Or those eyes shut, that makes thee answer ay.
If he be slain, say ay; or if not, no.
Brief sounds determine of my weal or woe.

NURSE
I saw the wound, I saw it with mine eyes,—
55   God save the mark!—here on his manly breast.
A piteous corse, a bloody piteous corse!
Pale, pale as ashes, all bedaub'd in blood,
All in gore-blood; I swounded at the sight.

JULIET
O, break, my heart! poor bankrupt, break at once!
60   To prison, eyes, ne'er look on liberty!
Vile earth, to earth resign; end motion here;
And thou and Romeo press one heavy bier!

NURSE
O Tybalt, Tybalt, the best friend I had!
O courteous Tybalt! honest gentleman!
65   That ever I should live to see thee dead!

JULIET
What storm is this that blows so contrary?
Is Romeo slaught'red, and is Tybalt dead?
My dearest cousin, and my dearer lord?
Then, dreadful trumpet, sound the general doom!
70   For who is living, if those two are gone?

NURSE
Tybalt is gone, and Romeo banished;
Romeo that kill'd him, he is banished.

JULIET
O God! did Romeo's hand shed Tybalt's blood?

---

48 *I* is also Elizabethan for yes.   49 *cockatrice* is a mythical serpent that killed with a glance.   69 *dreadful trumpet* refers to the religious belief that the sound of a trumpet will announce Judgment Day or the end of the world.

This torture should be announced in hell.
Has Romeo killed himself? If you say yes,
just the vowel "aye" will be more deadly
than a serpent's death-killing eye.
50   I'll no longer be an "I" if your answer is yes,
or if Romeo's closed eyes make you answer yes.
If Romeo has been killed, say yes. If he hasn't,
     say no.
One brief word will decided if I'm happy or sad.

NURSE
I saw the wound. I saw it with my eyes—
55   God forbid—here on his manly breast. (*Points*)
A pitiful body! A bloody pitiful body!
He was pale, pale as ashes, and all covered in
     blood—
all in clotted blood. I fainted at the sight.

JULIET
O, break my heart! You are bankrupt! Break at once!
60   Go to prison, eyes; never look upon freedom!
My wretched body will return to earth. I'll end my
     life here
and Romeo and I can share one grave.

NURSE
O Tybalt, Tybalt, the best friend I had.
O courteous Tybalt! Honest gentleman!
65   I didn't think I'd ever live to see you dead.

JULIET
What kind of terrible storm is this?
Has Romeo been killed and is Tybalt dead, too?
My dearest cousin and my dearer husband?
Then, dreadful trumpet, announce the end of the
     world.
70   Who is living, if these two men are gone?

NURSE
Tybalt is dead and Romeo is banished.
Romeo killed Tybalt and he is banished.

JULIET
O God! Did Romeo kill Tybalt?

NURSE
It did, it did; alas the day, it did!

JULIET

75
O serpent heart, hid with a flow'ring face!
Did ever dragon keep so fair a cave?
Beautiful tyrant! fiend angelical!
Dove-feather'd raven! wolvish ravening lamb!
Despised substance of divinest show!

80
Just opposite to what thou justly seem'st,
A damned saint, an honourable villain!
O nature, what hadst thou to do in hell,
When thou didst bower the spirit of a fiend
In mortal paradise of such sweet flesh?

85
Was ever book containing such vile matter
So fairly bound? O, that deceit should dwell
In such a gorgeous palace!

NURSE
There's no trust,
No faith, no honesty in men; all perjur'd,

90
All forsworn, all naught, all dissemblers.
Ah, where's my man? Give me some *aqua vita;*
These griefs, these woes, these sorrows make me old.
Shame come to Romeo!

JULIET
Blister'd be thy tongue

95
For such a wish! he was not born to shame.
Upon his brow shame is asham'd to sit;
For 'tis a throne where honour may be crown'd
Sole monarch of the universal earth.
O, what a beast was I to chide at him!

NURSE

100
Will you speak well of him that kill'd your cousin?

JULIET
Shall I speak ill of him that is my husband?
Ah, poor my lord, what tongue shall smooth thy name,
When I, thy three-hours wife, have mangled it?

NURSE
He did! He did! Alas, he did!

JULIET
75   O, how can he hide such an evil heart with such a
         beautiful face?
     Did ever an ugly dragon live in such a lovely place?
     Beautiful tyrant! Devilish angel!
     Dove-feathered raven! Wolf-killing lamb!
     Vile creature that looks so beautiful—
80   just opposite of what you seem.
     A damned saint! An honorable villain!
     O nature, what were you doing in hell
     when you admitted the devil
     into the sweet paradise of the Garden of Eden?
85   Was there ever such a vulgar book
     bound with such a beautiful cover? O, that deceit should live
     in such a gorgeous body!

NURSE
     There's no trust,
     no faith, no honesty in men. All men are liars,
90   all break their word, all are wicked, all are phonies.
     Where's my servant? Get me a drink.
     These griefs, these sorrows, these troubles make me old.
     Shame on Romeo!

JULIET
     I hope your tongue blisters
95   for saying such a thing! He was not born to feel shame.
     Shame is ashamed to sit upon his head.
     His head is a throne where honor may be crowned
     king of the universe.
     O, what a beast I was to speak against him.

NURSE
100   Will you speak well of the man who killed your cousin?

JULIET
     Shall I speak poorly of the man who is my husband?
     Alas, my poor husband, what tongue can clear your name
     when I, your wife of three hours, muddies it?

But, wherefore, villain, didst thou kill my cousin?
105   That villain cousin would have kill'd my husband.
Back, foolish tears, back to your native spring;
Your tributary drops belong to woe,
Which you, mistaking, offer up to joy.
My husband lives that Tybalt would have slain;
110   And Tybalt's dead that would have slain my husband.
All this is comfort; wherefore weep I then?
Some word there was, worser than Tybalt's death,
That murd'red me; I would forget it fain;
But, O, it presses to my memory
115   Like damned guilty deeds to sinners' minds:
"Tybalt is dead, and Romeo—banished."
That "banished," that one word "banished,"
Hath slain ten thousand Tybalts. Tybalt's death
Was woe enough, if it had ended there;
120   Or, if sour woe delights in fellowship
And needly will be rank'd with other griefs,
Why follow'd not, when she said, "Tybalt's dead,"
Thy father, or thy mother, nay, or both,
Which modern lamentation might have mov'd?
125   But with a rear-ward following Tybalt's death,
"Romeo is banished," to speak that word,
Is father, mother, Tybalt, Romeo, Juliet,
All slain, all dead. "Romeo is banished!"
There is no end, no limit, measure, bound,
130   In that word's death; no words can that woe sound.
Where is my father and my mother, nurse?

NURSE
Weeping and wailing over Tybalt's corse.
Will you go to them? I will bring you thither.

JULIET
Wash they his wounds with tears? Mine shall be spent,
135   When theirs are dry, for Romeo's banishment.
Take up those cords. Poor ropes, you are beguil'd,
Both you and I, for Romeo is exil'd.
He made you for a highway to my bed,

But why, villain, did you kill my cousin?
105   But my villainous cousin would have killed my husband!
Get back, foolish tears, back to your native spring.
Tear drops are for sorrows,
which you mistakenly offer when I feel happy.
My husband lives whom Tybalt would have killed.
110   And Tybalt, who would have killed my husband, is dead.
This is comforting—why then am I crying?
There was a word, worse than Tybalt's death,
that murdered me. I wish I could forget it,
but it tries to make me remember
115   like damning guilty deeds coming to sinners' minds.
"Tybalt is dead, and Romeo—banished."
"Banished." That one word "banished"
equals the death of ten thousand Tybalts. Tybalt's death
was sad enough, if that was the end of the bad news.
120   Or if misery loves company
and must be accompanied by other griefs,
why didn't my nurse tell me after she said "Tybalt's dead"
that my father was dead, or my mother, or even both.
Such news would have brought ordinary grief.
125   But following news of Tybalt's death
came the news "Romeo is banished." To say that
is the same as saying father, mother, Tybalt, Romeo
      and Juliet
are all killed, all dead! "Romeo is banished!"
There is no end, no limit, no meaning, no boundary
130   in that word. No words can describe that sorrow.
Where are my mother and father, nurse?

NURSE
They are crying and grieving over Tybalt's body.
Will you go to them? I'll take you.

JULIET
Are they washing his wounds with their tears? My
      tears will be shed,
135   when theirs are dry, for Romeo's banishment.
Take away those ropes. Poor ropes, you are tricked—
both you and I, for Romeo is exiled.
He wanted you to be a highway to my bed,

But I, a maid, die maiden-widowed.
140   Come, cords, come, nurse; I'll to my wedding-bed;
And death, not Romeo, take my maidenhead!

NURSE
Hie to your chamber. I'll find Romeo
To comfort you; I wot well where he is.
Hark ye, your Romeo will be here at night.
145   I'll to him; he is hid at Laurence' cell.

JULIET
O, find him! Give this ring to my true knight
And bid him come to take his last farewell.

[*Exeunt.*]

Scene iii: [*Friar Laurence's cell.*] *Enter* FRIAR LAURENCE,
ROMEO [*following*].

FRIAR LAURENCE
Romeo, come forth; come forth, thou fearful man:
Affliction is enamour'd of thy parts,
And thou art wedded to calamity.

ROMEO
Father, what news? What is the Prince's doom?
5   What sorrow craves acquaintance at my hand,
That I yet know not?

FRIAR LAURENCE
                    Too familiar
Is my dear son with such sour company.
I bring thee tidings of the Prince's doom.

ROMEO
10   What less than dooms-day is the Prince's doom?

FRIAR LAURENCE
A gentler judgement vanish'd from his lips,
Not body's death, but body's banishment.

but I, a virgin, will die a virgin-widow.
140   Come, ropes! Come, nurse! I'll go to my
          wedding bed.
      And death, not Romeo, will take my virginity!

NURSE
      Hurry to your room! I'll find Romeo
      to comfort you. I know where he is.
      Listen to me, your Romeo will be here tonight.
145   I'll go find him. He's hiding at Friar Laurence's cell.

JULIET
      O find him! Give this ring to my true knight
      and tell him to come to say his last goodbye.
          They exit.

Act III, Scene iii: Friar Laurence's cell. Enter FRIAR LAURENCE.

FRIAR LAURENCE
      Romeo, come out! Come out, you fearful man!
      Pain is in love with you,
      and you are married to trouble.
          Enter ROMEO.

ROMEO
      What's the news, father? What is the prince's
          sentence?
5   What sorrow am I going to learn about now
      that I don't already know?

FRIAR LAURENCE
      You are too familiar
      with unhappy things, my dear man.
      I bring you news of the prince's sentence.

ROMEO
10   What except death can the prince's sentence be?

FRIAR LAURENCE
      He gave a more gentle sentence—
      you'll not be executed, just banished.

ROMEO

Ha, banishment! Be merciful, say "death";
For exile hath more terror in his look,
15   Much more than death. Do not say "banishment"!

FRIAR LAURENCE

Here from Verona art thou banished.
Be patient, for the world is broad and wide.

ROMEO

There is no world without Verona walls,
But purgatory, torture, hell itself.
20   Hence "banished" is banish'd from the world,
And world's exile is death; then "banished"
Is death mis-term'd. Calling death "banishment,"
Thou cut'st my head off with a golden axe,
And smil'st upon the stroke that murders me.

FRIAR LAURENCE

25   O deadly sin! O rude unthankfulness!
Thy fault our law calls death; but the kind prince,
Taking thy part, hath rush'd aside the law,
And turn'd that black word "death" to "banishment."
This is dear mercy, and thou seest it not.

ROMEO

30   'Tis torture, and not mercy. Heaven is here,
Where Juliet lives; and every cat and dog
And little mouse, every unworthy thing,
Live here in heaven and may look on her;
But Romeo may not. More validity,
35   More honourable state, more courtship lives
In carrion-flies than Romeo; they may seize
On the white wonder of dear Juliet's hand
And steal immortal blessing from her lips,
Who, even in pure and vestal modesty,
40   Still blush, as thinking their own kisses sin;
But Romeo may not; he is banished.
This may flies do, when I from this must fly;
They are free men, but I am banished:

ROMEO
Banishment! Be merciful! Say, "death," instead.
Exile is worse than death,
15   much worse than death. Don't say, "banishment!"

FRIAR LAURENCE
You are banished from Verona.
Be patient. The world is broad and wide.

ROMEO
There's no world outside Verona!
There's only purgatory, torture, and hell itself!
20   To be banished from Verona is to be banished from the world,
and exile from the world is death! So to be banished
means death, in other words. By saying death is banishment,
you cut off my head with a golden axe,
and smile upon my murder.

FRIAR LAURENCE
25   You're speaking a deadly sin. You're rude and unthankful!
For your crime, the lawful punishment is death, but
    the kind prince
sided with you and put aside the law,
turning the black word "death" to "banishment."
He granted you mercy and you don't see it.

ROMEO
30   It's torture, not mercy! Heaven is here
where Juliet lives. Every cat and dog
and little mouse and every unworthy thing here
lives in heaven if they can look at her.
But Romeo may not. There's more value,
35   more honor, and more courtship
in flies than in Romeo. Flies may sit
on Juliet's white, wondrous hands
and steal heavenly blessings from her lips
which in pure and virginal modesty
40   always blush because they think it's a sinful kiss
    when they press together.
But Romeo may not kiss her lips because he's banished.
Flies may touch her, but I must fly away from her.
Flies are free, but I am banished.

And say'st thou yet that exile is not death?
45 Hadst thou no poison mix'd, no sharp-ground knife,
No sudden mean of death, though ne'er so mean,
But "banished" to kill me?—"Banished"?
O friar, the damned use that word in hell;
Howling attends it. How hast thou the heart,
50 Being a divine, a ghostly confessor,
A sin-absolver, and my friend profess'd,
To mangle me with that word "banished"?

FRIAR LAURENCE
Thou fond mad man, hear me a little speak.

ROMEO
O, thou wilt speak again of banishment.

FRIAR LAURENCE
55 I'll give thee armour to keep off that word;
Adversity's sweet milk, philosophy,
To comfort thee, though thou art banished.

ROMEO
Yet "banished"? Hang up philosophy!
Unless philosophy can make a Juliet,
60 Displant a town, reverse a prince's doom,
It helps not, it prevails not. Talk no more.

FRIAR LAURENCE
O, then I see that madmen have no ears.

ROMEO
How should they, when that wise men have no eyes?

FRIAR LAURENCE
Let me dispute with thee of thy estate.

ROMEO
65 Thou canst not speak of that thou dost not feel.
Wert thou as young as I, Juliet thy love,
An hour but married, Tybalt murdered,
Doting like me and like me banished,
Then mightst thou speak, then mightst thou tear thy hair,
70 And fall upon the ground as I do now,

And you still say exile is not death?
45   Don't you have some poison, or a sharp knife,
or some quick means of dying—no matter how crude—
other than the word "banished" to kill me? Banished?
O friar, the damned use that word in hell;
they howl when it is spoken! How can you have the heart,
50   being a holy man, a confessor,
a sin-forgiver, and my friend,
to tear me apart with that word banished?

FRIAR LAURENCE
You foolish madman, listen to me for just a moment.

ROMEO
No. You'll talk again of banishment.

FRIAR LAURENCE
55   I'll give you some armor to shield you from that word.
I'll give you the sweet milk of philosophy
to comfort you, though you are banished.

ROMEO
You say "banished" again? Hang your philosophy—
Unless philosphy can make a Juliet,
60   move Verona, or reverse the prince's sentence,
it won't help, it will be useless. Don't say any more.

FRIAR LAURENCE
O, I see, then, that madmen have no ears.

ROMEO
How can they, when wise men have no eyes?

FRIAR LAURENCE
Let me discuss your situation with you—

ROMEO
65   You can't talk about something you can't feel.
If you were as young as I am, Juliet your lover,
married only an hour, Tybalt killed,
as deeply in love as I am, and banished like me,
then you could speak. Then you would tear your hair out!
70   Then you would fall upon the ground, as I do now, and

Taking the measure of an unmade grave.

[*Knocking within.*]

FRIAR LAURENCE

Arise; one knocks. Good Romeo, hide thyself.

ROMEO

Not I; unless the breath of heart-sick groans,
Mist-like infold me from the search of eyes.

[*Knocking.*]

FRIAR LAURENCE

75   Hark, how they knock! Who's there? Romeo, arise;
Thou wilt be taken.—Stay a while!—Stand up;

[*Knocking.*]

Run to my study.—By and by!—God's will,
What simpleness is this!—I come, I come!

[*Knocking.*]

Who knocks so hard? Whence come you? What's your will?

Enter NURSE.

NURSE

80   Let me come in, and you shall know my errand.
I come from Lady Juliet.

FRIAR LAURENCE

                      Welcome, then.

NURSE

O holy friar, O, tell me, holy friar,
Where is my lady's lord, where's Romeo?

FRIAR LAURENCE

85   There on the ground, with his own tears made drunk.

NURSE

O, he is even in my mistress' case,
Just in her case! O woeful sympathy!
Piteous predicament! Even so lies she,
Blubb'ring and weeping, weeping and blubb'ring.

90   Stand up, stand up; stand, an you be a man.

measure your unmade grave.
>*There is a knock at the door.*

FRIAR LAURENCE
Get up, Romeo! Someone is knocking. Good Romeo, hide.

ROMEO
No, I won't—not unless the breath from my heartsick groans
wraps me in a mist to hide me from searching eyes.
>*There is another knock.*

FRIAR LAURENCE
75 Listen, they're knocking again. Who's there? Romeo, get up!
You'll be arrested! (*To the knocker*) Just a
minute! (*To Romeo*) Get up!
>*Knocking.*

Run to my study! (*To the knocker*) I'm coming!
(*To Romeo*) Why are you acting so foolishly?
(*To the knocker*) I'm coming, I'm coming!
>*Knocking.*

Who is knocking so hard? Where did you come from?
What do you want?
>*NURSE enters.*

NURSE
80 Let me come in and I'll tell you what I want.
I come from Lady Juliet.

FRIAR LAURENCE
Welcome, then.

NURSE
O holy friar. Tell me, holy friar,
where's my lady's lord? Where's Romeo?

FRIAR LAURENCE
85 He's lying there on the ground, drunk with his own tears.

NURSE
He's just like my mistress—
just like her! What a sorrowful echo of Juliet's grief!
It's a pitiful predicament. She lies just like him,
blubbering and crying, crying and blubbering.
90 Stand up, stand up! Stand if you're a man.

For Juliet's sake, for her sake, rise and stand;
Why should you fall into so deep an O?

ROMEO
Nurse!

NURSE
Ah sir! ah sir! Death's the end of all.

ROMEO
95   Spak'st thou of Juliet? How is it with her?
Doth not she think me an old murderer,
Now I have stain'd the childhood of our joy
With blood remov'd but little from her own?
Where is she? and how doth she? and what says
100   My conceal'd lady to our cancell'd love?

NURSE
O, she says nothing, sir, but weeps and weeps;
And now falls on her bed; and then starts up,
And Tybalt calls; and then on Romeo cries,
And then down falls again.

ROMEO
105   As if that name,
Shot from the deadly level of a gun,
Did murder her, as that name's cursed hand
Murder'd her kinsman. O, tell me, friar, tell me,
In what vile part of this anatomy
110   Doth my name lodge? Tell me, that I may sack
The hateful mansion.

     [*He offers to stab himself, and the Nurse snatches the
     dagger away.*]

FRIAR LAURENCE
              Hold thy desperate hand!
Art thou a man? Thy form cries out thou art;
Thy tears are womanish; thy wild acts denote
115   The unreasonable fury of a beast.
Unseemly woman in a seeming man,
And ill-beseeming beast in seeming both,

For Juliet's sake, for her sake, rise and stand.
Why should you fall into such a fit of grief?

ROMEO (*rises*)
Nurse!

NURSE
Alas, sir. Well, death ends everything.

ROMEO
95   Did you speak of Juliet? How is she?
Does she think I am a hardened murderer
now that I have stained the beginning of our joyful
    marriage
with the blood of her cousin.
Where is she? How is she? What does my
100   secretly-married wife say about our cancelled
    marriage?

NURSE
She says nothing, sir. She just cries and cries
and falls on her bed. Then she gets up
and calls Tybalt, and then she cries for Romeo,
and then she falls on her bed again.

ROMEO
105   It's just like my name
is a shot from a deadly gun
that murdered her, as my cursed hand
murdered her cousin. O, tell me, friar, tell me,
in what horrible part of my body
110   does my name lie? Tell me so I can destroy
that hateful part.
        ROMEO *tries to stab himself, but the* NURSE
        snatches the dagger out of his hand.

FRIAR LAURENCE
Stop your desperate hand!
Are you a man? Your body says you are,
but your tears are womanish and your wild actions
    are like
115   the irrational actions of an animal.
You're like an undignified woman in the body of a man—
an odd animal in seeming to be both man and woman.

Thou hast amaz'd me! By my holy order,
I thought thy disposition better temper'd.
120   Hast thou slain Tybalt? Wilt thou slay thyself,
And slay thy lady that in thy life lives,
By doing damned hate upon thyself?
Why rail'st thou on thy birth, the heaven, and earth?
Since birth, and heaven, and earth, all three do meet
125   In thee at once, which thou at once wouldst lose.
Fie, fie, thou sham'st thy shape, thy love, thy wit;
Which, like a usurer, abound'st in all,
And usest none in that true use indeed
Which should bedeck thy shape, thy love, thy wit.
130   Thy noble shape is but a form of wax,
Digressing from the valour of a man;
Thy dear love sworn but hollow purjury,
Killing that love which thou hast vow'd to cherish;
Thy wit, that ornament to shape and love,
135   Mis-shapen in the conduct of them both,
Like powder in a skilless soldier's flask,
Is set a-fire by thine own ignorance,
And thou dismemb'red with thine own defence.
What, rouse thee, man! thy Juliet is alive,
140   For whose dear sake thou wast but lately dead:
There art thou happy. Tybalt would kill thee,
But thou slewest Tybalt: there art thou happy.
The law that threat'ned death becomes thy friend
And turns it to exile: there art thou happy.
145   A pack of blessings light upon thy back;
Happiness courts thee in her best array;
But, like a misbehav'd and sullen wench,
Thou pout'st upon thy fortune and thy love.
Take heed, take heed, for such die miserable.
150   Go, get thee to thy love, as was decreed;
Ascend her chamber; hence, and comfort her.
But look thou stay not till the watch be set,
For then thou canst not pass to Mantua,
Where thou shalt live till we can find a time
155   To blaze your marriage, reconcile your friends,

---

124 *birth, and heaven, and earth*   Romeo's family background, soul, and body.   125 *at once wouldst lose*   since Friar Laurence is Catholic, he believes that Romeo would lose his soul as well as his earthly life if he committed suicide.

You amaze me! By my holy order,
I thought you had a more even-tempered disposition.
120 Have you killed Tybalt? Will you kill yourself?
And will you also kill the lady whose life is your life
by killing yourself?
Why are you ranting about your birth, the heavens,
and earth?
Birth, heaven, and earth—all three—are joined
125 in you at the same time. Now you want to desert all
of that at once.
For shame! You shame your body, your love, and your
intelligence.
You're like a moneylender who has countless riches
and yet uses none of that wealth properly
to honor your body, love, and intelligence.
130 Your handsome body is just a wax model
without manly virtues.
The love you have sworn is just a lie
and kills the love which you have vowed to cherish.
Your intelligence, that complement to your body and love,
135 poorly directs both of those.
Your intelligence is like gunpowder in a novice soldier's powder horn—
lit by your own ignorance
and blowing you apart with your own weapon.
Wake up man! Your Juliet is alive!
140 It was for her sake that you wanted to be dead just now.
You are fortunate. Tybalt wanted to kill you,
but you killed him. You are fortunate.
The law that threatened your death became your friend
and gave you exile. You are fortunate.
145 A pack of blessings have fallen on your back.
Happiness comes to you in her best clothes
but, like a badly behaved and sullen maid,
you frown at your good fortune and your love.
Listen to me, people like you die miserably.
150 Go, get to your love as your marriage decrees that you should do.
Climb to her room and comfort her.
But be sure you don't stay until the night guards
come on duty,
for then you can't escape to Mantua—
where you will live until we can find a time
155 to announce your marriage, reconcile your friends,

Beg pardon of the Prince, and call thee back
With twenty hundred thousand times more joy
Than thou went'st forth in lamentation.
Go before, nurse; commend me to thy lady;
160 And bid her hasten all the house to bed,
Which heavy sorrow makes them apt unto.
Romeo is coming.

NURSE
O Lord, I could have stay'd here all the night
To hear good counsel. O, what learning is!
165 My lord, I'll tell my lady you will come.

ROMEO
Do so, and bid my sweet prepare to chide.

[*Nurse offers to go in, and turns again.*]

NURSE
Here, sir, a ring she bid me give you, sir.
Hie you, make haste, for it grows very late.

ROMEO
How well my comfort is reviv'd by this!

[*Exit Nurse.*]

FRIAR LAURENCE
170 Go hence; good-night; and here stands all your state:
Either be gone before the watch be set,
Or by the break of day disguis'd from hence.
Sojourn in Mantua; I'll find out your man,
And he shall signify from time to time
175 Every good hap to you that chances here.
Give me thy hand; 'tis late. Farewell; good-night.

ROMEO
But that a joy past joy calls out on me,
It were a grief, so brief to part with thee.
Farewell.

[*Exeunt.*]

ask the prince's pardon, and bring you back home
with two million times more joy
than when you left in sorrow.
Go, nurse. Give my regards to your lady,
160   and tell her to hurry everyone in the house to bed.
Their heavy grief will make them want to go to bed,
       anyway.
Tell her Romeo is coming.

NURSE
O Lord, I could have stayed here all night
to hear such good advice. O, learning is wonderful!
165   My lord, I'll tell my lady you'll come.

ROMEO
Do so, and bid my sweet lady to prepare to scold me.
       The NURSE starts to leave but turns back.

NURSE
Here's a ring she asked me to give you, sir.
Hurry! Make haste, for it's getting very late.

ROMEO
I'm greatly comforted by this ring.
       The NURSE exits.

FRIAR LAURENCE (*to Nurse*)
170   Go, good night. (*To Romeo*) Here's your situation:
you must leave before the guards are posted at the
       gates,
or leave in a disguise at the break of day.
Stay in Mantua. I'll find your servant,
and he'll tell you from time to time
175   every good thing that occurs here.
Give me your hand. It's late. Farewell; good night.

ROMEO
If a joy to surpass all joys did not call me,
it would be sad to leave you so quickly.
Farewell!
       They exit.

Scene iv: [*A room in Capulet's house.*] *Enter* CAPULET,
LADY CAUPLET, *and* PARIS.

CAPULET
Things have fallen out, sir, so unluckily
That we have had no time to move our daughter.
Look you, she lov'd her kinsman Tybalt dearly,
And so did I. Well, we were born to die.
5   'Tis very late, she'll not come down to-night;
I promise you, but for your company,
I would have been a-bed an hour ago.

PARIS
These times of woe afford no times to woo.
Madam, good-night; commend me to your daughter.

LADY CAPULET
10   I will, and know her mind early to-morrow;
To-night she's mewed up to her heaviness.

CAPULET
Sir Paris, I will make a desperate tender
Of my child's love. I think she will be rul'd
In all respects by me; nay, more, I doubt it not.
15   Wife, go you to her ere you go to bed;
Acquaint her here of my son Paris' love;
And bid her—mark you me?—on Wednesday next—
But, soft! what day is this?

PARIS
                                    Monday, my lord.

CAPULET
20   Monday! ha, ha! Well, Wednesday is too soon,
O' Thursday let it be,—o' Thursday, tell her,
She shall be married to this noble earl.
Will you be ready? Do you like this haste?
We'll keep no great ado,—a friend or two;
25   For, hark you, Tybalt being slain so late,
It may be thought we held him carelessly,
Being our kinsman, if we revel much;

Act III, Scene iv: A room in Capulet's house. Enter CAPULET,
LADY CAPULET *and* PARIS.

CAPULET
>Because of recent unhappy events,
>we've had no time to talk to our daughter.
>You see, she loved her cousin Tybalt dearly,
>and so did I. Well, we're all born to die.
>5   It's very late; she won't come down tonight.
>I assure you, if you had not been here,
>I would have been to bed an hour ago.

PARIS
>This time of sorrow is not the time to court her.
>Madam, good night. Give my regards to your daughter.

LADY CAPULET
>10   I will. And I'll find out what she thinks, tomorrow.
>Tonight, she's shut up in her room with her grief.

CAPULET
>Sir, I'll make a rash offer
>of my daughter's love. I think she'll obey me
>in everything. No, I don't doubt that she'll listen to me.
>15   Wife, go to her before you go to bed
>and tell her of Paris' love.
>Also tell her—are you listening to me?—that next Wednesday—
>Wait! What day is this?

PARIS
>Monday, my lord.

CAPULET
>20   Monday! (*Laughs*) Well then, Wednesday is too soon.
>Let it be on Thursday! (*To Lady Capulet*) Tell
>   her that on Thursday
>she shall be married to this noble earl.
>(*To Paris*) Can you be ready? How do these speedy
>   arrangements strike you?
>We won't have a big wedding—just a friend or two.
>25   For really, since Tybalt was killed so recently,
>it could be thought that we didn't care much for him,
>one of our relatives, if we celebrated too much.

Therefore we'll have some half a dozen friends,
And there an end. But what say you to Thursday?

PARIS

30   My lord, I would that Thursday were to-morrow.

CAPULET

Well, get you gone; o' Thursday be it, then.
Go you to Juliet ere you go to bed;
Prepare her, wife, against this wedding-day.
Farewell, my lord. Light to my chamber, ho!
35   Afore me! it is so very late that we
May call it early by and by. Good-night.

[*Exeunt.*]

Scene v: [*Capulet's orchard.*] *Enter* ROMEO *and* JULIET,
aloft.

JULIET

Wilt thou be gone? it is not yet near day.
It was the nightingale, and not the lark,
That pierc'd the fearful hollow of thine ear;
Nightly she sings on yond pomegranate-tree.
5   Believe me, love, it was the nightingale.

ROMEO

It was the lark, the herald of the morn,
No nightingale. Look, love, what envious streaks
Do lace the severing clouds in yonder east.
Night's candles are burnt out, and jocund day
10   Stands tiptoe on the misty mountain tops.
I must be gone and live, or stay and die.

JULIET

Yond light is not day-light, I know it, I;
It is some meteor that the sun exhales
To be to thee this night a torch-bearer
15   And light thee on thy way to Mantua;
Therefore stay yet; thou need'st not to be gone.

Therefore, we'll invite just a half a dozen friends,
and that will be all. How is Thursday for you, Paris?

PARIS
30   My lord, I wish Thursday were tomorrow.

CAPULET
Well, go now. It will be on Thursday, then. (*To
his wife*) Go to Juliet before you go to bed,
and prepare her for her wedding day. (*To Paris*)
Goodbye, my lord. (*To servants*) Give me a light
to my bedroom.
35   By heaven, it's so late,
we'll soon have to call it early. Good night.
    They exit.

Act III, Scene v: Capulet's house. Enter ROMEO *and* JULIET *on the
balcony.*

JULIET
Do you have to go? It isn't day yet.
It was the nightingale, not the lark,
that sang in your apprehensive ear.
She sings every night on the pomegranate tree.
5   Believe me, love, it was the nightingale.

ROMEO
It was the lark, the herald of the morning,
not a nightingale. Look, love, see the envious streaks
of light that lace the scattering clouds in the east.
The stars are fading and cheerful day
10   stands on tiptoe on the foggy mountaintops.
If I want to live, I must go. If I stay, I will die.

JULIET
That light is not daylight. I know it.
It's just a meteor from the sun
which will be your torchbearer
15   tonight and light your road to Mantua.
Therefore, stay awhile; you don't need to go yet.

ROMEO

Let me be ta'en, let me be put to death;
I am content, so thou wilt have it so.
I'll say yon grey is not the morning's eye,
20   'Tis but the pale reflex of Cynthia's brow;
Nor that is not the lark, whose notes do beat
The vaulty heaven so high above our heads.
I have more care to stay than will to go.
Come, death, and welcome! Juliet wills it so.
25   How is't, my soul? Let's talk; it is not day.

JULIET

It is, it is! Hie hence, be gone, away!
It is the lark that sings so out of tune,
Straining harsh discords and unpleasing sharps.
Some say the lark makes sweet division;
30   This doth not so, for she divideth us.
Some say the lark and loathed toad change eyes;
O, now I would they had chang'd voices too,
Since arm from arm that voice doth us affray,
Hunting thee hence with hunt's-up to the day.
35   O, now be gone; more light and light it grows.

ROMEO

More light and light; more dark and dark our woes!

Enter NURSE [*from the chamber*].

NURSE

Madam!

JULIET

Nurse?

NURSE

Your lady mother is coming to your chamber.
40   The day is broke; be wary, look about.

[*Exit.*]

JULIET

Then, window, let day in, and let life out.

ROMEO

    Let them capture me, let them put me to death.

    I'm content if you are satisfied.

    I'll say that the grey I see in the sky isn't morning

20   but just a pale reflection of the moon.

    It's not the lark I hear singing whose song rises to

    the heavens high above our heads.

    I have more desire to stay than will to go.

    Come death! Welcome! Juliet wills it.

25   How are you, my soul? Let's talk; it's not day.

JULIET

    It is! It is! Hurry, go, away!

    It's the lark that sings so out of tune

    singing harsh, sour notes and unpleasant sharps.

    Some people say the lark sings a sweet melody,

30   but this bird does not because she separates us.

    Some people say the lark and the hated toad exchanged
        eyes.

    I wish they'd exchanged voices, too,

    since that voice frightens us out of each other's arms

    and chases you from here with the song that awakens
        hunters.

35   O, go now! It grows lighter and lighter.

ROMEO

    Lighter and lighter means our sorrow grows darker
        and darker.

        Enter NURSE *from the bedroom.*

NURSE

    Madam!

JULIET

    Nurse?

NURSE

    Your mother is coming to your bedroom.

40   Day is dawning. Be careful; watch out.

        She exits.

JULIET

    Then, window, let day in, and let my life out.

ROMEO
> Farewell, farewell! One kiss, and I'll descend.

> [*He goeth down.*]

JULIET
> Art thou gone so? Love, lord, ay, husband, friend!
> I must hear from thee every day in the hour,
45   For in a minute there are many days.
> O, by this count I shall be much in years
> Ere I again behold my Romeo!

ROMEO
> [*From below.*] Farewell!
> I will omit no opportunity
50   That may convey my greetings, love, to thee.

JULIET
> O, think'st thou we shall ever meet again?

ROMEO
> I doubt it not; and all these woes shall serve
> For sweet discourses in our times to come.

JULIET
> O God, I have an ill-divining soul!
55   Methinks I see thee, now thou art below,
> As one dead in the bottom of a tomb.
> Either my eyesight fails, or thou look'st pale.

ROMEO
> And trust me, love, in my eye so do you;
> Dry sorrow drinks our blood. Adieu, adieu!

JULIET
60   O Fortune, Fortune! all men call thee fickle;
> If thou art fickle, what dost thou with him
> That is renown'd for faith? Be fickle, Fortune;
> For then, I hope, thou wilt not keep him long,
> But send him back.

> *Enter* LADY CAPULET.

---

59 *dry sorrow* sorrow was believed to dry up blood and other body fluids.

ROMEO
> Goodbye, goodbye! One kiss, and I'll descend.
> *He climbs down.*

JULIET
> Are you gone? My love, my lord, my husband, and my
>   friend?
> I must hear from you every hour of the day,
45   for just one minute will be like many days.
> If I count this way, I'll be very old
> before I see Romeo again.

ROMEO (*from below*)
> Goodbye!
> I'll not miss a chance
50   to send my greetings to you, love.

JULIET
> Do you think we'll ever meet again?

ROMEO
> I'm sure we will. Then all of these sorrows will
>   serve
> as sweet conversation in the future.

JULIET
> O God, I have a feeling of doom!
55   I think I see you, as you are now,
> but like a dead person in the bottom of a tomb.
> Either my eyesight is failing or you look pale.

ROMEO
> Trust me, love. In my eyes, you look pale, too.
> Our sorrow makes us pale. Goodbye, goodbye!

JULIET
60   O, Fate. Fate! All men call you fickle!
> If you're fickle, what business can you have with him
> who is known for his faith? Be fickle, Fate.
> Then you will not keep him long,
> and you'll send him back to me.
>   *Enter* LADY CAPULET.

LADY CAPULET

65   Ho, daughter! are you up?

JULIET

    Who is't that calls? It is my lady mother.
    Is she not down so late, or up so early?
    What unaccustom'd cause procures her hither?

LADY CAPULET

    Why, how now, Juliet?

JULIET

70   Madam, I am not well.

LADY CAPULET

    Evermore weeping for your cousin's death?
    What, wilt thou wash him from his grave with tears?
    An if thou couldst, thou couldst not make him live;
    Therefore, have done. Some grief shows much of love,
75   But much of grief shows still some want of wit.

JULIET

    Yet let me weep for such a feeling loss.

LADY CAPULET

    So shall you feel the loss, but not the friend
    Which you weep for.

JULIET

                Feeling so the loss,
80   I cannot choose but ever weep the friend.

LADY CAPULET

    Well, girl, thou weep'st not so much for his death,
    As that the villain lives which slaughter'd him.

JULIET

    What villain, madam?

LADY CAPULET

               That same villain, Romeo.

JULIET

85   [*Aside.*] Villain and he be many miles asunder.—
    God pardon him! I do, with all my heart;
    And yet no man like he doth grieve my heart.

LADY CAPULET
65   Daughter, are you up?

JULIET
Who's calling? It's my mother.
Is she up late or up early?
What unusual occurrence brings her here?

LADY CAPULET
How are you, Juliet?

JULIET
70   Madam, I'm not well.

LADY CAPULET
Are you still crying for your cousin's death?
Will your tears wash him out of his grave?
Even if they did, you couldn't make him live.
So quit crying. Some grief reveals deep love,
75   but too much grief reveals a lack of intelligence.

JULIET
Let me cry over such a deeply-felt loss.

LADY CAPULET
Then you'll feel the loss,
but not the friend for whom you weep.

JULIET
Since I feel the loss,
80   I can't help crying for my friend.

LADY CAPULET
Well, girl, you're really not crying for his death,
but for the fact that the villain who killed him
    still lives.

JULIET
What villain, madam?

LADY CAPULET
The villain Romeo.

JULIET (*to herself*)
85   There is a big difference between Romeo and a villain.
(*To Lady Capulet*) God forgive him! I forgive him
    with all my heart.
And yet no man grieves my heart more than Romeo.

LADY CAPULET
That is, because the traitor murderer lives.

JULIET
Ay, madam, from the reach of these my hands.
90   Would none but I might venge my cousin's death!

LADY CAPULET
We will have vengeance for it, fear thou not;
Then weep no more. I'll send to one in Mantua,
Where that same banish'd runagate doth live,
Shall give him such an unaccustom'd dram
95   That he shall soon keep Tybalt company;
And then, I hope, thou wilt be satisfied.

JULIET
Indeed, I never shall be satisfied
With Romeo, till I behold him—dead—
Is my poor heart, so for a kinsman vex'd.
100   Madam, if you could find out but a man
To bear a poison, I would temper it
That Romeo should, upon receipt thereof,
Soon sleep in quiet. O, how my heart abhors
To hear him nam'd, and cannot come to him
105   To wreak the love I bore my cousin Tybalt
Upon his body that hath slaughter'd him!

LADY CAPULET
Find thou the means, and I'll find such a man.
But now I'll tell thee joyful tidings, girl.

JULIET
And joy comes well in such a needy time.
110   What are they, I beseech your ladyship?

LADY CAPULET
Well, well, thou hast a careful father, child;
One who, to put thee from thy heaviness,
Hath sorted out a sudden day of joy
That thou expects not nor I look'd not for.

97-106 *never, ff* Juliet uses double meanings in this speech. She is seconding her mother's opinion that Romeo should be punished and expressing her devotion to her lover at the same time.

LADY CAPULET
That's because that traitor and murderer still lives.

JULIET
I wish that only my hands
90 could avenge my cousin's death.

LADY CAPULET
We'll have revenge for his death, don't you fear.
So don't cry any more. I'll send a message to someone
    in Mantua
where that banished renegade lives,
and he'll give Romeo so much poison
95 that he'll soon keep Tybalt company in the grave.
Then I hope you'll be satisfied.

JULIET
I'll never be satisfied
with Romeo until I see him—dead—
is my poor heart, so upset am I about my cousin's death.
100 Madam, if you could find a man
to take the poison, I would mix it with my own hands
    so that
as soon as Romeo gets it,
he'll sleep quietly. O, how my heart hates
to hear his name and not be able to come to him
105 to pour the love I bore for Tybalt
upon the body of the man who killed him.

LADY CAPULET
You find the poison, and I'll find the poisoner.
But now I'll tell you some joyful news, girl.

JULIET
Joy would be very welcome right now.
110 What's your news? I beg, your ladyship, tell me.

LADY CAPULET
Well, you have a thoughtful father, child.
To help you get over your grief,
he's set a day of joy in the near future
which you did not expect and I did not anticipate.

JULIET

115   Madam, in happy time, what day is that?

LADY CAPULET

Marry, my child, early next Thursday morn
The gallant, young, and noble gentleman,
The County Paris, at Saint Peter's Church,
Shall happily make thee there a joyful bride.

JULIET

120   Now, by Saint Peter's Church and Peter too,
He shall not make me there a joyful bride.
I wonder at this haste that I must wed
Ere he that should be husband comes to woo.
I pray you, tell my lord and father, madam,
125   I will not marry yet; and when I do, I swear,
It shall be Romeo, whom you know I hate,
Rather than Paris. These are news indeed!

LADY CAPULET

Here comes your father; tell him so yourself,
And see how he will take it at your hands.

Enter CAPULET *and* NURSE.

CAPULET

130   When the sun sets, the air doth drizzle dew;
But for the sunset of my brother's son
It rains downright.
How now! a conduit, girl? What, still in tears?
Evermore show'ring? In one little body
135   Thou counterfeits a bark, a sea, a wind:
For still thy eyes, which I may call the sea,
Do ebb and flow with tears; the bark thy body is,
Sailing in this salt flood; the winds, thy sighs,
Who, raging with thy tears, and they with them,
140   Without a sudden calm, will overset
Thy tempest-tossed body. How now, wife!
Have you delivered to her our decree?

JULIET

115   Madam, how fortunate! What day is that?

LADY CAPULET
    My child, early next Thursday morning,
    the brave, young, and noble gentleman,
    Count Paris, will make you
    a joyful bride at St. Peter's church.

JULIET

120   By St. Peter's church and St. Peter, too,
    he won't make me a joyful bride!
    I don't understand what's all the rush to force me
       to marry
    my future husband before he even comes to court me.
    I beg you, tell my lord and father, madam,

125   that I'll not marry yet. And when I do get married,
    it will be to Romeo, whom you know I hate,
    rather than to Paris. Now that's a real piece of news!

LADY CAPULET
    Here comes your father. Tell him yourself,
    and see how well he'll take this news from you.
        Enter CAPULET *and* NURSE.

CAPULET

130   When the sun sets, the air drizzles dew,
    but the sunset for my brother's son,
    is downright rainy.
    What's going on? Are you a water pipe, girl? Are
       you still in tears?
    Are you always crying? In your one little body,

135   you imitate a ship, a sea, and a wind.
    Your eyes, which I might call a sea,
    are always ebbing and flowing with tears. The ship is your
    body sailing on this salty flood of tears. The
       winds are your sighs,
    raging with your tears and your tears raging with
       those sighs.

140   If we don't have a sudden calm, the storm will overturn
    your storm-tossed body. Well, wife?
    Have you told her about my decision?

LADY CAPULET

　　Ay, sir; but she will none, she gives you thanks.
　　I would the fool were married to her grave!

CAPULET

145　Soft! take me with you, take me with you, wife.
　　How! will she none? Doth she not give us thanks?
　　Is she not proud? Doth she not count her blest,
　　Unworthy as she is, that we have wrought
　　So worthy a gentleman to be her bride?

JULIET

150　Not proud you have; but thankful that you have.
　　Proud can I never be of what I hate;
　　But thankful even for hate that is meant love.

CAPULET

　　How how, how how, chop-logic! What is this?
　　"Proud," and "I thank you," and "I thank you not;"
155　And yet "not proud." Mistress minion, you,
　　Thank me no thankings, nor proud me no prouds,
　　But fettle your fine joints 'gainst Thursday next,
　　To go with Paris to Saint Peter's Church,
　　Or I will drag thee on a hurdle thither.
160　Out, you green-sickness carrion! Out you baggage!
　　You tallow-face!

LADY CAPULET

　　　　　　　　　　　　　Fie, fie! what, are you mad?

JULIET

　　Good father, I beseech you on my knees,
　　Hear me with patience but to speak a word.

CAPULET

165　Hang thee, young baggage! disobedient wretch!
　　I tell thee what: get thee to church o' Thursday,
　　Or never after look me in the face.
　　Speak not, reply not, do not answer me!
　　My fingers itch. Wife, we scarce thought us blest
170　That God had lent us but this only child;
　　But now I see this one is one too much,

---

159 *hurdle*　is a sledge or a heavy cart upon which criminals were dragged off to execution.

LADY CAPULET

    Yes, sir, but she says she won't marry Paris, but
      thanks you anyway.
    I wish this fool were married to her grave.

CAPULET

145   Wait a moment! Let me understand you, wife.
    What do you mean? She won't? Didn't she thank us?
    Isn't she proud? Doesn't she count herself lucky,
    unworthy as she is, that we've arranged for
    so worthy a gentleman to marry her?

JULIET

150   I'm not very pleased, but I'm thankful.
    I can never be proud of what I hate,
    but I'm thankful even for something hateful that is
      meant to be a gift of love.

CAPULET

    Are you splitting hairs? What is this?
    "Proud"? "I thank you"? "I thank you not"
155   and "not very pleased"? You spoiled child!
    Don't thank me with "no thank you" or give me any "not prouds."
    Just prepare your fine self to be ready next Thursday
    to marry Paris at St. Peter's church!
    If you don't, I'll drag you there on a cart.
160   Get out, you anemic thing! Out, you minx!
    You waxy-faced girl!

LADY CAPULET

    Are you crazy?

JULIET

    Good father, I beg you on my knees. (*She kneels*)
    Listen to me with patience. Just let me speak one word.

CAPULET

165   Hang you, you minx! You disobedient wretch!
    I'll tell you now: go to the church on Thursday,
    or never look on my face again.
    Don't speak, don't reply, don't answer me!
    My fingers itch (to hit you). Wife, we really
      didn't think we had been blessed
170   when God gave us just this one child.
    But now I think this one is too much

And that we have a curse in having her.
Out on her, hilding!

NURSE

                God in heaven bless her!
175   You are to blame, my lord, to rate her so.

CAPULET

And why, my lady Wisdom? Hold your tongue,
Good prudence; smatter with your gossips, go.

NURSE

I speak no treason.

CAPULET

              O, God ye god-den.

NURSE

180   May not one speak?

CAPULET

                 Peace, you mumbling fool!
Utter your gravity o'er a gossip's bowl;
For here we need it not.

LADY CAPULET

                You are too hot.

CAPULET

185   God's bread! it makes me mad.
Day, night, hour, tide, time, work, play,
Alone, in company, still my care hath been
To have her match'd; and having now provided
A gentleman of noble parentage,
190   Of fair demesnes, youthful and nobly train'd,
Stuff'd, as they say, with honourable parts,
Proportion'd as one's thought would wish a man;
And then to have a wretched puling fool,
A whining mammet, in her fortune's tender
195   To answer, "I'll not wed; I cannot love,
I am too young; I pray you, pardon me."
But, an you will not wed, I'll pardon you.
Graze where you will, you shall not house with me.

and that we have been cursed by having her.
Out with her, the wretch!

NURSE
God in heaven bless her!
175   You're to blame for speaking to her so horribly.

CAPULET
What, my Lady Wisdom? Shut your mouth,
Miss Prudence! Go gossip with your old cronies.

NURSE
I'm not speaking treason.

CAPULET
O, for God's sake!

NURSE
180   Isn't a person allowed to speak?

CAPULET
Quiet, you mumbling fool.
Save your wisdom for the gossipers, for we don't need
    it here.

LADY CAPULET
You're too angry.

CAPULET
By God's sacrament! It makes me so mad!
185   Day and night, early and late, at work or relaxing,
alone or with others, my one thought has been
to make her a good match. And now I've provided
for you a gentleman from noble parents,
of beautiful estates, youthful and well-trained,
190   full of honor, and as handsome and well-built
as any girl could wish a man to be.
And then to have a wretched, whining fool,
a crying doll, who when offered good fortune
says, "I won't marry him. I can't love him.
195   I'm too young. I beg you to excuse me."
If you don't marry, I'll "excuse" you to find
    another home.
Go where you want to—you won't live here.

Look to't, think on't, I do not use to jest.
200   Thursday is near; lay hand on heart, advise.
An you be mine, I'll give you to my friend;
An you be not, hang, beg, starve, die in the streets,
For by my soul, I'll ne'er acknowledge thee,
Nor what is mine shall never do thee good.
205   Trust to't, bethink you; I'll not be forsworn.

    [*Exit.*]

JULIET
Is there no pity sitting in the clouds,
That sees into the bottom of my grief?
O, sweet my mother, cast me not away!
Delay this marriage for a month, a week;
210   Or, if you do not, make the bridal bed
In that dim monument where Tybalt lies.

LADY CAPULET
Talk not to me, for I'll not speak a word.
Do as thou wilt, for I have done with thee.

    [*Exit.*]

JULIET
O God!—O nurse, how shall this be prevented?
215   My husband is on earth, my faith in heaven;
How shall that faith return again to earth,
Unless that husband send it me from heaven
By leaving earth? Comfort me, counsel me!
Alack, alack, that heaven should practise stratagems
220   Upon so soft a subject as myself!
What say'st thou? Hast thou not a word of joy?
Some comfort, nurse.

NURSE
               Faith, here it is.
Romeo is banish'd; and all the world to nothing
225   That he dares ne'er come back to challenge you;
Or, if he do, it needs must be by stealth.
Then, since the case so stands as now it doth,
I think it best you married with the County.

Take care! Think about it! I'm not one to joke.
Thursday isn't far away. Think about it carefully.
200 If you're my daughter, I'll be giving your hand in
marriage to my friend.
If you don't marry, you can hang, beg, starve, and
die in the streets,
for I swear, I'll never recognize you
as my daughter again.
And I'll never give you anything.
205 Count on that! Think about it. I won't go back on my word.
He exits.

JULIET
Is there no pity in heaven
that can understand my grief?
O, sweet mother, don't disown me!
Put off this wedding for a month—a week.
210 Or if you don't, make my bridal bed
in the tomb where Tybalt lies.

LADY CAPULET
Don't talk to me. I won't say a word.
Do as you want to. I'm done with you.

JULIET
O God! Nurse, how shall this marriage be prevented?
215 My husband is on earth. My marriage vow to him was
made in heaven.
How can my heavenly vow be broken
unless my husband's death
makes me a widow? Comfort me, advise me.
O God, that heaven should use such tricks
220 on a person as weak as I am.
What do you say? Don't you have a word of comfort?
Give me some comfort, nurse.

NURSE
Indeed, here it is.
Romeo is banished and I think it's safe to say
225 that he'll never dare to come back and claim you as his wife.
If he does, he'll have to come in secret.
So as the situation now stands,
I think you should marry Count Paris.

O, he's a lovely gentleman!
230 Romeo's a dishclout to him. An eagle, madam,
Hath not so green, so quick, so fair an eye
As Paris hath. Beshrew my very heart,
I think you are happy in this second match,
For it excels your first; or if it did not,
235 Your first is dead; or 'twere as good he were
As living here and you no use of him.

JULIET
Speak'st thou from thy heart?

NURSE
And from my soul too; else beshrew them both.

JULIET
Amen!

NURSE
240 What?

JULIET
Well, thou hast comforted me marvellous much.
Go in; and tell my lady I am gone,
Having displeas'd my father, to Laurence' cell,
To make confession and to be absolv'd.

NURSE
245 Marry, I will; and this is wisely done.

     [*Exit.*]

JULIET
Ancient damnation! O most wicked fiend!
Is it more sin to wish me thus forsworn,
Or to dispraise my lord with that same tongue
Which she hath prais'd him with above compare
250 So many thousand times? Go, counsellor;
Thou and my bosom henceforth shall be twain.
I'll to the friar, to know his remedy;
If all else fail, myself have power to die.

     [*Exit.*]

O, he's a lovely gentleman!
230   Romeo is a dishrag compared with him. An eagle, madam,
doesn't have as green, as quick, or as beautiful an eye
as Paris has. Curse my own heart,
but I think you'll be happy marrying Paris
for he's better than Romeo. Even if Paris weren't as
    good as Romeo,
235   your first husband is dead—it comes to the same thing
as Romeo still being among the living and you being
    separated from him.

JULIET
Are you speaking from your heart?

NURSE
And from my soul, too. Otherwise, may both be
    damned.

JULIET
Amen!

NURSE
240   What?

JULIET
Well, you've really comforted me.
Go in and tell my mother I've gone
to Friar Laurence's cell to confess
and be absolved for having displeased my father.

NURSE
245   Certainly, I will. Now you're acting wisely.
       She exits.

JULIET
Damnable old woman! Most wicked devil!
Is it more sinful to wish me to break my vow,
or to condemn my husband with the same tongue
with which she has praised him as above compare
250   so many times? Go, my adviser!
You and my real feelings are separated now forever.
I'll go to the friar and get his advice.
If everything else fails, I'll commit suicide.
       She exits.

Act IV, Scene i: [Friar Laurence's cell.] Enter FRIAR
LAURENCE *and* PARIS.

FRIAR LAURENCE
  On Thursday, sir? The time is very short.

PARIS
  My father Capulet will have it so,
  And I am nothing slow to slack his haste.

FRIAR LAURENCE
  You say you do not know the lady's mind.
5   Uneven is the course, I like it not.

PARIS
  Immoderately she weeps for Tybalt's death,
  And therefore have I little talk'd of love,
  For Venus smiles not in a house of tears.
  Now, sir, her father counts it dangerous
10   That she do give her sorrow so much sway,
  And in his wisdom hastes our marriage
  To stop the inundation of her tears;
  Which, too much minded by herself alone,
  May be put from her by society.
15   Now do you know the reason of this haste.

FRIAR LAURENCE
  [*Aside.*] I would I knew not why it should be slow'd.
  Look, sir, here comes the lady toward my cell.

      Enter JULIET.`

PARIS
  Happily met, my lady and my wife!

JULIET
  That may be, sir, when I may be a wife.

PARIS
20   That may be must be, love, on Thursday next.

JULIET
  What must be shall be.

Act IV, Scene i: Friar Laurence's cell. Enter FRIAR LAURENCE
and PARIS.

FRIAR LAURENCE
　Your wedding is Thursday, sir? That's a very short
　　time away.

PARIS
　My new father-in-law Capulet wants it that way,
　and I'll not slow his hasty arrangements by being
　　slow myself.

FRIAR LAURENCE
　You say you don't know what the young lady thinks
　　about the marriage.
5　That's unusual. I don't like it.

PARIS
　She cries all the time over Tybalt's death,
　so I haven't talked much about love.
　Love is not welcome in the midst of grief.
　Her father thinks it's dangerous
10　that she gives in so much to her sorrow.
　So in his wisdom, he's rushing the marriage
　to stop her grief
　which she thinks about too much when she's by herself.
　Being around people might help her get over her grief.
15　So now you know the reason for our haste.

FRIAR LAURENCE (*to himself*)
　I wish I didn't know why this wedding must be slowed
　　down.
　　(*To Paris*) Look, sir, here comes the lady now.
　　　Enter JULIET.

PARIS
　How happy I am to see you, my lady and my wife.

JULIET
　That may be, sir—when I become your wife.

PARIS
20　Your "may be" will be a "must," my love, on next Thursday.

JULIET
　What must be, shall be.

FRIAR LAURENCE
That's a certain text.

PARIS
Come you to make confession to this father?

JULIET
To answer that, I should confess to you.

PARIS
25   Do not deny to him that you love me.

JULIET
I will confess to you that I love him.

PARIS
So will ye, I am sure, that you love me.

JULIET
If I do so, it will be of more price,
Being spoke behind your back, than to your face.

PARIS
30   Poor soul, thy face is much abus'd with tears.

JULIET
The tears have got small victory by that,
For it was bad enough before their spite.

PARIS
Thou wrong'st it, more than tears, with that report.

JULIET
That is no slander, sir, which is a truth;
35   And what I spake, I spake it to my face.

PARIS
Thy face is mine, and thou hast slandered it.

JULIET
It may be so, for it is not mine own.
Are you at leisure, holy father, now;
Or shall I come to you at evening mass?

FRIAR LAURENCE
40   My leisure serves me, pensive daughter, now.
My lord, we must entreat the time alone.

FRIAR LAURENCE
> That's the truth.

PARIS
> Did you come to make your confession to this father?

JULIET
> In order to answer that, I'd have to confess to you.

PARIS
25 > Don't deny to him that you love me.

JULIET
> I'll confess to you that I love him.

PARIS
> I'm sure you will confess to him that you love me.

JULIET
> If I do, it will mean more
> if I say it behind your back rather than to your face.

PARIS
30 > Poor soul, your face is very stained with tears.

JULIET
> The tears have made little difference
> for my face was unattractive enough before I cried.

PARIS
> You do more injustice to your face with that
>   statement than those tears did.

JULIET
> It's not slander, sir, to speak the truth.
35 > And what I said, I said to my own face.

PARIS
> Your face is mine, and you have slandered it.

JULIET
> You may be right because my face is not my own.
> Are you free now, holy father,
> or should I come to you at evening mass?

FRIAR LAURENCE
40 > I'm free to see you now, my thoughtful daughter.
> (*To Paris*) My lord, I must beg you to leave us alone.

PARIS
> God shield I should disturb devotion!
> Juliet, on Thursday early will I rouse ye;
> Till then, adieu; and keep this holy kiss.

> [*Exit.*]

JULIET
45
> O, shut the door! and when thou hast done so,
> Come weep with me, past hope, past care, past help!

FRIAR LAURENCE
> O Juliet, I already know thy grief;
> It strains me past the compass of my wits.
> I hear thou must, and nothing may prorogue it,
50
> On Thursday next be married to this County.

JULIET
> Tell me not, friar, that thou hear'st of this,
> Unless thou tell me how I may prevent it.
> If, in thy wisdom, thou canst give no help,
> Do thou but call my resolution wise,
55
> And with this knife I'll help it presently.
> God join'd my heart and Romeo's, thou our hands;
> And ere this hand, by thee to Romeo's seal'd,
> Shall be the label to another deed,
> Or my true heart with treacherous revolt
60
> Turn to another, this shall slay them both.
> Therefore, out of thy long-experienc'd time,
> Give me some present counsel, or, behold,
> 'Twixt my extremes and me this bloody knife
> Shall play the umpire, arbitrating that
65
> Which the commission of thy years and art
> Could to no issue of true honour bring.
> Be not so long to speak; I long to die
> If what thou speak'st speak not of remedy.

FRIAR LAURENCE
> Hold, daughter! I do spy a kind of hope,
70
> Which craves as desperate an execution
> As that is desperate which we would prevent.

PARIS

> God forbid that I should disturb a confession.
> Juliet, I'll awaken you early Thursday morning.
> Until then, goodbye, and keep this holy kiss.
> *He kisses her and exits.*

JULIET

45
> O, close the door, and when you have done so,
> come cry with me! I'm beyond hope, beyond cure,
>   beyond help!

FRIAR LAURENCE

> O Juliet, I already know your grief.
> It drives me past my wit's end.
> I hear you must be married to this count
50
> next Thursday and that nothing can postpone it.

JULIET

> Don't tell me that you have heard about this, friar,
> unless you can tell me how to prevent it.
> If even you and your wisdom can't help me,
> just say that my way of solving the problem is wise—
55
> and with this knife, I'll put my plan into action at once.
> God joined my heart and Romeo's, and you joined our hands.
> And before this hand, which you joined to Romeo's,
> can seal another deal
> or before my faithful heart could turn in
>   treacherous revolt
60
> to another man, this hand will destroy both my hand
>   and my heart.
> Therefore, out of your great experience,
> give me some advice. Otherwise,
> between me and my distress, this bloody knife
> will determine whether I live or die, deciding that
65
> which your experience and skill
> could not honorably resolve.
> Don't wait long to speak. I want to die
> if what you speak can't help me.

FRIAR LAURENCE

> Wait, daughter! I see some hope.
70
> But it's as dangerous as the danger
> we're trying to prevent.

If, rather than to marry County Paris,
Thou hast the strength of will to slay thyself,
Then is it likely thou wilt undertake
75   A thing like death to chide away this shame,
That cop'st with Death himself to scape from it;
And, if thou dar'st, I'll give thee remedy.

JULIET
O, bid me leap, rather than marry Paris,
From off the battlements of any tower,
80   Or walk in thievish ways, or bid me lurk
Where serpents are; chain me with roaring bears,
Or hide me nightly in a charnel-house,
O'er-cover'd quite with dead men's rattling bones,
With reeky shanks and yellow chapless skulls;
85   Or bid me go into a new-made grave
And hide me with a dead man in his shroud,—
Things that, to hear them told, have made me tremble;
And I will do it without fear or doubt,
To live an unstain'd wife to my sweet love.

FRIAR LAURENCE
90   Hold, then. Go home, be merry, give consent
To marry Paris. Wednesday is to-morrow.
To-morrow night look that thou lie alone;
Let not the nurse lie with thee in thy chamber.
Take thou this vial, being then in bed,
95   And this distilled liquor drink thou off;
When presently through all thy veins shall run
A cold and drowsy humour; for no pulse
Shall keep his native progress, but surcease;
No warmth, no breath shall testify thou livest;
100   The roses in thy lips and cheeks shall fade
To paly ashes, thy eyes' windows fall,
Like death when he shuts up the day of life;
Each part, depriv'd of supple government,
Shall, stiff and stark and cold, appear like death:
105   And in this borrowed likeness of shrunk death
Thou shalt continue two and forty hours,

If rather than marrying Count Paris,
you have the strength of will to kill yourself,
then you'd probably be willing to risk
75 something like death to avoid this shame
that requires you to deal with Death himself in
    order to escape this marriage.
If you have the courage, I'll give you the remedy.

JULIET
O, tell me to leap off the top of that tower,
rather than marry Paris.
80 Rather than marry Paris, tell me to walk on a road
    where robbers hide,
or tell me to linger where snakes are, or chain me up
    with roaring bears,
or lock me in a vault with old bones every night,
completely covering me with dead men's rattling bones,
stinking leg bones, and yellow, jawless skulls.
85 Rather than marry Paris, tell me to lie in a
    newly-made grave
and hide me with a dead man in his burial cloth.
Things that, to hear them spoken of have frightened me,
I'll do without fear or doubt,
in order to remain a faithful wife to my sweet love.

FRIAR LAURENCE
90 All right, then. Go home, be happy, give your consent
to marry Paris. Tomorrow is Wednesday.
Tomorrow night, be sure to sleep alone.
Don't let the nurse sleep in your room.
Take this bottle, and when you're in bed,
95 drink this distilled liquor.
Immediately, a cold and quieting liquid
shall run through all your veins. Your pulse
will stop.
There'll be no warmth or breath to prove that you're alive.
100 The color in your lips and cheeks will fade
to pale ashes; your eyelids will close
like death when he shuts up the last day of your life.
Each part of your body, stripped of its ability to move,
shall be stiff and rigid and cold, as in death.
105 And in this imitation of death,
you'll remain forty-two hours,

And then awake as from a pleasant sleep.
Now, when the bridegroom in the morning comes
To rouse thee from thy bed, there art thou dead.
110 Then, as the manner of our country is,
In thy best robes uncovered on the bier
Thou shall be borne to that same ancient vault
Where all the kindred of the Capulets lie.
In the mean time, against thou shalt awake,
115 Shall Romeo by my letters know our drift,
And hither shall he come; and he and I
Will watch thy waking, and that very night
Shall Romeo bear thee hence to Mantua.
And this shall free thee from this present shame;
120 If no inconstant toy, nor womanish fear,
Abate thy valour in the acting it.

JULIET
Give me, give me! O, tell not me of fear!

FRIAR LAURENCE
Hold; get you gone, be strong and prosperous
In this resolve. I'll send a friar with speed
125 To Mantua, with my letters to thy lord.

JULIET
Love give me strength! and strength shall help afford.
Farewell, dear father!

　　　[Exeunt.]

Scene ii: [Hall in Capulet's house.] Enter CAPULET, LADY
CAPULET, NURSE, *and* SERVING-MEN, *two or three.*

CAPULET
So many guests invite as here are writ.

　　　[Exit 1. Servant.]

Sirrah, go hire me twenty cunning cooks.

and then you'll awake as if from a pleasant sleep.
When Paris comes on Thursday morning
to rouse you from your bed, you will seem dead.
110 Then, as is customary,
dressed in your best clothes and with an uncovered
     face, you'll be carried on a bier
to the ancient vault
where all of the Capulets are buried.
In the meantime, before you awake,
115 Romeo will learn through a letter from me what we're
     doing.
He'll return here, and he and I
will watch for you to awake. Then that very night
     when you do awake,
Romeo will take you to Mantua.
This will let you escape your present shame
120 if no fickle whim or womanish fears
sap your courage to go through with it.

JULIET
Give it to me! Give it to me! Don't talk of fear!

FRIAR LAURENCE
Enough! Go, and be strong and prosperous
in this plan. I'll send a friar to speed
125 to Mantua with letters to Romeo.

JULIET
Love will give me strength, and strength will help
     me through.
Goodbye, dear father.
          They exit.

Act IV, Scene ii: A hall in Capulet's house. Enter CAPULET,
LADY CAPULET, NURSE, *and servingmen.*

CAPULET (*to servants*)
Invite all the guests whose names are written here.
          SERVANT *exits.*
Servant, go and hire twenty skillful cooks.

2. SERVANT

You shall have none ill, sir; for I'll try if they can lick their fingers.

CAPULET

How canst thou try them so?

2. SERVANT

5   Marry, sir, 'tis an ill cook that cannot lick his own fingers;
therefore he that cannot lick his fingers goes not with me.

CAPULET

Go, be gone.

       [*Exit 2. Servant.*]

We shall be much unfurnish'd for this time.
What, is my daughter gone to Friar Laurence?

NURSE

10   Ay, forsooth.

CAPULET

Well, he may chance to do some good on her.
A peevish self-will'd harlotry it is.

       Enter JULIET.

NURSE

See where she comes from shrift with merry look.

CAPULET

How now, my headstrong! where have you been gadding?

JULIET

15   Where I have learn'd me to repent the sin
Of disobedient opposition
To you and your behests, and am enjoin'd
By holy Laurence to fall prostrate here
And beg your pardon. Pardon, I beseech you!

20   Henceforward I am ever rul'd by you.

CAPULET

Send for the County; go tell him of this.
I'll have this knot knit up to-morrow morning.

SECOND SERVANT
　You shall have none that aren't good, sir, for I'll
　　test them by seeing if they will lick their fingers.

CAPULET
　What kind of test is that?

SECOND SERVANT
5　Well, sir, a bad cook won't lick his fingers (i.e.
　　because his own cooking tastes so bad).
　Therefore, the cook who won't lick his fingers
　　won't be hired by me.

CAPULET
　Go, on your way.
　　　　SECOND SERVANT *exits.*
　We're not stocked up for this wedding celebration.
　Has my daughter gone to Friar Laurence's?

NURSE
10　Yes.

CAPULET
　Well, he may be able to do some good with her.
　She's a silly good-for-nothing.
　　　　Enter JULIET.

NURSE
　See! She's coming from confession with a happy
　　look on her face.

CAPULET
　Hello, my headstrong daughter. Where have you been
　　running about?

JULIET
15　I've been where I learned to repent of the sin
　of disobedience
　to you and your orders. I've been advised
　by holy Friar Laurence to fall on my knees
　and beg your pardon. Please forgive me, I beg you.
20　From now on, I'll be ruled by you.

CAPULET
　Send for the count. Tell him about this.
　I'll have the wedding tomorrow morning.

JULIET

I met the youthful lord at Laurence' cell
And gave him what becomed love I might,
25   Not stepping o'er the bounds of modesty.

CAPULET

Why, I am glad on't; this is well; stand up.
This is as't should be. Let me see the County;
Ay, marry, go, I say, and fetch him hither.
Now, afore God! this reverend holy friar,
30   All our whole city is much bound to him.

JULIET

Nurse, will you go with me into my closet
To help me sort such needful ornaments
As you think fit to furnish me to-morrow?

LADY CAPULET

No, not till Thursday; there is time enough.

CAPULET

35   Go, nurse, go with her; we'll to church tomorrow.

[*Exeunt Juliet and Nurse.*]

LADY CAPULET

We shall be short in our provision;
'Tis now near night.

CAPULET

                    Tush, I will stir about,
And all things shall be well, I warrant thee, wife;
40   Go thou to Juliet, help to deck up her.
I'll not to bed to-night; let me alone;
I'll play the housewife for this once. What, ho!
They are all forth. Well, I will walk myself
To County Paris, to prepare up him
45   Against to-morrow. My heart is wondrous light,
Since this same wayward girl is so reclaim'd.

[*Exeunt.*]

JULIET
I met the youthful lord at Friar Laurence's cell
and gave him the most fitting love I could
25   without overstepping the bounds of modesty.

CAPULET
I'm glad. This is good. Stand up.
This is as it should be. Let me see Count Paris.
Indeed, go and bring him here.
Now, before God, the whole city owes a great deal
30   to this holy reverend father.

JULIET
Nurse, will you go with me to my room
to help me choose the ornaments
that you think are fitting for me to wear tomorrow?

LADY CAPULET
No, not until Thursday. That's soon enough.

CAPULET
35   Go, nurse, go with her. The wedding will be tomorrow.
      JULIET and NURSE exit.

LADY CAPULET
We'll be short of provisions.
It's almost night now.

CAPULET
Nonsense, I'll get busy
and everything will go well, I promise you, wife.
40   Go to Juliet and help dress her up.
I won't go to bed tonight! Leave me alone.
I'll play the housewife this one time. Servants!—
They're all gone. Well, I'll go to see
Count Paris myself, to prepare him
45   for tomorrow. My heart is wonderfully light
since this unruly daughter of mine has come to her
      senses.
      He exits.

Scene iii: [*Juliet's chamber.*] *Enter* JULIET *and* NURSE.

JULIET
Ay, those attires are best; but, gentle nurse,
I pray thee, leave me to myself to-night;
For I have need of many orisons
To move the heavens to smile upon my state,
5   Which, well thou know'st is cross and full of sin.
        Enter LADY CAPULET.

LADY CAPULET
What, are you busy, ho? Need you my help?

JULIET
No, madam; we have cull'd such necessaries
As are behoveful for our state to-morrow.
So please you, let me now be left alone,
10   And let the nurse this night sit up with you;
For, I am sure, you have your hands full all,
In this so sudden business.

LADY CAPULET
                                    Good-night.
Get thee to bed, and rest; for thou hast need.
        [*Exeunt Lady Cauplet and Nurse*].

JULIET
15   Farewell! God knows when we shall meet again
I have a faint cold fear thrills through my veins,
That almost freezes up the heat of life.
I'll call them back again to comfort me.
Nurse!—What should she do here?
20   My dismal scene I needs must act alone.
Come, vial.
What if this mixture do not work at all?
Shall I be married then to-morrow morning?
No, no; this shall forbid it. Lie thou there.

Act IV, Scene iii: Juliet's bedroom. Enter JULIET *and the* NURSE.

JULIET
    Yes, those dresses are best, but gentle nurse,
    I beg you, leave me alone tonight.
    I must pray many prayers
    to move heaven to smile upon my situation,
5   which, as you well know, is wrong and full of sin.
        Enter LADY CAPULET.

LADY CAPULET
    Are you busy? Do you need my help?

JULIET
    No, madam. We have gathered those necessities
    I'll need for my wedding tomorrow.
    So, please, leave me alone now.
10   Let the nurse sit up with you tonight.
    I'm sure you have your hands full
    since the wedding has been moved up a day.

LADY CAPULET
    Good night.
    Go to bed and rest; you'll need it.
        LADY CAPULET *and the* NURSE *exit.*

JULIET
15   Goodbye! God only knows when we'll meet again.
    I feel a dizzying, cold fear running through my
      veins
    that almost freezes up the warmth of my life.
    I'll call them back to comfort me.
    Nurse!—But why should she be here?
20   I'll have to act out this dreadful scene alone.
    Come, bottle!
    What if this mixture doesn't work at all?
    Will I be married, then, tomorrow morning?
    No! This will see that doesn't happen. Lie there.

[*Laying down her dagger.*]

25   What if it be a poison, which the friar
     Subtly hath minist'red to have me dead,
     Lest in this marriage he should be dishonour'd
     Because he married me before to Romeo?
     I fear it is; and yet, methinks, it should not,
30   For he hath still been tried a holy man.
     How if, when I am laid into the tomb,
     I wake before the time that Romeo
     Come to redeem me? There's a fearful point!
     Shall I not then be stifled in the vault,
35   To whose foul mouth no healthsome air breathes in,
     And there die strangled ere my Romeo comes?
     Or, if I live, is it not very like
     The horrible conceit of death and night,
     Together with the terror of the place,—
40   As in a vault, an ancient receptacle,
     Where, for this many hundred years, the bones
     Of all my buried ancestors are pack'd;
     Where bloody Tybalt, yet but green in earth,
     Lies fest'ring in his shroud; where, as they say,
45   At some hours in the night spirits resort;—
     Alack, alack, is it not like that I,
     So early waking,—what with loathsome smells,
     And shrieks like mandrakes' torn out of the earth,
     That living mortals, hearing them, run mad;—
50   O, if I wake, shall I not be distraught,
     Environed with all these hideous fears,
     And madly play with my forefathers' joints,
     And pluck the mangled Tybalt from his shroud,
     And, in this rage, with some great kinsman's bone
55   As with a club, dash out my desperate brains?
     O, look! methinks I see my cousin's ghost
     Seeking out Romeo, that did spit his body
     Upon a rapier's point. Stay, Tybalt, stay!
     Romeo, I come! This do I drink to thee.

     [*She falls upon her bed, within the curtains.*]

---

48 mandrakes'   the root of the mandrake was said to have a human-like form. Superstitious belief reported that the mandrake screamed horrible cries when its roots were pulled out of the ground, driving listeners mad.

She lays down a dagger.
25 What if this is a poison which the friar
has secretly given me to kill me
so that he won't be dishonored by this marriage
since he married me to Romeo earlier?
I'm afraid that's the case. And yet, I don't think so
30 because he's always shown himself to be a holy man.
What if, when I am laid in the tomb,
I awake before Romeo
comes to save me? That's a terrifying thought!
Won't I be stifled in the tomb
35 where no wholesome air circulates?
Won't I suffocate there before my Romeo comes?
Or if I can breathe, isn't it likely that I'll feel
the horrible idea of death and night,
along with the terror of the place?
40 That vault is an ancient tomb
where for hundreds of years the bones
of all my buried ancestors have been stored;
where bloody Tybalt, so recently buried,
lies rotting in his burial cloth; where, so they say,
45 at some hours in the night, ghosts live.
Alas, alas, isn't it likely that waking there,
I'll encounter horrible smells
and shrieks like the uprooted mandrakes'
which drive people insane?
50 Or if I wake, won't I be driven mad,
closed in with all these hideous fears,
and play like a madwoman with my ancestors' bones,
and pluck battered Tybalt from his burial cloth,
and in this fit, take one of my great relative's bones
55 to use as a club and dash out my desperate brains?
Look! I think I see my cousin's ghost
looking for Romeo who stabbed him
with a rapier. Stay there, Tybalt!
Romeo, I'm coming. I drink to you!
She drinks and falls upon her bed, which is
enclosed in curtains.

Scene iv: [*Hall in Capulet's house.*] *Enter* LADY CAPULET *and* NURSE.

LADY CAPULET
  Hold, take these keys and fetch more spices, nurse.

NURSE
  They call for dates and quinces in the pastry.

  Enter CAPULET.

CAPULET
  Come, stir, stir, stir! the second cock hath crow'd,
  The curfew-bell hath rung, 'tis three o'clock.
5 Look to the bak'd meats, good Angelica;
  Spare not for cost.

NURSE
                    Go you cot-quean, go,
  Get you to bed. Faith, you'll be sick to-morrow
  For this night's watching.

CAPULET
10 No, not a whit! What! I have watch'd ere now
  All night for lesser cause, and ne'er been sick.

LADY CAPULET
  Ay, you have been a mouse-hunt in your time;
  But I will watch you from such watching now.

  [*Exeunt Lady Capulet and Nurse.*]

CAPULET
  A jealous-hood, a jealous-hood!

  Enter three or four SERVING-MEN, *with spits, logs, and baskets.*

15   Now, fellow,
  What's there?

1. SERVANT
  Things for the cook, sir; but I know not what.

Act IV, Scene iv: A hall in Capulet's house. Enter LADY CAPULET
and the NURSE.

LADY CAPULET
  Wait, take these keys and bring me more spices, nurse.

NURSE
  The cooks in the pantry are calling for dates and quinces.
      Enter CAPULET.

CAPULET
  Come on! Get busy! The second rooster has crowed
      already.
  The curfew bell has rung. It's three o'clock.
5 Check on the meat pies, good Angelica.
  Don't worry about the cost.

NURSE (*to Capulet*)
  Go to bed, little housewife.
  Go on, go to bed. Really, you'll be sick tomorrow
  from staying up all night.

CAPULET
10 No I won't, not one bit. Why, I've stayed up
  all night before for more trivial reasons, and I was never sick.

LADY CAPULET
  Yes, you've been a woman-chaser in your day,
  but I'll see that you don't keep those kinds of late
      hours anymore.
      LADY CAPULET *and the* NURSE *exit*.

CAPULET
  She's a jealous woman, a jealous woman.
      *Enter three or four servants with cooking
          rods, logs and a basket.*
15 Now, fellow,
  what's that?

FIRST SERVANT
  These are things for the cook, sir, but I don't know
      what they are.

CAPULET
　Make haste, make haste.

　　　　[*Exit I. Servant.*]

　Sirrah, fetch drier logs:
20　Call Peter, he will show thee where they are.

2. SERVANT
　I have a head, sir, that will find out logs,
　And never trouble Peter for the matter.

CAPULET
　Mass, and well said; a merry whoreson, ha!
　Thou shalt be logger-head.

　　　　[*Exit 2. Servant.*]

25　Good faith, 'tis day.
　The County will be here with music straight,
　For so he said he would. I hear him near.

　　　　[*Music within.*]

　Nurse! Wife! What, ho! What, nurse, I say!

　　　　Re-enter NURSE.

　Go waken Juliet, go and trim her up;
30　I'll go and chat with Paris. Hie, make haste,
　Make haste; the bridegroom he is come already.
　Make haste, I say.

　　　　[*Exeunt.*]

Scene v: [*Juliet's chamber.*] *Enter* NURSE.

NURSE
　Mistress! what, mistress! Juliet!—Fast, I warrant her, she.—
　Why, lamb! why, lady! fie, you slug-a-bed!
　Why, love! I say, madam! sweetheart! why, bride!
　What, not a word? You take your penny-worths now;
5　Sleep for a week; for the next night, I warrant,
　The County Paris hath set up his rest

---

21 *logs* the servant's comment reflects ironically on his own head—it is wooden, too.

CAPULET
>Hurry up! Hurry up!
>>FIRST SERVANT *exits*.
>Servant, get some drier logs.
20 Call Peter, he'll show you where they are.

SECOND SERVANT
>I never have trouble finding logs, sir.
>I don't have to bother Peter.

CAPULET
>By the mass, that's clever. You're a happy rascal.
>You're a blockhead.
>>*Exit* SECOND SERVANT.
25 Good heavens, day has dawned!
>Count Paris will be here with the musicians right
>>away,
>as he said he would. I hear him now.
>>*Music is heard*.
>Nurse! Wife! Where are you? Nurse, I say!
>>*Re-enter* NURSE.
>Go wake Juliet. Go and get her dressed.
30 I'll go and talk with Paris. Hurry, make haste!
>Make haste! The bridegroom has already arrived.
>Hurry, I say!
>>*They exit*.

Act IV, Scene v: Juliet's bedroom. Enter NURSE.

NURSE
>Mistress! Mistress! Juliet—I'll bet she's fast
>>asleep.
>Lamb! Lady! For shame, you sleepyhead.
>Well, love! I say, madam! Sweetheart! Bride!
>What, not a word? Take your little naps now.
5 Sleep for a week because I'll bet you tonight
>Count Paris is determined

That you shall rest but little. God forgive me!
Marry, and amen, how sound is she asleep!
I needs must wake her. Madam, madam, madam!
10   Ay, let the County take you in your bed;
He'll fright you up, i' faith. Will it not be?

> [*Draws back the curtains.*]

What, dress'd, and in your clothes! and down again!
I must needs wake you. Lady! lady! lady!
Alas, alas! Help, help! my lady's dead!
15   O, well-a-day, that ever I was born!
Some *aqua vitae,* ho! My lord! my lady!

> *Enter* LADY CAPULET.

LADY CAPULET
What noise is here?

NURSE

O lamentable day!

CAPULET
What is the matter?

NURSE
20   Look, look! O heavy day!

LADY CAPULET
O me, O me! My child, my only life,
Revive, look up, or I will die with thee!
Help, help! Call help.

> *Enter* CAPULET.

CAPULET
For shame, bring Juliet forth; her lord is come.

NURSE
25   She's dead, deceas'd, she's dead; alack the day!

LADY CAPULET
Alack the day, she's dead, she's dead, she's dead!

CAPULET
Ha! let me see her. Out, alas! she's cold;

that you won't rest very much. God forgive me, I
  shouldn't say that.
How sound asleep she is.
I must wake her. Madam, madam, madam!
10   Are you going to let the Count Paris find you in bed?
He'll frighten you, I guarantee. Will nothing wake you?
  She draws back the curtains.
What, already dressed and gone back to bed?
I must wake you. Lady, lady, lady!
Alas! Help! Help! My lady is dead!
15   I wish I'd never been born.
Some liquor, here! My lord! My lady!
  Enter LADY CAPULET.

LADY CAPULET
  What's all this noise?

NURSE
  O awful day!

LADY CAPULET
  What's the matter?

NURSE
20   O look, look! O horrible day!

LADY CAPULET
  O no! O no! My child! My only child!
  Revive! Look up, or I'll die with you.
  Help! Help! Call for help!
  Enter CAPULET.

CAPULET
  For shame. Bring Juliet here. Her lord has arrived.

NURSE
25   She's dead, deceased; she's dead! Curse this day.

LADY CAPULET
  Horrible day! She's dead. She's dead! She's dead!

CAPULET
  Let me see her. Alas, she's cold,

Her blood is settled, and her joints are stiff;
Life and these lips have long been separated.
30 Death lies on her like an untimely frost
Upon the sweetest flower of all the field.

NURSE
O lamentable day!

LADY CAPULET
                        O woeful time!

CAPULET
Death, that hath ta'en her hence to make me wail,
35 Ties up my tongue, and will not let me speak.

> *Enter* FRIAR LAURENCE *and* PARIS, *with*
> MUSICIANS.

FRIAR LAURENCE
Come, is the bride ready to go to church?

CAPULET
Ready to go, but never to return.—
O son! the night before thy wedding-day
Hath Death lain with thy wife. There she lies,
40 Flower as she was, deflowered by him.
Death is my son-in-law, Death is my heir;
My daughter he hath wedded. I will die
And leave him all; life, living, all is Death's.

PARIS
Have I thought long to see this morning's face,
45 And doth it give me such a sight as this?

LADY CAPULET
Accurs'd, unhappy, wretched, hateful day!
Most miserable hour that e'er Time saw
In lasting labour of his pilgrimage!
But one, poor one, one poor and loving child,
50 But one thing to rejoice and solace in,
And cruel Death hath catch'd it from my sight!

NURSE
O woe! O woeful, woeful, woeful day!

---

40 *deflowered*   stripped of virginity (and her life).

her blood is settled, and her joints are stiff.
Life left her lips a long time ago.
30 Death lies on her like an untimely frost
on the sweetest flower of all the fields.

NURSE
O sorrowful day!

LADY CAPULET
O woeful time—

CAPULET
Death, who has taken her away to make me cry,
35 ties up my tongue and will not let me speak.
Enter FRIAR LAURENCE *and* PARIS *with musicians.*

FRIAR LAURENCE
Is the bride ready to go to the church?

CAPULET
She is ready to go but never to return. (*To
Paris*) O son, the night before your wedding day
Death slept with your wife. See, there she lies,
40 the flower that she was, deflowered by Death.
Death is my son-in-law, Death is my heir;
he has married my daughter. I'll die
and leave Death everything. Life, living—all is Death's.

PARIS
I've thought of nothing else but to see this day dawn.
45 Why does morning give me such a sight as this?

LADY CAPULET
Damned, unhappy, wretched, hateful day!
This is the most miserable hour that Time ever saw
in his ceaseless journey.
Only one—just one, one poor and loving child,
50 only one child in which to rejoice and find comfort—
and cruel Death has snatched her from my sight.

NURSE
O sad! Sad, sad, sad day,

Most lamentable day, most woeful day,
That ever, ever, I did yet behold!
55   O day! O day! O day! O hateful day!
Never was seen so black a day as this.
O woeful day, O woeful day!

PARIS
Beguil'd, divorced, wronged, spited, slain!
Most detestable Death, by thee beguil'd,
60   By cruel cruel thee quite overthrown!
O love! O life! not life, but love in death!

CAPULET
Despis'd, distressed, hatred, martyr'd, kill'd!
Uncomfortable time, why cam'st thou now
To murder, murder our solemnity?
65   O child! O child! my soul, and not my child!
Dead art thou! Alack! my child is dead;
And with my child my joys are buried.

FRIAR LAURENCE
Peace, ho, for shame! Confusion's cure lives not
In these confusions. Heaven and yourself
70   Had part in this fair maid; now heaven hath all,
And all the better is it for the maid.
Your part in her you could not keep from death,
But heaven keeps his part in eternal life.
The most you sought was her promotion,
75   For 'twas your heaven she should be advanc'd;
And weep ye now, seeing she is advanc'd
Above the clouds, as high as heaven itself?
O, in this love, you love your child so ill
That you run mad, seeing that she is well.
80   She's not well married that lives married long;
But she's best married that dies married young.
Dry up your tears, and stick your rosemary
On this fair corse; and, as the custom is,
In all her best array bear her to church;
85   For though fond nature bids us all lament,
Yet nature's tears are reason's merriment.

---

82 *rosemary*   an evergreen shrub, symbolized remembrance to the Elizabethans.

most sorrowful day, saddest day
that I've ever seen!
55   O day! O day! O hateful day!
There's never been such a black day as this!
O sad day! O sad day!

PARIS
Seduced, divorced, wronged, spited, killed!
You detestable Death, you have seduced her.
60   You've cruelly destroyed her.
O my love! My life!—No longer alive, but at least
    I'll love you in death.

CAPULET
Despised, distressed, hated, martyred, killed!
Discomforting time, why did you come now
to murder our celebration?
65   O child! Child! My soul, and not my child!
You're dead, dead! Alas, my child is dead.
And with you, my child, my joys are buried.

FRIAR LAURENCE
Peace! For shame! The remedy to disaster is not
in this commotion. Both you and heaven
70   had a part in this beautiful maiden. Now heaven has all of her,
and it's all the better for the maiden.
The body you gave her was mortal and had to die,
but heaven gives her soul eternal life.
The best thing you could think of was to try to
    marry her to a nobleman.
75   That was your notion of heaven—to see her position raised.
So why do you cry now, seeing that she is raised
above the clouds, as high as heaven itself?
With this kind of love, you love your child so foolishly
that you go crazy when you know she's better off.
80   Any woman is not well married when she lives a long married life.
The woman is best married who dies a young bride.
Dry your tears and pin rosemary
on this lovely corpse. And as is the custom,
dress her in her best clothes and carry her to the church.
85   For though our foolish human nature tells us all to grieve,
reason gives up cause to rejoice that she is in heaven.

CAPULET
>All things that we ordained festival,
>Turn from their office to black funeral;
>Our instruments to melancholy bells,
>90   Our wedding cheer to a sad burial feast,
>Our solemn hymns to sullen dirges change,
>Our bridal flowers serve for a buried corse,
>And all things change them to the contrary.

FRIAR LAURENCE
>Sir, go you in; and, madam, go with him;
>95   And go, Sir Paris; every one prepare
>To follow this fair corse unto her grave.
>The heavens do lour upon you for some ill;
>Move them no more by crossing their high will.

>>[*Exeunt Capulet, Lady Capulet, Paris, and Friar*].

1. MUSICIAN
>Faith, we may put up our pipes and be gone.

NURSE
>100   Honest good fellows, ah, put up, put up;
>For well you know, this is a pitiful case.

>>[*Exit.*]

1. MUSICIAN
>Ay, by my troth, the case may be amended.

>>*Enter* PETER.

PETER
>Musicians, O, musicians, "Heart's ease, Heart's ease!" O, an you will have me live, play "Heart's ease."

1. MUSICIAN
>105   Why "Heart's ease"?

PETER
>O, musicians, because my heart itself plays "My heart is full of woe." O, play me some merry dump to comfort me.

1. MUSICIAN
>Not a dump we; 'tis no time to play now.

---

102 *case*   means both situation and a musical case.   103 *"Heart's Ease"*   or "My Heart is Full of Woe" is an old ballad.

CAPULET
　　Everything that we planned for the wedding feast
　　will now be used instead for the sad funeral.
　　The dancing music will become melancholy bells,
90　　our wedding party will become a sad burial feast,
　　our celebration hymns will change to solemn funeral marches,
　　our wedding flowers will serve as funeral flowers.
　　Change everything to its opposite (for the funeral).

FRIAR LAURENCE
　　Sir, go inside. Madam, go with him.
95　　You, too, Paris. Everyone is to prepare
　　to follow this beautiful corpse to her grave.
　　The heavens frown on you for some sin you have committed.
　　Don't anger the heavens more by disobeying their will.
　　　　LADY CAPULET, CAPULET, PARIS, *and*
　　　　FRIAR LAURENCE *exit.*

FIRST MUSICIAN
　　We might as well put away our instruments and leave.

NURSE
100　　Honest fellows, put them away, put them away.
　　You can see that this is a pitiful situation.
　　　　She exits.

FIRST MUSICIAN
　　Yes, this certainly could be a better case.
　　　　Enter PETER.

PETER
　　Musicians! O musicians, play "Heart's Ease."
　　　"Heart's Ease"! O, if you
　　want me to live, play "Heart's Ease"!

FIRST MUSICIAN
105　　Why "Heart's Ease"?

PETER
　　O musicians, because my heart itself is playing, "My heart is full
　　of sorrow." O, play me a merry sad song to comfort me.

FIRST MUSICIAN
　　We're not going to play a sad song! This is no time
　　to play.

PETER
You will not, then?

1. MUSICIAN
110   No.

PETER
I will then give it you soundly.

1. MUSICIAN
What will you give us?

PETER
No money, on my faith, but the gleek; I will give you the minstrel.

1. MUSICIAN
Then will I give you the serving-creature.

PETER
115   Then will I lay the serving-creature's dagger on your pate. I will carry no crotchets; I'll *re* you, I'll *fa* you. Do you note me?

1. MUSICIAN
An you *re* us and *fa* us, you note us.

2. MUSICIAN
Pray you, put up your dagger, and put out your wit.

PETER
Then have at you with my wit! I will dry-beat you with an iron
120   wit, and put up my iron dagger. Answer me like men:
   "When griping griefs the heart doth wound,
      And doleful dumps the mind oppress,
   Then music with her silver sound"—
why "silver sound"? Why "music with her silver sound"? What
125   say you, Simon Catling?

1. MUSICIAN
Marry, sir, because silver hath a sweet sound.

PETER
Pretty! What say you, Hugh Rebeck?

---

116 *crochets* besides meaning whim, is also a quarter note in music.
121-23 *When...sounds* this is a song from Richard Edward's "In the Commendation of
Music." 125 *Catling* Peter calls the musician a "catstring." Lute strings were made of
catgut. 127 *rebeck* is a three-stringed fiddle.

PETER
>You won't play one then?

FIRST MUSICIAN
110   No.

PETER
>Then I'll give it to you good.

FIRST MUSICIAN
>What will you give us?

PETER
>No money, I swear, but a mocking speech. I'll call
>you a two-bit player.

FIRST MUSICIAN
>Then I'll call you a lackey.

PETER
115   Then I'll crack you over the head with my lackey's dagger. I'll
>not put up with your whims. I'll "re" you and I'll
>"fa" you. Understand me?

FIRST MUSICIAN
>If you "re" us and "fa" us, you'll set us to music.

SECOND MUSICIAN
>Please put away your dagger and use your intelligence.

PETER
>Then I'll have a go at you with my intelligence.
>I'll beat you with an iron
120   intelligence and put away my iron dagger. Answer me
>like men. *(Sings)*
>>*When terrible griefs wound the heart,*
>>*and sad sorrows trouble the mind.*
>>*Then music with her silver sound—*
>Why "silver sound?" Why "music with her silver
>sound?" What
125   do you say, Simon Catling?

FIRST MUSICIAN
>Well, sir, because silver has a sweet sound.

PETER
>Nicely put! What do you say, Hugh Rebeck?

2. MUSICIAN

I say, "silver sound," because musicians sound for silver.

PETER

Pretty too! What say you, James Soundpost?

3. MUSICIAN

130 Faith, I know not what to say.

PETER

O, I cry you mercy; you are the singer; I will say for you. It is "music with her silver sound," because musicians have no gold for sounding:

"Then music with her silver sound
135 With speedy help doth lend redress."

[*Exit.*]

1. MUSICIAN

What a pestilent knave is this same!

2. MUSICIAN

Hang him, Jack! Come, we'll in here, tarry for the mourners, and stay dinner.

[*Exeunt.*]

Act V, Scene i: [Mantua. A street.] Enter ROMEO.

ROMEO

If I may trust the flattering truth of sleep,
My dreams presage some joyful news at hand.
My bosom's lord sits lightly in his throne,
And all this day an unaccustom'd spirit
5 Lifts me above the ground with cheerful thoughts.
I dreamt my lady came and found me dead—
Strange dream, that gives a dead man leave to think!—
And breath'd such life with kisses in my lips
That I reviv'd and was an emperor.
10 Ah me! how sweet is love itself possess'd,
When but love's shadows are so rich in joy!

---

129 *Soundpost* is a wooden peg used to brace and support a violin.

SECOND MUSICIAN
I say "silver sound" because musicians sound (play) for silver.

PETER
That's nicely put, too. What do you say, James Soundpost?

THIRD MUSICIAN
130   Really, I don't know what to say.

PETER
O, well excuse me. You're the singer (and can only
    sing). I'll speak for you. The line goes
"music with her silver sounds" because musicians get
    no gold
for playing. (*Sings*)
    Then music with her silver sound
135   *with speedy help gives relief.*
    He exits singing.

FIRST MUSICIAN
What a pest that rascal is.

SEDOND MUSICIAN
Hang him, Jack! Come on, we'll go in here, wait for
    the mourners,
and stay for dinner.
    They exit.

Act V, Scene i: A street in Mantua. Enter ROMEO.

ROMEO
If I may trust the truth of sleep's illusions,
my dreams predict I'm about to receive some joyful news.
My heart feels light in my breast,
and all day an unusual spirit has
5   lifted me above the ground with cheerful thoughts.
I dreamed my lady came and found me dead—
it's a strange dream that lets a dead man think—
and breathed such life with her kisses
that I revived and became an emperor.
10   Ah me, how sweet is real love
when just love's images are so joyful.

Enter BALTHASAR, *his man, booted.*

News from Verona!—How now, Balthasar!
Dost thou not bring me letters from the friar?
How doth my lady? Is my father well?
15   How fares my Juliet? that I ask again;
For nothing can be ill, if she be well.

BALTHASAR
Then she is well, and nothing can be ill.
Her body sleeps in Capel's monument,
And her immortal part with angels lives.
20   I saw her laid low in her kindred's vault,
And presently took post to tell it you.
O, pardon me for bringing these ill news,
Since you did leave it for my office, sir.

ROMEO
Is it even so? Then I defy you, stars!
25   Thou know'st my lodging; get me ink and paper
And hire post-horses; I will hence to-night.

BALTHASAR
I do beseech you, sir, have patience.
Your looks are pale and wild, and do import
Some misadventure.

ROMEO
30   Tush, thou art deceiv'd:
Leave me, and do the thing I bid thee do.
Hast thou no letters to me from the friar?

BALTHASAR
No, my good lord.

ROMEO
                No matter; get thee gone
35   And hire those horses; I'll be with thee straight.

    [*Exit Balthasar.*]

Well, Juliet, I will lie with thee to-night.
Let's see for means. O mischief, thou art swift
To enter in the thoughts of desperate men!

>   *Enter* BALATHASAR, *his servant.*
>   News from Verona! Well, Balthasar?
>   Didn't you bring me letters from the friar?
>   How's my lady? Is my father well?
> 15   How's Juliet? I ask that again
>   because nothing can be bad if she's well.

BALATHASAR

>   Then she is well, so nothing can be bad.
>   Her body sleeps in the Capulet's tomb,
>   and her soul is with the angels.
> 20   I saw her laid down in her ancestor's vault,
>   and I immediately hired horses to ride here to tell
>   you.
>   O, forgive me for bringing this bad news,
>   since you made it my duty, sir.

ROMEO

>   Is this true? Then I defy you, fate! (*To*
>   *Balathasar*)
> 25   You know where I live. Get me some ink and paper,
>   and hire me some horses. I'll leave tonight.

BALTHASAR

>   I beg you, sir, be patient.
>   Your face is pale and wild, and you look like
>   you're heading for trouble.

ROMEO

> 30   Nonsense, you're mistaken.
>   Leave me, and do what I asked you to do.
>   Don't you have any letters for me from the friar?

BALTHASAR

>   No, my good lord.

ROMEO

>   It doesn't matter. Go
> 35   and hire the horses. I'll be with you right away.
>   BALTHASAR *exits.*
>   Well, Juliet, I'll lie with you tonight.
>   Let's see, what method shall I use? O mischief,
>   you're quick
>   to enter the thoughts of desperate men.

I do remember an apothecary,—
40 And hereabouts 'a dwells,—which late I noted
In tatt'red weeds, with overwhelming brows,
Culling of simples; meagre were his looks,
Sharp misery had worn him to the bones;
And in his needy shop a tortoise hung,
45 An alligator stuff'd and other skins
Of ill-shap'd fishes; and about his shelves
A beggarly account of empty boxes,
Green earthen pots, bladders and musty seeds,
Remnants of packthread and old cakes of roses
50 Were thinly scattered, to make up a show.
Noting this penury, to myself I said,
"And if a man did need a poison now,
Whose sale is present death in Mantua,
Here lives a caitiff wretch would sell it him."
55 O, this same thought did but forerun my need;
And this same needy man must sell it me.
As I remember, this should be the house.
Being holiday, the beggar's shop is shut.
What, ho! apothecary!

Enter APOTHECARY.

APOTHECARY
60   Who calls so loud?

ROMEO
Come hither, man. I see that thou art poor.
Hold, there is forty ducats. Let me have
A dram of poison, such soon-speeding gear
As will disperse itself through all the veins
65 That the life-weary taker may fall dead,
And that the trunk may be discharg'd of breath
As violently as hasty powder fir'd
Doth hurry from the fatal cannon's womb.

APOTHECARY
Such mortal drugs I have; but Mantua's law
70 Is death to any he that utters them.

I remember a pharmacist
40   who lives near here. I noticed him recently,
with his tattered clothes and overhanging eyebrows,
as he sorted medicinal herbs. He was very thin.
Sharp misery had worn him to skin and bones.
In his poor shop hung a tortoise,
45   a stuffed alligator, and other skins
of misshapen fish. On his shelves
were a few empty boxes,
green clay pots, bladders, musty seeds,
bits of twine, and old packets of rose petals—
50   all thinly scattered for show.
Noticing how poor he was, I said to myself,
"If a man should need poison now—
when its sale here in Mantua is punishable by
    death—
then here lives a miserable wretch who would sell it
    to him."
55   This thought came to me before I ever thought about
    needing poison,
and this same needy man must sell it to me.
If I remember, this should be his house.
Since this is a holiday, the poor man's shop is closed.
(*He calls*) Hello! Pharmacist!
    Enter PHARMACIST.

PHARMACIST
60   Who calls so loudly?

ROMEO
Come here, man. I see that you're poor.
There are forty gold coins. Let me have
a vial of poison of such quick-working stuff
that it will flow all through the veins
65   and make the life-weary taker fall dead.
Then the body may be discharged of breath
as violently as fired gunpowder
speeds from the deadly cannon's barrel.

PHARMACIST
I have deadly drugs, but Mantua's law
70   states that anyone who sells them will be executed.

ROMEO
Art thou so bare and full of wretchedness,
And fear'st to die? Famine is in thy cheeks,
Need and oppression starveth in thy eyes,
Contempt and beggary hangs upon thy back;
75 The world is not thy friend nor the world's law,
The world affords no law to make thee rich;
Then be poor, but break it, and take this.

APOTHECARY
My poverty, but not my will, consents.

ROMEO
I pay thy poverty, and not thy will.

APOTHECARY
80 Put this in any liquid thing you will,
And drink it off; and, if you had the strength
Of twenty men, it would dispatch you straight.

ROMEO
There is thy gold, worse poison to men's souls,
Doing more murder in this loathsome world,
85 Than these poor compounds that thou mayst not sell.
I sell thee poison; thou hast sold me none.
Farewell! Buy food, and get thyself in flesh.
Come, cordial and not poison, go with me
To Juliet's grave; for there must I use thee.
    [*Exeunt.*]

Scene ii: [*Verona. Friar Laurence's cell.*] *Enter* FRIAR JOHN.

FRIAR JOHN
Holy Franciscan friar! brother, ho!
    Enter FRIAR LAURENCE.

FRIAR LAURENCE
This same should be the voice of Frair John.
Welcome from Mantua! What says Romeo?
Or, if his mind be writ, give me his letter.

ROMEO
>You're so poor and wretched—
>and yet you're still afraid of death (by execution)?
>There's poverty in your cheeks,
>need and oppression starving in your eyes,
>and contempt and beggary hangs on your back.
>75 The world is not your friend or the world's law.
>The world has no law to make you rich.
>Then be poor, but break the law and take this gold.

PHARMACIST
>My poverty, but not my will, agrees.

ROMEO
>Then I'll pay your poverty, not your will.

PHARMACIST
>80 Put this drug in any kind of liquid you wish,
>and drink it all, and even if you had the strength
>of twenty men, it would kill you immediately.

ROMEO
>There's your gold—which is a worse poison to men's souls
>since it causes more murder in this hateful world
>85 than these poor drugs that you're not allowed to sell.
>I sell you poison—you haven't sold me any.
>Goodbye. Buy food and get some flesh on your bones.
>Come, restoring drug, you are not poison. Go with me
>to Juliet's grave, for that is where I'll use you.
>>ROMEO *and the* PHARMACIST *exit.*

Act V, Scene ii: Verona. Friar Laurence's cell. Enter FRIAR JOHN.

FRIAR JOHN
>Holy Franciscan friar! Brother, hello!
>>*Enter* FRIAR LAURENCE.

FRIAR LAURENCE
>That voice should be Friar John's.
>Welcome back from Mantua. What did Romeo say?
>Or if he wrote, give me his letter.

FRIAR JOHN

5   Going to find a bare-foot brother out,
One of our order, to associate me,
Here in this city visiting the sick,
And finding him, the searchers of the town,
Suspecting that we both were in a house
10   Where the infectious pestilence did reign,
Seal'd up the doors and would not let us forth,
So that my speed to Mantua there was stay'd.

FRIAR LAURENCE

Who bare my letter, then, to Romeo?

FRIAR JOHN

I could not send it,—here it is again,—
15   Nor get a messenger to bring it thee,
So fearful were they of infection.

FRIAR LAURENCE

Unhappy fortune! By my brotherhood,
The letter was not nice but full of charge
Of dear import, and the neglecting it
20   May do much danger. Friar John, go hence;
Get me an iron crow, and bring it straight
Unto my cell.

FRIAR JOHN

Brother, I'll go and bring it thee.

      [*Exit.*]

FRIAR LAURENCE

Now must I to the monument alone;
25   Within this three hours will fair Juliet wake.
She will beshrew me much that Romeo
Hath had no notice of these accidents;
But I will write again to Mantua,
And keep her at my cell till Romeo come;
30   Poor living corse, clos'd in a dead man's tomb!

      [*Exit.*]

FRIAR JOHN

5   I went to find another friar
       from our order to accompany me.
       He was here in the city visiting the sick.
       I found him, but the health officials of the town,
       suspecting that we both were in a house
10   where plague victims lived,
       sealed the doors and would not let us leave.
       So, my journey to Mantua to see Romeo was stopped.

FRIAR LAURENCE
       Who took my letter to Romeo, then?

FRIAR JOHN
       I couldn't send it. Here it is.
15   I couldn't find a messenger to bring it to you
       because they were so afraid of the plague.

FRIAR LAURENCE
       Unhappy fate! By the Franciscans,
       this was not just a trivial letter but one full of news
       of great importance. Failure to deliver it
20   could do much damage. Friar John, go and
       get me a crowbar and bring it here right away
       to my cell.

FRIAR JOHN
       Brother, I'll go get it and bring it to you.
           He exits.

FRIAR LAURENCE
       Now I must go to the tomb alone.
25   Within three hours, beautiful Juliet will awake.
       She'll blame me that Romeo
       hasn't been told about what's going on.
       But I'll write another letter to Mantua
       and keep her at my cell until Romeo comes.
30   Poor living body, shut up in a dead man's tomb!
           He exits.

Scene iii: [*A churchyard; in it a tomb belonging to the Capulets.*]
Enter PARIS, *and his* PAGE *with flowers and sweet water and a
torch.*

PARIS

Give me thy torch, boy. Hence, and stand aloof.
Yet put it out, for I would not be seen.
Under yond yew-tree lay thee all along,
Holding thine ear close to the hollow ground;
5   So shall no foot upon the churchyard tread,
Being loose, unfirm, with digging up of graves,
But thou shalt hear it. Whistle then to me,
As signal that thou hear'st something approach.
Give me those flowers. Do as I bid thee, go.

PAGE

10   [*Aside.*] I am almost afraid to stand alone
Here in the churchyard; yet I will adventure.

[*Retires.*]

PARIS

Sweet flower, with flowers thy bridal bed I strew,—
O woe! thy canopy is dust and stones—
Which with sweet water nightly I will dew,
15   Or, wanting that, with tears distill'd by moans.
The obsequies that I for thee will keep
Nightly shall be to strew thy grave and weep.

[*The Page whistles.*]

The boy gives warning something doth approach.
What cursed foot wanders this way to-night,
20   To cross my obsequies and true love's rite?
What, with a torch! Muffle me, night, a while.

[*Retires.*]

Enter ROMEO *and* BALTHASAR, *with a torch, a mattock, and a crow of iron.*

ROMEO

Give me that mattock and the wrenching iron.

Act V, Scene iii: A churchyard in which is a tomb belonging to the Capulet family. Enter PARIS *and his* PAGE *with flowers, perfumed water, and a torch.*

PARIS
    Give me your torch, boy. Go stand over there.
    Put out the torch, for I don't want to be seen.
    Go lie under that yew tree,
    and keep your ear close to the ground.
5   No foot will walk about the churchyard—
    since the soil is loose and not firm due to the
        digging of graves—
    that you won't be able to hear it. Whistle
    to signal me if you hear someone coming.
    Give me those flowers. Do as I tell you. Go!

PAGE (*to himself*)
10 I'm almost afraid to be alone
    here in this churchyard, but I'll chance it.
        He hides.

PARIS
    Sweet Juliet, my flower, with these flowers, I'll
        cover your bridal bed.
        He scatters flowers around tomb.
    O sorrow! Your bed is dust and stones—
    which I'll sprinkle with perfume every night.
15 Or if I don't have perfume, I'll use tears mixed
        with my moans.
    The funeral rites that I'll keep for you
    every night will be to sprinkle flowers on your
        grave and weep.
        The PAGE *whistles.*
    That's the boy's signal that someone is approaching.
    What damned foot wanders this way tonight
20 to interrupt the ritual for my true love?
    What—someone with a torch? Hide me, night, for awhile.
        He hides.
        Enter ROMEO *and* BALTHASAR *with a torch, a
        pickaxe, and a crowbar.*

ROMEO
    Give me that pickaxe and the crowbar.

Hold, take this letter; early in the morning
See thou deliver it to my lord and father.
25 Give me the light. Upon thy life I charge thee,
Whate'er thou hear'st or seest, stand all aloof,
And do not interrupt me in my course.
Why I descend into this bed of death
Is partly to behold my lady's face,
30 But chiefly to take thence from her dead finger
A precious ring, a ring that I must use
In dear employment; therefore hence, be gone.
But if thou, jealous, dost return to pry
In what I farther shall intend to do,
35 By heaven, I will tear thee joint by joint
And strew this hungry churchyard with thy limbs.
The time and my intents are savage-wild,
More fierce and more inexorable far
Than empty tigers or the roaring sea.

BALTHASAR
40 I will be gone, sir, and not trouble ye.

ROMEO
So shalt thou show me friendship. Take thou that;
Live, and be prosperous; and farewell, good fellow.

BALTHASAR
[*Aside.*] For all this same, I'll hide me hereabout.
His looks I fear, and his intents I doubt.

[*Retires.*]

ROMEO
45 Thou detestable maw, thou womb of death,
Gorg'd with the dearest morsel of the earth,
Thus I enforce thy rotten jaws to open,
And, in despite, I'll cram thee with more food!

[*Opens the tomb.*]

PARIS
This is that banish'd haughty Montague,
50 That murd'red my love's cousin, with which grief,

Wait! Take this letter and deliver it
to my lord and father early in the morning.
25 Give me the light. Upon your life, I order you,
whatever you hear or see, to stand aside
and don't try to stop me.
I'm going into this tomb
partly to see my lady's face,
30 but mostly to take from her dead finger
a precious ring—a ring that I must use
in important business. Therefore, go away!
But if you become curious and return to pry
into what I intend to do,
35 by heaven, I'll tear you limb from limb
and cover this hungry churchyard with your body.
The time and my plans are savage and wild,
far more fierce and more relentless
than hungry tigers or the roaring sea.

BALTHASAR
40 I'll go, sir, and not bother you.

ROMEO
By doing so, you'll prove you're my friend. Take
 this. (*Gives him money*)
Live and be prosperous. Goodbye, good fellow.

BALTHASAR (*to himself*)
Despite what he said, I'll hide close by.
His looks are frightening and I am suspicious about
 what he intends to do.
  He hides.

ROMEO (*looking at the tomb*)
45 You detestable stomach. You womb of death.
You are gorged with the dearest morsel on earth.
So I'll force your rotten jaws to open,
and to spite you, I'll cram you with more food!
  Opens the tomb.

PARIS
There's that banished, haughty Montague
50 who murdered my love's cousin. It was from grieving
 for Tybalt,

It is supposed, the fair creature died;
And here is come to do some villainous shame
To the dead bodies. I will apprehend him.

    [Comes forward.]

Stop thy unhallowed toil, vile Montague!
55   Can vengeance be pursued further than death?
Comdemned villain, I do apprehend thee.
Obey, and go with me; for thou must die.

ROMEO
I must indeed; and therefore came I hither.
Good gentle youth, tempt not a desperate man.
60   Fly hence, and leave me; think upon these gone,
Let them affright thee. I beseech thee, youth,
Put not another sin upon my head,
By urging me to fury: O, be gone!
By heaven, I love thee better than myself;
65   For I come hither arm'd against myself.
Stay not, be gone; live, and hereafter say
A madman's mercy bid thee run away.

PARIS
I do defy thy conjurations
And apprehend thee for a felon here.

ROMEO
70   Wilt thou provoke me? Then have at thee, boy!

    [They fight.]

PAGE
O Lord, they fight! I will go call the watch.

    [Exit.]

PARIS
O, I am slain! *[Falls.]* If thou be merciful,
Open the tomb, lay me with Juliet.

    [Dies.]

ROMEO
In faith, I will. Let me peruse this face.

it's said, that my beautiful love died.
And now he's come to do some villainous dishonor to
the dead bodies. I'll stop him.
> *He comes forward.*
Stop your unholy work, evil Montague!
55   Can you demand any further revenge than death?
Condemned villain, I'll stop you.
Obey and go with me, for you must die.

ROMEO

I must die, indeed, and that is why I came here.
Good gentle youth, don't tempt a desperate man.
60   Fly away and leave me. Think about those who are
        dead.
Let them frighten you. I beg you, youth,
don't lay another sin on my head
by making me angry. Go away!
By heaven, I love you better than I love myself,
65   for I came here with weapons to hurt myself.
Don't stay; go! Live, and later you can say that
a madman's mercy told you to run away.

PARIS

I reject your appeals,
and I arrest you as a criminal.

ROMEO

70   You want to start something? Then take that, boy.
> *They fight.*

PAGE

O Lord, they're fighting! I'll go call the guards.
> *He exits.*

PARIS

O, I'm dying. (*He falls*) If you are merciful,
open the tomb and lay me beside Juliet!
> *He dies.*

ROMEO

Truly, I will. Let me look at his face.

75   Mercutio's kinsman, noble County Paris!
        What said my man, when my betossed soul
        Did not attend him as we rode? I think
        He told me Paris should have married Juliet.
        Said he not so? Or did I dream it so?
80   Or am I mad, hearing him talk of Juliet,
        To think it was so? O, give me thy hand,
        One writ with me in sour misfortune's book!
        I'll bury thee in a triumphant grave.
        A grave? O, no! a lantern, slaught'red youth,
85   For here lies Juliet, and her beauty makes
        This vault a feasting presence full of light.
        Death, lie thou there, by a dead man interr'd.

        [*Laying Paris in the tomb.*]

        How oft when men are at the point of death
        Have they been merry! which their keepers call
90   A lightning before death. O, how may I
        Call this a lightning? O my love! my wife!
        Death, that hath suck'd the honey of thy breath,
        Hath had no power yet upon thy beauty.
        Thou art not conquer'd; beauty's ensign yet
95   Is crimson in thy lips and in thy cheeks,
        And death's pale flag is not advanced there.
        Tybalt, li'st thou there in thy bloody sheet?
        O, what more favour can I do to thee,
        Than with that hand that cut thy youth in twain
100   To sunder his that was thine enemy?
        Forgive me, cousin! Ah, dear Juliet,
        Why art thou yet so fair? Shall I believe
        That unsubstantial Death is amorous,
        And that the lean abhorred monster keeps
105   Thee here in dark to be his paramour?
        For fear of that, I still will stay with thee,
        And never from this palace of dim night
        Depart again. Here, here will I remain
        With worms that are thy chamber-maids; O, here
110   Will I set up my everlasting rest,

---

84 *lantern*   is a room on top of a tower designed with many windows to admit light and air.

75   This is Mercutio's relative, the noble Count Paris!
      What was it my servant said when my disturbed soul
      did not listen to him as we rode? I think
      he told me Paris was supposed to have married Juliet.
      Isn't that what he said? Or did I dream it?
80   Or am I crazy, hearing him talk of Juliet,
      to believe it? O, give me your hand.
      We've both been written about in sour misfortune's book.
      I'll bury you in a triumphant grave.
      A grave? O, no, rather a lantern, slain youth,
85   because Juliet lies here, and her beauty makes
      this tomb a state banquet hall full of light.
      Dead man, lie there, buried by a dead man.
            He lays PARIS *in the tomb.*
      Often when men are at the point of death,
      they have been happy. Their nurses call this
90   a revival before death. O, how may I
      call this a revival? O my love! My wife!
      Death, that has sucked the honey from your breath,
      has no power yet over your beauty.
      You are not conquered. Beauty's flag is
95   still crimson in your lips and cheeks,
      and death's pale flag has not advanced there.
      Tybalt, is that you lying there in your bloody sheet?
      O, what greater favor can I do for you
      than, with this hand that killed you,
100   kill the one who was your enemy?
      Forgive, me, cousin.—Ah, dear Juliet,
      why are you still so beautiful? Shall I believe
      that the phantom Death is passionate
      and that the thin, hateful monster keeps
105   you here in the dark to be his mistress?
      For fear of that, I'll stay with you
      and never again leave this palace of
      dim night. Here, here I'll remain
      with worms that are your servingmaids. O, here
110   I'll take my eternal rest,

And shake the yoke of inauspicious stars
From this world-wearied flesh. Eyes, look your last!
Arms take your last embrace! and, lips, O you
The doors of breath, seal with a righteous kiss
115   A dateless bargain to engrossing death!
Come, bitter conduct, come, unsavoury guide!
Thou desperate pilot, now at once run on
The dashing rocks thy sea-sick weary bark!
Here's to my love! [*Drinks.*] O true apothecary!
120   Thy drugs are quick. Thus with a kiss I die.

　　　　[*Dies.*]

　　　　Enter FRIAR LAURENCE, *with lantern, crow, and
　　　　spade.*

FRIAR LAURENCE
Saint Francis be my speed! how oft tonight
Have my old feet stumbled at graves! Who's there?

BALTHASAR
Here's one, a friend, and one that knows you well.

FRIAR LAURENCE
Bliss be upon you! Tell me, good my friend,
125   What torch is yond, that vainly lends his light
To grubs and eyeless skulls? As I discern,
It burneth in the Capels' monument.

BALTHASAR
It doth so, holy sir; and there's my master,
One that you love.

FRIAR LAURENCE
130　　　　　　　　　　　　Who is it?

BALTHASAR
　　　　　　　　　　　　　Romeo.

FRIAR LAURENCE
How long hath he been there?

BALTHASAR
　　　　　　　　　　　Full half an hour.

---

122 *stumbled at graves*　this was considered a bad omen.

and shake off the grip of unkind fate
from my world-wearied body. Eyes, take your last look!
Arms, take your last embrace! And lips—O you lips
that are the doors of breath—seal with a fitting kiss
115   an eternal bargain to all-consuming death!
Come, bitter poison, come distasteful guide.
You desperate pilot, crash my seasick, tired body
against the dashing rocks at once.
Here's to my love! (*He drinks the poison*)
   O, faithful pharmacist!
120   Your drugs are quick. With this kiss, I die.
         ROMEO *kisses* JULIET *and dies.*
         Enter FRIAR LAURENCE, *with a lantern, a*
           crowbar, and a spade.

FRIAR LAURENCE
     Saint Francis, help me! How often tonight
     have my old feet stumbled over graves. Who's there?

BALTHASAR
     A friend and one who knows you well.

FRIAR LAURENCE
     Bless you. Tell me, my friend,
125   what torch is that over there that vainly lights up
     the worms and eyeless skulls? As best as I can see,
     it burns in the Capulets' tomb.

BALTHASAR
     It does, holy sir; and that's where my master is,
     one that you love.

FRIAR LAURENCE
130   Who's that?

BALTHASAR
     Romeo.

FRIAR LAURENCE
     How long has he been there?

BALTHASAR
     At least half an hour.

FRIAR LAURENCE
Go with me to the vault.

BALTHASAR
135   I dare not, sir.
My master knows not but I am gone hence;
And fearfully did menace me with death
If I did stay to look on his intents.

FRIAR LAURENCE
Stay, then; I'll go alone. Fear comes upon me:
140   O, much I fear some ill unthrifty thing.

BALTHASAR
As I did sleep under this yew-tree here,
I dreamt my master and another fought,
And that my master slew him.

FRIAR LAURENCE
                                   Romeo!
        [*Advances.*]

145   Alack, alack, what blood is this, which stains
The stony entrance of this sepulchre?
What mean these masterless and gory swords
To lie discolour'd by this place of peace?

        [*Enters the tomb.*]

Romeo! O, pale! Who else? What, Paris too?
150   And steep'd in blood? Ah, what an unkind hour
Is guilty of this lamentable change!
The lady stirs.

        [*Juliet rises.*]

JULIET
O comfortable friar! where is my lord?
I do remember well where I should be,
155   And there I am. Where is my Romeo?

        [*Noise within.*]

FRIAR LAURENCE
I hear some noise. Lady, come from that nest

FRIAR LAURENCE
Go with me to the tomb.

BALTHASAR
135   I don't dare, sir.
My master doesn't know that I haven't left.
With frightening words, he threatened me with death
if I stayed to see what he did.

FRIAR LAURENCE
Stay here then; I'll go alone. I'm beginning to
    feel frightened.
140   I'm afraid something terribly unlucky has happened.

BALTHASAR
As I slept under this yew tree here,
I dreamed my master and another man fought,
and that my master killed him.

FRIAR LAURENCE
Romeo!
        He advances toward the tomb.
145   Alas, alas, whose blood is this that stains
the stone entrance of this tomb?
What's the meaning of these unclaimed, bloody swords
that lie here, stained with blood, in this peaceful place?
        He enters the tomb.
Romeo! How pale he is! Who else is here? What,
    Paris, too?
150   And he's covered in blood? The hour that saw this
sad turn of events occur is tragic, indeed!
The lady is waking up.
        JULIET *rises.*

JULIET
O comforting friar, where is my lord?
I remember quite well where I am supposed to be,
155   and here I am. But where is my Romeo?
        There is a noise.

FRIAR LAURENCE
I hear some noise. Lady, come from that bed

Of death, contagion, and unnatural sleep.
A greater power than we can contradict
Hath thwarted our intents. Come, come away.
160   Thy husband in thy bosom there lies dead;
And Paris too. Come, I'll dispose of thee
Among a sisterhood of holy nuns.
Stay not to question, for the watch is coming;
Come, go, good Juliet [*Noise again*], I dare no longer stay.

　　　[Exit Friar Laurence.]

JULIET
165   Go, get thee hence, for I will not away.
What's here? A cup, clos'd in my true love's hand?
Poison, I see, hath been his timeless end.
O churl! drunk all, and left no friendly drop
To help me after? I will kiss thy lips;
170   Haply some poison yet doth hang on them,
To make me die with a restorative.
Thy lips are warm.

　　　Enter WATCH, *with the* PAGE *of Paris.*

1. WATCH
Lead, boy; which way?

JULIET
Yea, noise? Then I'll be brief. O happy dagger!

　　　[Snatching Romeo's dagger.]

175   This is thy sheath (*Stabs herself*); there rust, and let me die.

　　　[Falls on Romeo's body, and dies].

PAGE
This is the place; there, where the torch doth burn.

1. WATCH
The ground is bloody; search about the churchyard.
Go, some of you, whoe'er you find attach.

　　　[Exeunt some.]

Pitiful sight! here lies the County slain;
180   And Juliet bleeding, warm, and newly dead,

of death, contamination, and unnatural sleep.
A greater power than we can argue with
has ruined our plans. Come, come away.

160   Your dear husband lies dead—
and Paris, too. Come, I'll hide you
in a convent of nuns.
Don't stop to ask questions because the guards are coming.
Come, let's go, good Juliet. (*The noise is heard
again*) I don't dare stay any longer.
       FRIAR LAURENCE *exits.*

JULIET

165   Go, go away. I'll stay.
What's this? A bottle, clutched in my true love's hand?
Poison, I see, has brought him to his untimely end.
O, the rascal drank it all and didn't leave one good drop
to help me follow him. I'll kiss your lips, then.

170   Perhaps some drop of poison still hangs on them
to make me die from that life-giving kiss.
Your lips are warm!
       Enter GUARDS *and Paris'* PAGE.

FIRST GUARD

Lead the way, boy. Which direction?

JULIET

Noise! Then I'll be brief. What luck—a dagger!
       She snatches ROMEO'S *dagger.*

175   This is your holder. (*She stabs herself*) Rest
there and let me die.
       JULIET *falls on* ROMEO'S *body and dies.*

PAGE

That's the place—there where the torch burns.

FIRST GUARD

The ground is bloody. Search the churchyard.
Go, some of you, and whoever you find, arrest.
       Some of the guards exit.
This is a pitiful sight! Here lies Count Paris, killed.

180   And there lies Juliet, bleeding, warm and just dead,

Who here hath lain this two days buried.
Go, tell the Prince; run to the Capulets;
Raise up the Montagues; some others search.

　　[*Exeunt others.*]

　　We see the ground whereon these woes do lie;
185　But the true ground of all these piteous woes
　　We cannot without circumstance descry.

　　　　Re-enter some of the WATCH, *with* BALTHASAR.

2. WATCH
Here's Romeo's man; we found him in the churchyard.

1. WATCH
Hold him in safety till the Prince come hither.

　　　　Re-enter another WATCHMAN, *with* FRIAR
　　　　LAURENCE.

3. WATCH
Here is a friar, that trembles, sighs, and weeps.
190　We took this mattock and this spade from him,
As he was coming from this churchyard's side.

1. WATCH
A great suspicion. Stay the friar too.

　　　　Enter the PRINCE *and* Attendants.

PRINCE ESCALUS
What misadventure is so early up,
That calls our person from our morning rest?

　　　　Enter CAPULET, LADY CAPULET, *and others.*

CAPULET
195　What should it be, that they so shriek abroad?

LADY CAPULET
Oh! the people in the street cry Romeo,
Some Juliet, and some Paris; and all run,
With open outcry, toward our monument.

PRINCE ESCALUS
What fear is this which startles in our ears?

though she has lain here buried for two days.
Go, tell the prince. Run to the Capulets.
Wake up the Montagues. Others of you, search the
area!
> *Other guards exit.*

We see the ground where these sorrows lie.
185   But the true cause of all these pitiful sorrows
we can't tell without more details.
> *Re-enter some of the guards with* BALTHASAR.

SECOND GUARD
Here's Romeo's servant. We found him in the
churchyard.

FIRST GUARD
Keep him under guard until the prince comes.
> *Re-enter another guard with* FRIAR LAURENCE.

THIRD GUARD
Here's a friar who shakes, sighs, and weeps.
190   We took this pickaxe and this spade from him,
as he was coming from the side of this churchyard.

FIRST GUARD
This is very suspicious. Keep the friar, too.
> *Enter the* PRINCE, *and attendants.*

PRINCE
What trouble is up so early
that wakes me from my morning sleep?
> *Enter* CAPULET, LADY CAPULET, *and others.*

CAPULET
195   What could it be that people are shouting in the
streets?

LADY CAPULET
The people in the street shout, "Romeo,"
some shout, "Juliet," and some shout, "Paris." And
all of them are running
with noisy shouts toward our tomb.

PRINCE
What news has alarmed everyone?

1. WATCH

200   Sovereign, here lies the County Paris slain;
And Romeo dead; and Juliet, dead before,
Warm and new kill'd.

PRINCE ESCALUS

Search, seek, and know how this foul murder comes.

1. WATCH

Here is a friar, and slaughter'd Romeo's man,
205   With instruments upon them, fit to open
These dead men's tombs.

CAPULET

O heavens! O wife, look how our daughter bleeds!
This dagger hath mista'en,—for, lo, his house
Is empty on the back of Montague,—
210   And it mis-sheathed in my daughter's bosom!

LADY CAPULET

O me! this sight of death is as a bell,
That warns my old age to a sepulchre.

Enter MONTAGUE *and others.*

PRINCE ESCALUS

Come, Montague; for thou art early up
To see thy son and heir more early down.

MONTAGUE

215   Alas, my liege, my wife is dead to-night;
Grief of my son's exile hath stopp'd her breath.
What further woe conspires against mine age?

PRINCE ESCALUS

Look, and thou shalt see.

MONTAGUE

O thou untaught! what manners is in this,
220   To press before thy father to a grave?

PRINCE ESCALUS

Seal up the mouth of outrage for a while,
Till we can clear these ambiguities,

FIRST GUARD

200   Your majesty, here lies Count Paris, killed.
Romeo is also dead, and Juliet, who was dead before,
is still warm and newly killed.

PRINCE

Search, investigate, and find out how this foul
murder happened.

FIRST GUARD

Here's a friar, and Romeo's servant,
205   carrying tools that could be used to open
these dead men's tombs.

CAPULET

O heavens! Wife, see how our daughter bleeds!
This dagger has missed the right victim. See,
    Romeo's dagger sheath
is empty, and the dagger has been
210   mistakenly placed in our daughter's breast.

LADY CAPULET

Alas! This sight of death is like a bell
that summons my aged body to my grave.
    Enter MONTAGUE *and others.*

PRINCE

Come, Montague. You are up early
to see your son and heir who just retired even
    earlier.

MONTAGUE

215   Alas, prince, my wife died tonight!
Grief over my son's exile killed her.
What further sorrow schemes against me in my old age?

PRINCE

Look and you will see.

MONTAGUE

O you rude boy. What kind of manners is this
220   to hurry before your father to a grave?

PRINCE

No more of your violent grieving for awhile
until we can clear up these strange events

And know their spring, their head, their true descent;
And then will I be general of your woes
225   And lead you even to death. Meantime forbear,
And let mischance be slave to patience.
Bring forth the parties of suspicion.

FRIAR LAURENCE
I am the greatest, able to do least,
Yet most suspected, as the time and place
230   Doth make against me, of this direful murder;
And here I stand, both to impeach and purge
Myself condemned and myself excus'd.

PRINCE ESCALUS
Then say at once what thou dost know in this.

FRIAR LAURENCE
I will be brief, for my short date of breath
235   Is not so long as is a tedious tale.
Romeo, there dead, was husband to that Juliet;
And she, there dead, that Romeo's faithful wife.
I married them; and their stol'n marriage-day
Was Tybalt's dooms-day, whose untimely death
240   Banish'd the new-made bridegroom from this city,
For whom, and not for Tybalt, Juliet pin'd.
You, to remove that siege of grief from her,
Betroth'd and would have married her perforce
To County Paris. Then comes she to me,
245   And, with wild looks, bid me devise some mean
To rid her from this second marriage,
Or in my cell there would she kill herself.
Then gave I her, so tutor'd by my art,
A sleeping potion; which so took effect
250   As I intended, for it wrought on her
The form of death. Meantime I writ to Romeo,
That he should hither come as this dire night
To help to take her from her borrowed grave,
Being the time the potion's force should cease.
255   But he which bore my letter, Friar John,
Was stay'd by accident, and yesternight

and know how and why they started and how they
   really occurred.
Then I'll be your leader in mourning
225   and lead you even to death. But in the meantime, no more.
Bear your sorrows with patience.
Bring here the people under suspicion.

FRIAR LAURENCE
   I'm the most important suspect, least likely to do
      something wrong,
   yet I'm most suspected since the time and place
230   stands as evidence against me and seems to prove me
      guilty of this shocking murder.
   And here I stand, both to charge myself and clear myself,
   condemn myself and excuse myself.

PRINCE
   Then tell us at once what you know about this.

FRIAR LAURENCE
   I'll be brief because the span of my remaining years
235   is not as long as a long tale.
   Romeo, who lies dead there, was Juliet's husband.
   And she, who lies dead there, was Romeo's faithful wife.
   I married them, and their secret wedding day
   was Tybalt's last day. His untimely death
240   banished the new bridegroom from this city.
   It was for him—not for Tybalt—that Juliet grieved.
   You, Lord Capulet, to shake her out of her depression,
   arranged for her to marry Count Paris
   right away. Then she came to me,
245   and with wild looks, begged me to think of some way
   to get her out of this second marriage.
   If I didn't, she said she'd kill herself there in my cell.
   Then I gave her, from my knowledge of medicine,
   a sleeping potion. It worked
250   as I intended it to do since it made her
   seem like she was dead. Meanwhile, I wrote to Romeo
   that he should come here tonight
   to help free her from this borrowed grave
   as tonight was the time the potion would wear off.
255   But Friar John, who was to take my letter to Romeo,
   was detained by accident, and last night,

Return'd my letter back. Then all alone
At the prefixed hour of her waking,
Came I to take her from her kindred's vault;
260 Meaning to keep her closely at my cell,
Till I conveniently could send to Romeo;
But when I came, some minutes ere the time
Of her awak'ning, here untimely lay
The noble Paris and true Romeo dead.
265 She wakes; and I entreated her come forth
And bear this work of heaven with patience.
But then a noise did scare me from the tomb;
And she, too desperate, would not go with me,
But, as it seems, did violence on herself.
270 All this I know; and to the marriage
Her nurse is privy; and, if aught in this
Miscarried by my fault, let my old life
Be sacrific'd, some hour before his time,
Unto the rigour of severest law.

PRINCE ESCALUS
275 We still have known thee for a holy man.
Where's Romeo's man? What can he say to this?

BALTHASAR
I brought my master news of Juliet's death;
And then in post he came from Mantua
To this same place, to this same monument.
280 This letter he early bid me give his father,
And threat'ned me with death, going in the vault,
If I departed not and left him there.

PRINCE ESCALUS
Give me the letter; I will look on it.
Where is the County's page, that rais'd the watch?
285 Sirrah, what made your master in this place?

PAGE
He came with flowers to strew his lady's grave;
And bid me stand aloof, and so I did.
Anon comes one with light to ope the tomb,

---

273 *some hour before his time* Friar Laurence is implying he is so old that his
life will not last much longer in any case.

he brought my letter back. Then all alone,
at the time I estimated Juliet would awaken,
I came to take her from her relatives' tomb.
260   I intended to keep her hidden in my cell
until I could conveniently get word to Romeo.
But when I came some minutes before
she was to awaken, here lay
the noble Paris and true Romeo, dead before their time.
265   Juliet awoke and I begged her to come out
and patiently accept these events willed by heaven.
But then a noise scared me away from the tomb,
and she, too deep in despair, wouldn't go with me.
She stayed, and it seems she committed suicide.
270   This is all I know. Her nurse was in on the secret
about Juliet's marriage. And if any of this
went wrong because of me, let my old life
be sacrificed, some hour before my time,
according to the severity of the strictest laws.

PRINCE
275   I've always known you to be a holy man.
Where's Romeo's servant? What can he add to this?

BALTHASAR
I brought my master news of Juliet's death.
And then, in haste, he came from Mantua
to this same place and this same tomb.
280   He told me to deliver this letter to his father early
    in the morning,
and as he went into the tomb, he threatened me with death
if I didn't go away and leave him there.

PRINCE
Give me the letter; I want to look at it.
Where is Count Paris' page—the one who called the guards?
285   Servant, what made your master come to this place?

PAGE
He came with flowers to scatter at his lady's grave.
He asked me to stay away, so I did.
Soon, someone came with a light to open the tomb.

And by and by my master drew on him;
290   And then I ran away to call the watch.

PRINCE ESCALUS
This letter doth make good the friar's words,
Their course of love, the tidings of her death.
And here he writes that he did buy a poison
Of a poor 'pothecary, and therewithal
295   Came to this vault to die, and lie with Juliet.
Where be these enemies? Capulet! Montague!
See what a scourge is laid upon your hate,
That Heaven finds means to kill your joys with love.
And I for winking at your discords too
300   Have lost a brace of kinsmen. All are punish'd.

CAPULET
O brother Montague, give me thy hand.
This is my daughter's jointure, for no more
Can I demand.

MONTAGUE
                              But I can give thee more;
305   For I will raise her statue in pure gold;
That whiles Verona by that name is known,
There shall no figure at such rate be set
As that of true and faithful Juliet.

CAPULET
As rich shall Romeo's by his lady's lie,
310   Poor sacrifices of our enmity!

PRINCE ESCALUS
A glooming peace this morning with it brings;
   The sun, for sorrow, will not show his head.
Go hence, to have more talk of these sad things;
   Some shall be pardon'd, and some punished:
315   For never was a story of more woe
Than this of Juliet and her Romeo.

            [*Exeunt.*]

290   After awhile, my master drew his sword on him,
    and I ran away to call the guard.

PRINCE
    This letter proves the truth of the friar's words.
    It tells the course of their love and the news of her death.
    Here he writes of how he bought poison
    from a poor pharmacist and then
295   came to this tomb to die and lie with Juliet.
    Where are these enemies? Capulet, Montague!
    See what a curse is laid upon your hatred.
    Heaven finds the means to kill your joys with love.
    And I, for overlooking your feud,
300   have lost two relatives, too. We've all been punished.

CAPULET
    O my brother Montague, give me your hand.
    This is my daughter's dowry, for I can ask
    for nothing more.

MONTAGUE
    But I'll give you more,
305   for I'll put up a statue to her in pure gold.
    So as long as Verona is called Verona,
    there'll be no other figure valued
    like that of the true and faithful Juliet.

CAPULET
    I'll put up an equally rich statue of Romeo beside Juliet's.
310   They are the poor sacrifices of our feud.

PRINCE
    This morning brings a cloudy peace.
      The sun, out of sorrow, will not show its head.
    Go! We'll talk more about these sad things.
      Some of you will be pardoned and some of you will
      be punished.
315   There never was a story of more sorrow
    than this one of Juliet and her Romeo.
        They exit.

THE PLAY IN REVIEW:

A Teacher and Student Supplement

The Curtain Rises: Prereading Questions

Act I

1. The prologue to Act I suggests that the relationship of Romeo and Juliet is doomed from the start. Do you believe some things are fated to happen, no matter what? Or do you believe that your actions can change the course of your life? Explain your answer.

2. What events might you expect to take place in a story about feuding families?

3. What role do you think one's family should have in the selection of one's wife or husband?

4. The play is set in Verona, Italy, during the Renaissance. What images do you have of Renaissance Italy? How accurately do you think Shakespeare will portray Verona in this play?

Act II

5. Do you believe in love at first sight? In your opinion, are young teenagers capable of experiencing true and lasting love?

6. What do you expect to become of Romeo's love for Rosaline now that he's met Juliet?

7. What do you think Romeo and Juliet ought to do now that they've discovered each other's identities?

8. After Tybalt's behavior at the ball, what role do you expect him to play in the rest of the story?

Act III

9. Do you expect Romeo to tell Benvolio and Mercutio about his love for Juliet? Why or why not?

10. At this point in the play, which character strikes you as more vivid and compelling, Romeo or Juliet? Explain.

11. Judging from the play, how were gender roles different in the Renaissance from gender roles today?

12. What kind of long-term marriage would you expect Romeo and Juliet to have?

13. Which character would you expect to give unwanted advice to either Romeo or Juliet during Act III?

Act IV

14. How have your feelings about Romeo changed because of his role in the deaths of Mercutio and Tybalt?

15. What options remain open to Romeo and Juliet? What advice would you give them?

16. How do you expect Friar Laurence and the Nurse to affect the play's outcome? Which of them do you expect to play a more important role in the last two acts? Explain.

Act V

17. What do you think of Friar Laurence's decision to give Juliet the potion?

18. Take another look at the prologue to Act I. What does it tell you about how the play is going to end, beyond the fact that the lovers will die?

19. If the parents of Romeo and Juliet had learned of their children's marriage at the end of Act IV, what do you think they would have done?

Between Acts: Study Questions

Act I

1. What dramatic functions are served by the prologue to Act I?

2. What feelings are created by the play's first scene, prior to Prince Escalus's entrance?

3. What does the first scene of the play reveal about Romeo's behavior?

4. Describe the relationship between Capulet and his daughter, as it is shown during Scene ii.

5. What complications arise in Scene ii?

6. What concepts of love are presented by the female characters in Scene iii?

7. Characterize Mercutio as he appears in Scene iv.

8. In what ways does Capulet prove himself a good host?

9. Describe Romeo and Juliet's discoveries of each other's identity.

Act II

10. How does Mercutio try to draw Romeo out of hiding, and what is Romeo's response?

11. What images of light and fire does Juliet inspire in Romeo?

12. What concerns does Juliet express in Act II, Scene ii?

13. What examples of dramatic irony are in Act II, Scene ii?

14. What philosophical observations does Friar Laurence make in Act II, Scene iii?

15. What is Friar Laurence's reaction to Romeo's request in Act II, Scene iii?

16. How does Mercutio respond to the news of Tybalt's challenge to Romeo?

17. Describe the interview between Juliet's nurse and Romeo in Act II, Scene iv.

18. How does the nurse inform Juliet of Romeo's plans? How does Juliet react?

19. What elements in Scene vi foreshadow a fatal end to Romeo and Juliet's love?

Act III

20. Structurally, how does Act III, Scene i, resemble Act I, Scene i?

21. Describe Mercutio's dying remarks in Scene i.

22. Explain why Romeo chooses to fight Tybalt after all.

23. Compare Juliet's soliloquy in Act II, Scene v, with her soliloquy of Act III, Scene ii.

24. How does the nurse reveal the details of Romeo's banishment? What is Juliet's reaction?

25. Describe Romeo's emotions during the first part of Scene iii.

26. What admonition does Friar Laurence give Romeo in Scene iii?

27. Discuss the rash offer that Capulet makes Paris in Scene iv.

28. Compare the parting of the lovers in Act II, Scene ii, with their farewells in Act III, Scene v.

29. What occurs in Scene v to put distance between Juliet and her family and nurse?

Act IV

30. What plan does Friar Laurence propose to Juliet?

31. What worries does Juliet express in her soliloquy at the end of Scene iii? How does she dispense with each?

32. Describe the reactions to Juliet's apparent death in Scene v.

Act V

33. What preparations does Romeo make in Scene i when he is mistakenly informed of Juliet's death?

34. Describe Paris's actions in Scene iii. How does his presence influence your feelings about what might happen next?

35. Summarize Romeo's last soliloquy in Scene iii.

36. Describe Juliet's awakening and death.

37. How does the prince investigate the deaths?

38. Summarize the prince's thoughts once he fully understands what has happened.

39. What memorial will be built for Romeo and Juliet?

The Play's the Thing: Discussion Questions

Act I

1. Why do you think Shakespeare "gives away" the plot of his play in the prologue to Act I?

2. How and why do Romeo's feelings for Juliet differ from his feelings for Rosaline?

3. Why do you think Shakespeare portrayed Romeo as being initially infatuated with Rosaline? Do you think it was a good dramatic decision? Explain.

4. In your opinion, why are Romeo and Juliet so drawn to one another when they first meet at the masked ball?

Act II

5. The prologue to Act II ends with the lines, "But passion lends them power, time means, to meet, / Temp'ring extremities with extreme sweet." Discuss this statement in relation to this act and the entire story.

248

6. Juliet is the first to propose marriage between herself and Romeo during Act II, Scene ii. When does Romeo seem to agree to this proposal, and when does Juliet know of his acceptance? Explain.

7. What is the purpose of the verbal duel between Romeo and Mercutio in Scene iv?

8. In Scene vi, Friar Laurence advises Romeo, "Therefore love moderately…" Evaluate the wisdom of this advice at this moment in the play.

Act III

9. Before the fight in Scene i, Mercutio tells Tybalt that he wants one of Tybalt's "nine lives." What do you think Mercutio means by this?

10. How do you feel about Romeo's actions leading up to the deaths of Mercutio and Tybalt?

11. What are your impressions of the marriage between Lord and Lady Capulet? How do their feelings for one another affect their behavior toward their daughter?

12. How did you react to the nurse's suggestion that Juliet marry Paris? Do you think that this is really consistent with her character? Explain.

13. Describe Juliet's reactions to the nurse's suggestion that she marry Paris, both before and after the nurse's exit.

Act IV

14. What do you think motivates Friar Laurence throughout this act? Comment on whether his motivations remain the same throughout the play.

15. How do you feel about Juliet at the moment when she takes the potion?

16. Why do you think Shakespeare included Scene iv in the play?

17. Why do you think Shakespeare included the dialogue between Peter and the musicians at the end of Scene v?

Act V

18. Why do you think Shakespeare thought it important to have Paris die?

19. Do you think that fate or the characters themselves are most responsible for the outcome of the play? Explain.

20. What do you think of the action that takes place after Romeo and Juliet are both dead—particularly Friar Laurence's summary of prior events?

The Play as a Whole

1. In Act II, Scene iii, Friar Laurence speaks about the dual nature of his herbs. He then continues, "Two such opposed kings encamp them still/In man as well as herbs, grace and rude will…" Discuss how this comment reflects on the action of the play.

2. In what ways do the characters of Romeo and Juliet change and grow during the story?

3. Identify some situations in today's world where two lovers might find obstacles because of their membership in feuding groups.

4. Judging from the play, how do you think gender roles have changed since the Renaissance?

5. In what ways have popular stories of romantic love remained unchanged since *Romeo and Juliet* was written? In what ways have they changed? State some examples.

Encore: Vocabulary Words

The main words in the groups below are taken from *Romeo and Juliet.* Mark the lettered word that comes closest in meaning to each word in bold type.

Act I

1. **civil**
   "Where **civil** blood makes civil hands unclean."

   a. uncontrolled
   b. enemies'
   c. citizens'
   d. relative

2. **star-crossed**
   "A pair of **star-crossed** lovers take their life…"

   a. oath-swearing
   b. ill-destined
   c. swift-moving
   d. moon-struck

3. **ancient**
   "At this same **ancient** feast of Capulet's…"

   a. for the elderly
   b. out of style
   c. traditional
   d. long lasting

4. **wax**
   "Why, he's a man of **wax**."

   a. model qualities
   b. strong character
   c. easily-shaped nature
   d. burning promise

5. **chinks**
   "I tell you, he that can lay hold of her / Shall have the **chinks**."

   a. children
   b. envy
   c. misfortune
   d. money

6. **prodigious**
   "**Prodigious** birth of love it is to me / That I must love a loathed enemy."

   a. abnormal

   b. unexpected

   c. full of good hope

   d. long-awaited

Act II

7. **wherefore**
   "O Romeo, Romeo! **wherefore** art thou Romeo?"

   a. where

   b. who

   c. why

   d. when

8. **let**
   "Therefore thy kinsmen are no **let** to me."

   a. help

   b. relation

   c. obstacle

   d. friends

9. **properer**
   "Paris is the **properer** man…"

   a. more handsome

   b. better behaved

   c. wealthier

   d. more romantic

10. **countervail**

"But come what sorrow can, / It cannot **countervail** the exchange of joy."

   a. hide
   b. cry out for
   c. protest
   d. outweigh

11. **confounds**

"The sweetest honey…in the taste **confounds** the appetite."

   a. destroys
   b. confuses
   c. increases
   d. recognizes

12. **conceit**

"**Conceit,** more rich in matter than in words, / Brags of his substance, not of ornament."

   a. vanity
   b. fate
   c. understanding
   d. promises

Act III

13. **villain**

"No better term than this: thou art a **villain**."

   a. overbearing youth
   b. rat catcher
   c. criminal
   d. of low birth

14. **peppered**

"I am **peppered,** I warrant, for this world. / A plague o' both your houses!"

    a. hot-tempered

    b. confused

    c. completely finished

    d. disappointed

15. **respective lenity**

"Away to heaven, **respective lenity,** / And fire-eyed fury be my conduct now!"

    a. indecision

    b. thoughtful mercy

    c. fear of death

    d. brotherly love

16. **railst on**

"Why **railst** thou **on** thy birth, the heaven, and earth?"

    a. rely upon

    b. complain against

    c. risk

    d. fight for

17. **temper**

"Madam, if you could find out but a man / To bear a poison, I would **temper** it…"

    a. give

    b. take

    c. approve

    d. change

18. **practice stratagems**

"Alack, alack, that heaven should **practice stratagems** / Upon so soft a subject as myself!"

a. attempt to trap

b. act out tragedies

c. play sour notes

d. be at war with

Act IV

19. **charnel-house**

"Or hide me nightly in a **charnel-house**…"

a. insane asylum

b. skeletal storehouse

c. debtors' prison

d. nun's cloister

20. **supple government**

"Like death when he shuts up the day of life; / Each part, deprived of **supple government**…"

a. legal restrictions

b. common sense

c. ability to move

d. honorable behavior

21. **drift**

"Shall Romeo by my letters know our **drift**…"

a. dread

b. mistake

c. misfortune

d. intention

22. **orisons**

"For I have need of many **orisons** / To move the heavens to smile upon my state…"

   a. prayers

   b. visions

   c. sorrows

   d. miracles

23. **solemnity**

"Uncomfortable time, why camest thou now / To murder, murder our **solemnity?**"

   a. festivity

   b. confession

   c. romance

   d. confusion

24. **put out**

"Pray you put up your dagger, and **put out** your wit."

   a. banish

   b. exhibit

   c. silence

   d. pardon

Act V

25. **office**

"O, pardon me for bringing these ill news, / Since you did leave it for my **office, sir.**"

   a. place of work

   b. favor

   c. duty

   d. offense

26. **ducats**
   "Hold, there is forty **ducats.** Let me have / A dram of poison."

   a. kisses
   b. gold coins
   c. promises
   d. hours

27. **nice**
   "The letter was not **nice,** but full of charge…"

   a. important
   b. kind
   c. brief
   d. trifling

28. **dateless**
   "A **dateless** bargain to engrossing death!"

   a. unmemorable
   b. eternal
   c. cleanse
   d. tardy

29. **impeach**
   "And here I stand, both to **impeach** and purge / Myself condemned and myself excused."

   a. accuse
   b. remove from office
   c. cleanse
   d. advance

30. **privy**
   "…and to the marriage / Her nurse is **privy**…"

   a. guilty of
   b. ignorant of
   c. secretly aware
   d. blameless

Improvisation: Student Enrichment

Research:

1. Compare *West Side Story* with *Romeo and Juliet* in terms of setting, characters, conflict, plot, and theme. You might read the novel *West Side Story* by Irving Shulman or view the musical production.

2. Investigate "The Novel of Juliet" by Luigi da Porto in *Great Italian Short Stories*, selected by P.M. Pasinetti. Compare this version of the story with Shakespeare's play.

3. Read Richard Armour's madcap version of *Romeo and Juliet* contained in his *Twisted Tales from Shakespeare*. Determine what criticisms of the play or the playwright are made through humor. What instructive insights does Armour provide?

4. Read Shakespeare's other love-tragedy, *Anthony and Cleopatra*. Compare Cleopatra's role with Juliet's as co-protagonist in the respective plays.

5. Read Herman Raucher's novel *Summer of '42*. Compare Hermie's concept of love with Romeo's. Compare the relationship of love and maturation presented in *Romeo and Juliet* with that in *Summer of '42*.

Reaction:

1. With which of the young male characters do you most closely identify: Romeo, Mercutio, Benvolio, Tybalt, or Paris? Compare that character's behavior with action you might take in comparable situations.

2. Several characters express their philosophy of life in this play. Whom would you choose for an adviser—the nurse, Juliet, Mercutio, or Friar Laurence? Comment on how that character influences others in the play and why that character's philosophy appeals to you.

3. In an essay or visual organizer, explore the contrasting concepts of love in this play. What is gained dramatically through the presentation of more than one view of love? Which concept seems most like your own? What views of love are held by people you know?

4. Argue for or against this statement: The force of "over-whelming love" purifies and matures the protagonists of *Romeo and Juliet*. Support your arguments with specifics from the play.

5. Argue that Romeo and Juliet are either (a) tragic figures, or (b) pathetic figures. Research definitions of each term. Then state your position and support it with examples from the play.

Creation/Composition:

1. Select one of the following scenes; then paraphrase it in contemporary dialogue: Act I, Scene iii; Act I, Scene v; Act II, Scene ii; Act III, Scene i; Act III, Scene v; Act IV, Scene iii; or Act IV, Scene v.

2. Rewrite Act V, Scene iii, as a short story.

3. Consider the hypothesis that the three letters (Tybalt's challenge to Romeo, Friar Laurence's explanation to Romeo, and Romeo's explanation to his father) are essential to the tragedy because the delivery of any of them could have prevented catastrophe. Rewrite each of the letters in contemporary language or compose one of the letters in Shakespearean verse.

4. In Edgar Lee Masters' *Spoon River Anthology*, former inhabitants of Spoon River speak from the graves of a Midwestern cemetery; they deliver their own epitaphs, discovering and confessing the real motivations of their lives. Using Masters' concept and style, have the following Shakespearean characters speak from their tombs: Mercutio, Tybalt, Paris, Lady Montague, Romeo, and Juliet.

5. Rewrite *Romeo and Juliet* as a short story in which the central conflict is one of race relations.

6. Write a short story or skit entitled "Benvolio and Rosaline."

7. Read Shakespeare's "Sonnet 130." Contrast the sonnet with Romeo's comments on Rosaline and Juliet. Then compare the sonnet to Mercutio's remarks about love. Write a satirical sonnet such as Mercutio might have written. Shakespeare's sonnet begins:

> My mistress' eyes are nothing like the sun;
> Coral is far more red than her lips' red:
> If snow be white, why then her breasts are dun;
> If hairs be wires, black wires grow on her head...

Between the Lines: Essay Test

Literal Level

1. Contrast Romeo's feelings for Rosaline with his love for Juliet.

2. Describe how Juliet changes during the play.

3. List three obstacles that come between the young lovers. Explain how each obstacle affects their relationship.

Interpretive Level

1. Choose one character who shows rash, impetuous behavior. Comment on how this impetuosity affects the outcome of the play.

2. Select one comic element from *Romeo and Juliet* and describe how it functions in the play.

3. Who or what do you think is most responsible for the deaths of Romeo and Juliet?

Final Curtain: Objective Test

I. Matching

Match each character with the proper description.

_____ 1. Tybalt

_____ 2. Mercutio

a. fights to preserve Capulet name

b. banishes Romeo from Verona

_____	3. Romeo	c.	carries message between lovers
_____	4. the nurse	d.	receives confessions of lovers
_____	5. Paris	e.	apologizes to parents for disobedience
_____	6. Juliet	f.	promises to erect a statue of Juliet
_____	7. Friar John	g.	dies by Tybalt's sword
_____	8. Friar Laurence	h.	fails to reach Romeo with message
_____	9. Montague	i.	seeks parental consent to marry
_____	10. Escalus	j.	dies from drinking poison

II. True–False

Mark each statement _T_ for True or _F_ for False.

_____ 11. Romeo and Juliet fall in love before they know each other's names.

_____ 12. Romeo takes a risk by going to the Capulets' party.

_____ 13. Romeo wishes to marry Juliet at once, but she insists on having her father's consent.

_____ 14. Friar Laurence hopes that the marriage between Romeo and Juliet will bring peace to Verona.

_____ 15. Mercutio is fatally wounded when Romeo attempts to stop his fight with Tybalt.

_____ 16. Romeo kills Tybalt because Tybalt insults him.

_____ 17. Romeo at first feels that banishment is a merciful sentence.

_____ 18. Juliet's father threatens to disinherit her if she refuses to marry Paris.

_____ 19. Juliet experiences no fear as she drinks the friar's potion.

_____ 20. Friar Laurence's letter reaches Romeo, but he refuses to read it.

_____ 21. Romeo buys poison so he can avenge Juliet's death.

_____ 22. Paris asks to be buried beside Juliet, and Romeo agrees.

_____ 23. Juliet awakens as Romeo is dying.

_____ 24. Juliet stabs herself with Romeo's dagger.

_____ 25. Friar Laurence conceals his role in the tragic deaths of the young lovers.

III. Multiple Choice

Choose the best answer.

26. Most of the action in this play takes place in

    a. Venice.

    b. Mantua.

    c. Verona.

27. The prince warns Montague and Capulet that if they renew their quarrel, they will be

    a. exiled.

    b. put to death.

    c. placed under house arrest.

28. When the play opens, Juliet's age is not yet

    a. twelve.

    b. fourteen.

    c. nineteen.